A FATHER

If a sportsman true you'd be
Listen carefully to me

Never, never let your gun
Pointed be at anyone
That it might unloaded be
Matters not the least to me

When a ditch or fence you cross
Though of time it cause you loss
From your gun the cartridge take
For the greater safety sake

If 'twixt you and neighbouring gun
Bird may fly or beast may run
Let this maxim e're be thine ~
Follow not across the line

Stops and beaters oft unseen
Lurk behind some leafy screen
Calm and steady always be
Never shoot where you can't see

Keep your place and silent be
Game can hear and game can see
Don't be greedy, better spared
Is a pheasant than one shared

You may kill or you may miss
But at all times think of this
All the pheasants ever bred
Won't repay for one man dead

Birds, Boots
& Barrels

Birds, Boots & Barrels

GAME SHOOTING IN THE 21st CENTURY

GILES CATCHPOLE

Illustrated by Bryn Parry

SWAN·HILL PRESS

Many thanks are due to Mike Barnes,
editor and publisher of The Shooting Gazette,
for his original painting of the Doodler and the Scribbler
and his unstinting support of them both, singly and together.

For all those who have taught me this important stuff,
shot with me or invited me to shoot
and put up with the consequences

GREC – July 2002

Copyright © 2002 Giles Catchpole (Text) and
Bryn Parry (Illustrations)
First published in the UK in 2002 by Swan Hill Press,
an imprint of Quiller Publishing Ltd.
Reprinted 2005

British Library Cataloguing-in-Publication Data
A catalogue record for this book
is available from the British Library

ISBN 1 904057 04 7

Printed in Italy

Swan Hill Press
an imprint of Quiller Publishing Ltd.
Wykey House, Wykey, Shrewsbury, SY4 1JA, England
Tel: 01939 261616 Fax: 01939 261606
E-mail: info@quillerbooks.com
Website: www.swanhillbooks.com

CONTENTS

Comparisons are odious

1

THE PREMISE

When I started to write this book, I intended that it should be a no frills guide to modern shooting which should help the aspiring Shot and perhaps amuse those occasional experienced shooters into whose hands it fell. I hoped that I could provide a step by step primer for young and old alike who had it in mind to take up a shotgun and do something constructive and life enhancing with it.

I did not intend to set out some kind of moral philosophy or to seek to encapsulate all the tiny details which go to make up a shooting day and which make what seems to all too many people today to be an archaic throwback to times irrevocably associated with formality and restraint and bristly moustaches and as much snobbery and elitism as you could shake a stick at.

My brave plan did not last terribly long.

In every chapter, from the moment when I pictured in my mind's eye the man or woman, boy or girl, first hefting a gun and feeling the tingle of anticipation at the thought of letting it off, I found myself trying to answer their inevitable questions frankly and honestly and without recourse to comments such as 'Because I say so.' or 'Because that's the way it has always been done.' There is a tremendous amount of nonsense talked about shooting and most of it disguises the fact that much, indeed most, of what shooting is about has to do with things which are not very popular today: self control, discipline, manners, courtesy, respect. We live in a world where everything moves at a tremendous pace. We hurtle about the place in cars which go from 0-60 mph faster than ever before, and far faster than anyone could possibly need to achieve and then sit for frustrated hours in traffic jams all going together at a snail's pace. We fly from country to country at unthinkable heights while watching movies and trying to confront the awful realities of airline food that fails to achieve the simplest test of edibility. Through our mobile phones and our laptop computers we are never alone, never out of touch, never free. Aggression in business and sport is applauded and promoted and is aped by the young in schools and on street corners by incivility, foul language and fouler behaviour. And yet shooting is more popular than ever.

Is it perhaps because game shooting has been observed to be the pastime of the fabulously wealthy and glamorous? After all, shooting is also widely thought to be about elitism, snobbery, exclusivity, disdain, huge numbers of servants and vast amounts of money; all of which are endlessly fascinating to a very great number of people.

Throughout this book I find myself constantly referring back to the Edwardians, to whom, for better or worse, we owe the shape and form of our modern organised shooting whether it involves game or artificial targets. They have a good deal to answer for so perhaps it is as well to take a brief look at what it was they were about.

The Edwardians

Basically it boils down to this, Edward, Prince of Wales, elder son of the Queen Empress Victoria, was pretty much of a louche bounder. His mother had every intention of living forever and denying him the opportunity to reign and so he never really had a proper job. Like many a feckless young man with too much money and time on his hands, he took to having a good life - a very good life indeed. And like any immensely wealthy and determinedly dissolute chap, he quickly accumulated a goodly supply of mates to help him pass the time; and a fair number of very agreeable girls, actresses and singers mostly, to provide a spot of arm candy during the day, dancing partners of an evening and a willingness to while away the rest of the time with enthusiasm and generally athletic gusto. And those on the inside of the royal circle seemed to be having a very good time indeed - although there were a number of conspicuous fallers who went bankrupt and died, broke, miserable and alone, and unmentioned in the glossies of the day - and the wider world just lapped it up.

Nothing very much seems to have changed, when you think about it, except that the princes and dukes of then are movie actors and software magnates now and the girls are television presenters on the remoter satellite channels. And they still seem to have a very good time - though there are still a few who overdose, lose it in the tabloids or the casinos, punch a photographer and end up broke, miserable, alone and dead, and glossed over in the unmentionables - and the world is still fascinated. And the Empire has become corporate rather than military. A hundred years in a couple of paragraphs. How about that?

However, the Marlborough House set was absolutely the *Hello!* fodder of their day, and the paparazzi duly took a deep and abiding interest in how they conducted themselves. And since they spent the summer racing thoroughbred horses or yachts and the winter shooting each other's pheasants and since everyone, despite very Victorian pursed lips and raised eyebrows, would really rather be a dissolute prince than, say, a clump press minder or an accountant, racing and shooting became very fashionable things indeed to be seen doing, along with some mates, a spot of arm candy and prodigious amounts of champagne and truffles.

And then he became Edward VII, and not only carried on much as before, but made a lot of it compulsory. And there, I'm afraid, the whole social development of a large chunk of this country pretty much ground to a halt. Two World Wars, any number of social and industrial revolutions, mobile phones and cars that go nowhere at a zillion miles an hour and the British are still wearing top hats for Ascot and weddings, getting sozzled and falling in the water at Henley and Cowes and shooting pheasants in the winter. Or at least those who can and want to still are.

The rest of the world has moved on; and today's princes and their cliques go to grand prix, and film premieres and islands off Thailand and New York nightclubs and weddings in Vegas where the bride wears a gold lamé bikini and the groom wears a dress and there isn't a top hat in sight and then there is a huge party paid for by *Hello!* and it's all just fabulous. The two groups almost certainly roundly despise one another and the rest of us look on bemused and get on pressing clumps and accounting. And that's the Edwardians for you.

What the Edwardians bequeathed to us, however, and I mean by us those who have an urge to undertake shooting as a pastime, is the format of shooting as it is presently disposed. They did not invent shooting. People have been hunting forever. Initially for food, then for the protection of their herds and flocks and crops from marauding animals and finally for sport, because life without the thrill of hunting was so tedious that without any specific need to hunt, they had to invent one.

All the Edwardians did was to undertake hunting, or more specifically shooting, on such a scale that what had been a pretty ad hoc mooch with intent to pursue something as and when it arose, perhaps with a dog or two in tow, became a hugely complex organisation involving the entire population of the vast swathes of countryside which certain Edwardians conveniently owned and preparation for which began each season before even the previous season was over. And a very efficient, if costly, organisation it was too. And you don't go dismantling something which works as well as game shooting overnight. What you do is find someone else to pay for it, once the princes have moved on. Which is where we come in.

An Edwardian cove

Us

Having discarded the Edwardians, we come to us. I am often accused of wanting to be an Edwardian. I don't think it's true really. I would not have been a prince or a duke and accordingly I would have been a clerk or stuck up a chimney. I don't even want to be a prince today, because I've been to a grand prix and it was not to my taste. Lots of champagne and very pretty girls; but otherwise just very fast cars, very noisy, going round in circles.

I do like to shoot though. I would like to have the opportunity to shoot as much as the Edwardians did. I'd like to have a software fortune today. Lacking both I will spend what I have on shooting and if I can delude myself that I am doing anything other than deluding myself, then I can perhaps satisfy that urgent need within me to hunt on the one hand, and to lose myself in a world where time is governed not by electronics and data packets, but by the light and the seasons, and form is dictated by function rather than fashion and where courtesies and rituals have to do with an appreciation for the efforts of others and the important issue of not being shot by your neighbour.

This is why, I think, shooting is as popular today as it is. It is no longer necessary to be a prince or a duke to do it. There are those who insist that this remains the case, but, as a matter of fact, dukes and princes are permitted to do it just like the rest of us and savour their invitations and pay their money with the same enthusiasm. It remains true that some dukes and princes have estates and money now as ever, but if you think this means that they get their shooting for free, you are sadly mistaken. These days everybody pays. It's not really that glamorous though. Too much rain and cold and and mud and blood and hard work, and you never saw a *Hello!* spread on the Skipton and District Retriever Club Working Test. The rules are very simple and involve not shooting people and dogs which makes them quite easy to understand. The roles of all those present are clearly defined: beaters beat; birds fly; Guns shoot; pickers-up and their dogs pick up; headkeepers govern everything. And in the midst of all this is Death. Let us not skirt round this issue. Stuff dies here. Pheasants definitely, partridges and grouse certainly, perhaps hares and rabbits, ducks, jays and magpies if anyone gets the chance; pigeons. Dozens, perhaps hundreds, killed for our pleasure and sport. Why is that? I cannot justify it, other than to say that I have an instinctive urge to hunt which is satisfied by shooting. I enjoy shooting. I relax in and relish its forms and I appreciate its organisational and administrative intricacies. I consider that killing under such circumstances is not morally reprehensible. As long as I have regard for the fact that each bird or beast that I shoot has been deprived of its life in order that mine may be enhanced, I don't think that the hundredth head in a day to my own gun would be any more reprehensible than the first. If I could afford it.

The moment, however, that I lose sight of the sacrifice of that sentient being and begin to consider the birds to be just so many targets, then I believe that I am lost. If the birds are mere targets then I should be shooting clay pigeons and am not to be trusted in the field with live game.

I believe that the criticisms which are levelled against game shooting through the accumulation of big bags concern, as the consequence, not the size of the bags themselves, but the disregard of this fundamental rule. When Punters, for they are not Guns in the sense I understand the term, blaze away and kill hundreds of birds in a drive and then simply troop back to their transport without a backward look, to move onto the next killing field, it is appalling. When dead game is thrown casually onto the ground or into carts or in heaps or left where it falls, it is a disgrace. If a wounded bird is left without having been thoroughly sought after, not least by the person responsible, merely in order to join others in time for a drink, those who leave it rank as low as it is possible to sink.

If there is no respect for the quarry, then there is no respect for the keeper who reared it for your pleasure and no respect for the beaters who ushered it in your direction or for the host who invited

Sporting development

you on the one hand or who permitted you to rent his estate on the other, and who should, even now, be bitterly regretting doing so. And there is no regard for the other Guns who are tainted by your action, as surely as if you had shot the keeper or the keeper's dog or your neighbour. And if all this is giving you an impression of my approach to shooting and you reckon it's a bit old fashioned or finicky or if you just don't agree or don't think that the friend for whom you are buying this book will agree, then you'd best put it down right now, because everything that comes later is based on that.

Dealings with keepers, beaters, hosts, pickers-up, fellow Guns; finding or hiring shooting; joining syndicates, and equipping yourself to address the shooting day; even the bits about clay pigeon shooting, none of it will make any sense flat, unless you can see the point of this bit of a rant. For which I duly apologise.

Now perhaps we can get on with teaching folks some basics.

2

THE SHOTGUN CERTIFICATE

B oring. Boring. Boring. Where are the guns? The smell of cordite in the nostrils? The tweed and the glamour? Well, 'Coming up' is the answer, and if you want to flip quickly there I'm sure you can and will. However, you are not going to get very far with all of this unless the issue of the Law is confronted at some point, and given the length of time that can be involved with securing a Shotgun Certificate you may as well start early to save disappointment.

It is strange to think now that when I started shooting as a boy of eleven – Arghhhh! Avuncularity overload! Alarm! Alarm! – I was lent a .410 shotgun, which is a very tiny gun indeed, and good for almost nothing out of doors, which was kept on top of my father's wardrobe, to be inaccessible to me rather than to any burglar, and when invited by the local gamekeeper, one of my father's patients, to join him for an afternoon, I would go down to the ironmonger's shop and buy a box of cartridges. Then I would tie the gun to the crossbar of my bike and bicycle the three miles or so to the keeper's cottage. I can't begin to think how many offences my father, the ironmonger, the keeper and I have just committed during the last paragraph under the current firearms and shotguns legislation.

In fact it wasn't a .410 at all, but a .400 big game rifle, bored out to .410. It was by Dickson of Edinburgh and it had two great hammers and a lovely stock. I was lent it by a farmer friend who had no business issuing eleven year olds with guns, and to whom I am eternally grateful, and back to whom, in due season, I returned it when I moved on to bigger, and as I thought, better things. I doubt actually if I have ever owned or used a gun quite as good as that little .410. Had I had a greater appreciation of the gun, rather than its function, then I might have researched its history more closely and enjoyed its company even more.

However, today I wouldn't be enjoying it at all because I would be in some young offenders institution for not having the requisite licence. When I did finally get round to getting a Shotgun Certificate, it was a rather flimsy piece of paper which cost, as I recall, about a fiver and involved toddling down to the local police station with two letters of reference from respectable bods. In those far off days I had a doctor and a bank manager, both of whom were content to vouch for me, the one because he had delivered me, and the other because he had all my money. The sergeant at the police station knew who I was too and where I lived and so after a brief lecture about boys, guns and windows, he breathed heavily and formally upon his stamp and brought it crashing down upon my licence, the number of which he entered in a big ledger. I was street, or perhaps field, legal.

Compare that with the rigmarole I went through last year, in order to renew my Certificate. Today you are still required to have two referees, and they are still required to be JP, MP, doctor, lawyer, vicar, bank manager or someone of similar standing. Let's just look at these in a little more detail. The only JP I know fined me £75 and three points for jumping a red light on a scooter. I don't know any MPs and I doubt if I would admit it if I did. I have been to the local surgery, sorry Community Health Centre, once in the last decade where a child with a stethoscope who purported to be a doctor told me that rest would cure all. I do know a couple of consultants but they are not real doctors, because they go back to being Mr once they reach a certain level. My bank manager is a combination of a computer and a hole in the wall. I did offer up the chairman of a large international banking group as a referee, but he was rejected. He wasn't a bank manager, he was a bank chairman. Not the same thing at all; which rather knocked the 'similar standing' part on the head. On that basis the Archbishop of Canterbury would fall down for not being a vicar. Not that it makes any difference since I do not attend church. Fortunately I know numerous lawyers who will referee me for a pint, or less, so it's not a problem for me, but make a note, it's not getting any easier. Lawyer, incidentally, means solicitor. Barristers, in the opinion of the police, perhaps understandably, are not lawyers. Briefs, maybe? Scum? The lawyers also have to annotate and sign the back of two passport photographs with the immortal words 'I confirm that this is a true current likeness of [insert name of applicant]' which, if the applicant's name is Neville Fortesque Hartley Bagshott-Smyth and the referee's signature has a bit of a flourish about it, as many lawyers' signatures do, makes for not a whole lot of space on a thing the size of a passport photo, but there you go. You also have to fill in a largish form which asks if you are either a criminal or mad. So if you answer yes to the one, you must be the other. Then it is into the post to the local constabulary with £50. Don't imagine for moment that that is that. That isn't. The next step is that the Firearms Enquiry Unit of the local constabulary will pay you a visit. The irony about this is that some FEUs are perfectly charming and sensible and polite and helpful and obliging and confirm your belief that the British police are the best in the world. Some.

Others are snide and shirty and make you want to start looking for a convenient half brick to throw at something. Or so I've heard. Not only will they turn up and ask you a lot impertinent questions about your domestic life and drinking habits but they will also require to see your security arrangements; although a security arrangement does not necessarily mean a safe – which many FEUs think it does; and if you have a safe already, many FEUs think that it must be approved to British Standard No.7558, which it does not, and be bolted to a load-bearing wall, which it doesn't either.

If you want a BS 7558 safe and you want to bolt it to a load-bearing wall, all well and good, and I couldn't be happier for you. But, for those of us who have safes which pre-date the British Standards Agency by a century or so and which require to be moved by crane when moving house and who remember, for example, what happened to my mate's flat when a burglar started jemmying the safe away from the load bearing wall; and recall the burglar's comment as they dragged him from the rubble of the whole building – this adherence to the suggestion as if it was the law, instead of guidance, is very irritating. Under the Act, you are required to show 'reasonable security' for your gun or guns. And that's it.

Having said which, a safe is far and away the best thing for the job, as long as you can restrain the rest of the household from filling it with jewellery and silver teapots.

The FEU will also ask you where the keys to the safe are kept. This is a trick question. A safe is only as safe as its keys are safe and if you don't want to find yourself arguing the toss about keeping your safe keys in a safe, the key to which is in a safe, etc…etc; you had better say firmly and clearly that the keys are in a safe place. And shut up. Bad FEUs are rare but not unheard of. If you are a shooter already, but not a gun owner, you should be a member of the British Association for Shooting and Conservation (BASC) or the Countryside Alliance (CA) or better still both, either of which organisations have legal departments who will support you if you get into real difficulties. Sadly, they are spending more and more time doing exactly this sort of thing.

After all of which the FEU takes itself off and considers the whole application for a number of weeks and in due course issues you with a Shotgun Certificate of your very own. With your picture on it. Which means that we can finally go shopping for shooters.

3

THE SHOTGUN

Once armed, if that is the right word, with the all important Shotgun Certificate, it is now possible to amble down the high street and procure the shotgun of your dreams. Actually there is no reason why you cannot start this process even without the Certificate. Window-shopping, with or without the paperwork, is not against the law after all, and your gunsmith or dealer will, if he is a reasonable person, happily keep your choice, for a while at least, until your Certificate comes through.

How long though is a piece of string? If the question 'What gun should I buy and how much should I pay?' has been asked once it has been asked a million times; and the response is always likely to be the same. 'What do you want and how much are you prepared to pay for it?'

The choice is bewildering. Gunmaking has progressed a long way since the days of the arquebus and the matchlock, although it must be admitted that in design terms the whole area reached a frenzied peak between the two World Wars, and then stayed there. Not for want of inventiveness or ingenuity, but because the designs that had been arrived at by that period had achieved, if not perfection, then at least a fairly adjacent approximation of it. Since that time there has been some fiddling with the basic designs and a degree of tinkering with features such as the ribs and the ejectors, but on the whole shotguns today are, to the untutored eye, almost indistinguishable from their elders and many of the guns regularly in use today were built early in the last century, if not before. The key development in manufacturing between then and now has been the use of machinery and technology to accelerate the production process and to make guns more quickly and therefore less expensively. John Moses Browning, the American designer and gunmaker who patented all sorts of guns from a repeating shotgun to a .50 calibre machine gun and who worked extensively with Winchester and Sam Colt, was more responsible than most for taking gunmaking out of the workshop and into the factory and the success of his business and the fact that many hundreds of thousands of Browning guns are still made and used today, both in the field and in helicopter gunships, is testament to the enduring nature of his designs and production methods.

However, the key issue confronted by the aspiring owner today, before the issues of budget and performance are even addressed, will be 'What is the gun going to be used for?'

Today's shooter will probably undertake a mix of sport comprising some game shooting in a relatively formal setting; a bit of rough shooting, if he is fortunate; and the occasional foray after clay targets, more or less depending on his enthusiasm and opportunity. Certainly there will be those who only ever do one or the other. There are even those who will affect to despise utterly any discipline but their own choice; but for these folks there are any number of high quality instructional books dealing with the intricacies of every kind of shooting.

We are trying to lend a helping hand to a keen and ignorant novice generalist, so we should take a keen and generalist approach. Let's start with size. Is it important? Is it ever not? The bore of a shotgun describes the scale of the hole at the business end. Ironically, and in a typically confusing and deliberately obfuscatory way, the bigger the hole in the end of the barrel the lower the number used to describe it. Thus a twenty-eight bore is tiny, while a four bore is so colossal that it can scarcely be lifted by a strong man and should probably never be discharged from the shoulder without medical supervision. The factual origin of this anomaly is that the bore describes the number of balls of pure lead of a diameter the same as that of the barrel as will constitute a weight of one Imperial Pound (1lb). Hence a twelve bore implies twelve lumps and a twenty bore twenty lumps and so forth, and these days twelve bores and twenty bores are far and away the most popular sizes. In fact twenty bores are probably outstripping twelve bores in sales of both new and second hand guns. Why? Any number of reasons. Probably the fact that cartridge and ammunition design and technology have moved on further than gun design, if the truth be known. Fifty years ago everybody used twelve bores for more or less all purposes as being the most reasonable compromise between weight and effectiveness. At around 6½lb to carry, the twelve bore was not unfeasible, and with an ounce of shot per cartridge it would deal with most things confronted on a shooting day at a reasonable range fairly effectively. Also it was what all the nobby types in the Edwardian era, when game shooting was immensely fashionable and unutterably chic, used and the general view was that if it was good enough for them, then it was good enough for the rest of us. Other bores, twenties, sixteens, tens and so forth were made in some numbers but the twelve bore became, by weight of numbers, the bore or gauge of choice.

Today however, the improved smaller twenty bore cartridge loads will happily deal with whatever the normal shooting day sends your way. If confronting exceptional game, extreme pheasants for example, or geese or duck, then it might be the case that the bigger gun is better suited for the purpose; but even then it is the case that there are twenty bore cartridge loads designed for such adventures which will do the job as well if pointed in the right direction. There are, though, what scientists are known to refer to as side effects. The principal side effects of letting off any kind of gun are noise and recoil. The noise is commensurate with the size of the cartridge being discharged and will be dealt with specifically later, but recoil is different and since it is the one thing which all novices associate with shooting, it may be as well to think about it now.

The key to recoil is physics. Not a subject I know much about. Never liked it at school. However Newton's Third Law is, I think, the rule we are looking for. Every action has an equal and opposite reaction. $E=(\frac{1}{2})mV^2$ or perhaps that's the recipe for gunpowder. I'm never sure. Be that as it may, what it means is that if you shoot a little thing (1oz of shot) really fast out of the front end, then the big thing (the 6½lb gun you are holding) will come backwards at approximately 1/100th or thereabouts, of the pace of the departing speeding bullet. Which is several feet per second. Hence recoil. Now since guns and cartridges these days vary a good deal, and you can have light guns and heavy guns and very powerful cartridges and not so powerful cartridges it does not follow that big guns have more recoil than little guns. In fact the reverse is true. It is the case that if you use a little gun you will certainly get bashed about by the recoil if you insist on using immensely powerful cartridges. If you wish to use heavyweight cartridges then you should equip yourself with the heaviest gun you can handle and you will scarcely feel the consequences. If you are of more modest ambitions cartridge-wise then you can put them through a big gun with virtually no recoil at all, or through a smaller gun with no more than a shove in the shoulder. Is any of this clear?

Furthermore it should be remembered that if the gun is firmly bedded in your shoulder when you let it off, your weight is effectively added to that of the gun and accordingly the distance and pace at which you and the gun move backwards together become really quite small. If the gun is being held away from the body when it goes off though, it has a miserable 6½ lb to counteract the aforesaid speeding bullet and duly comes belting back into your collarbone at some great speed. And it hurts.

The impact of recoil

Everybody has heard how someone went shooting and came back with their shoulder black and blue with recoil. First up, they were probably using a gun that was all round too little for them, on the basis that the little one would be less hurty than a great big one. Wrong. Then they held it almost at arm's length well away from their shoulder when they let it off. Wrong. And finally they were using too strong a cartridge for the size of the gun and for their stage of shooting experience. Wrong.

All of which leaves us where exactly, in relation to buying a gun? Probably with a bigger choice than ever. We came in looking for a little beginner's gun, thinking to save the big ones for later, and Lo! The world is once again our oyster, thanks to physics.

Calibres, bores and gauges apart, let us for a moment consider that other great debate. The side-by-side versus the over-and-under. Now no one who is reading this should be such a novice as to not know what we are talking about. OK, you are. In short, side-by-side (or S/S as they say in the small ads) shotguns have two barrels set in horizontal juxtaposition – side-by-side; while over-and-under shotguns (O/U, startlingly) have two barrels set one above the other in the vertical axis. All clear? And why is there a debate about which is superior? Why is there a debate about anything? What else would shooters have to talk about except fishing and sex?

Oh, very well, let's get the thing sorted. At the root of the whole issue there is a basic snobbery. Back to those famous Edwardians. They didn't use O/Us, did they? And there is a very good reason why not. The modern sporting shotgun derives, essentially, from the old muskets and flintlocks of the seventeenth and eighteenth centuries where the shooter rammed a certain amount of powder and shot down the front of his gun, shoved an additional pinch into the flash pan and pulled the trigger. Spark from flint and steel fell into pan, fizzed through a little hole into the chamber, ignited the main charge and Goodnight Vienna! Now when advancing the concept to the level of a second barrel, the issue arises where do you put it? On top? Underneath? Beside? Given the difficulty of keeping little dibbles of powder in flash pans which were upside-down and the problems of getting sparks to fall upwards, gun makers went with logic and gravity and put the second barrel alongside the first in what was a resolutely sensible development. Purists of gun design will doubtless roar that there were flintlock O/Us and that I'm talking through my hat, but this is the story in essence and not a treatise on eighteenth century gun design. And when the flintlock gave way to percussion and the muzzleloader gave way to the breechloader, where the gun breaks open and the cartridge goes in at the back, it was still the case that each cartridge was struck by a spring loaded external hammer and it was these double-barrelled breech-loading side-by-side hammer guns which were in use at that particular juncture in English fashion history when the Edwardians hit. And there, more or less, it has stayed ever since. If you are interested, the whole history of that period, social, fashionable, political and sporting is adequately documented by J.G. Ruffer in his excellent book *The Big Shots* (Quiller Press).

Broadly speaking then, the side-by-side was dominant because the Prince of Wales and his mates used them and so everybody else followed suit. He also left his bottom waistcoat button undone because he couldn't find it under his great girth and everybody followed suit. Some still do today. He also seduced a considerable number of young actresses and drank too much. I guess you can see where this is going? To compound matters, and this was and remains frightfully important, O/Us, once they were developed by the leading gunsmiths of the day, were used in, of all things, competitions; between professionals; for money. Lawks! How vulgar. The early O/Us were indeed used for the purpose. Gunmakers very often used competitions as an advertising medium for their new products and many of the leading makers used to participate regularly in the competitions from which the modern clay pigeon disciplines derive. Except they used live pigeons and huge wagers were bet on the outcomes too. And to some extent the arguments have persisted. O/Us are for the clay target shooters;

professionals; not quite sportsmen or princes. It makes you weep in this day and age, really it does. There are however practical reasons why today's gun owner might prefer one to the other.

The side-by-side is, generally speaking, lighter than its superposed cousin. A gunsmith could tell you why. I can't. Across the gauges the O/U will always be the heavier of the two. Under most circumstances this will not be disadvantageous to the O/U user, who will experience less recoil throughout his shooting days and may find that the extra weight gives a more definitive point of aim and an agreeable momentum when swinging onto targets. The extra weight may also reduce irritating muzzle flip when the first shot is discharged permitting a quicker aim on the second target of a pair. All well and good. On the other hand the side-by-side owner will argue that the lighter gun is faster onto the first target, less weight to lug about all day, more manageable in the shot and easier to swing effectively.

It may also be the case that the O/U, with its single flat sighting plane is easier and more accurate to aim, and it is certainly true that no top flight clay shooter has been seen with anything other than an O/U and it is the gun of choice for the top game shooters too. But it is also certainly true that when you open a side-by-side you can pop a shell into either chamber – left or right – with exactly equal facility; whereas in the superposed version, while the top barrel is seldom a problem the underneath hole can be an issue and in moments of stress has been known to lead to hard words.

One might as well argue the toss about long and short barrels. And plenty of people do. Again the whole thing is rather fanciful. In the olden, golden days what propelled the shot out of their guns was your basic gunpowder. It didn't go off with a 'BANG!', it rather went 'whooooossshhh!' as it burned out along the barrel to the point where it delivered maximum propulsion. This took time and required a longish tube, thirty inches minimum, perhaps more. Shortly before the Great War, and certainly after it, the new nitro propellants were in common use and they required much less distance to complete their propellant burn. The 'BANG!' had arrived. Using the new powders meant that barrel length was a matter of choice rather than necessity. Gunmaker Robert Churchill quickly advertised his XXV guns with twenty-five inch barrels as being faster handling, quicker to aim and generally all round, up to the minute, cutting edge, wonder guns. And he demonstrated them in live pigeon matches to prove the point and achieved some prodigious records using the new guns. And several people bought them and declared them everything Robert Churchill said in the ads. It wasn't snake oil exactly, but it is a matter of fact that a short-barrelled gun will tend to shoot high. If I had the maths I could probably prove it, but I don't, so you will just have to take this on trust. About a foot high at thirty-five yards. So an average sort of a Shot is going to be a foot up on a rising bird going away from the shooter. Shooting live pigeon in competitions or grouse walked up or modern clay target disciplines such as trap or trench, all experiences where the bird zooms away from the shooter, a foot up at thirty-five yards, or a bit more for choice, is exactly where you want to be. Hence when Mr Churchill took a punter and gave him the gun to try on an average pigeon from a trap at thirty-five paces, guess what? The punter got it every time. Every one a winner and every winner a sale for Mr Churchill and his magic short barrels. Of course, if the same punter happened to use his new gun against driven grouse, for example, which come towards you, and where you really want your shot about a foot under the oncoming bird's beak at forty yards, it was a somewhat different story and many a reasonable grouse shooter found himself unaccountably off form. Churchill, naturally had the answer to that too and introduced the all new, singing and dancing, raised rib; which has the effect of dropping the point of aim by, would you believe it, a foot or so at thirty-five yards. So bingo, the shot goes where you are pointing. All of which is very well for chaps who are in a position to have one gun for birds going away and another for incomers, but no help for the rest of us. It is a story though. Anyway, the point is that long or short, up and down or side-by-side the issue is largely subjective and mostly a fashion thing and you needn't worry your confused little heads about it.

Anyway side-by-sides are prettier. Ooops! There; it's out. Well, I think they are. Certainly in my price range they are. Not at the top of the tree, it is true. Up there in the stratosphere where money is no object, beyond £20,000 a gun, the world is populated by O/Us - not least from Italy, but also home grown - which are elegant beyond compare and make me go quite weak at the knees. Down here with the rest of us it is not quite the same and in my view the side-by-side wins in the looks division. And that, when all is said and done, is what is important. We can look at things like fit and function, and we will, now and later; but what the whole buying thing comes down to in practice is whether you, the buyer, are prepared to part with the price asked for the piece concerned. And if you don't like the look of it then, chances are, you won't.

And price? Guns vary in price from £50 to £50,000 and beyond. Way beyond. What should you pay? Somewhere in between. It is such a difficult question. I am of the view however that there is little virtue in cheapness. What you see is what you get. Pay peanuts and you get peanuts. Or in this case you get a stick; a smokepole; a danger more to yourself than to your quarry be it flying or flung.

Rule of thumb, OK? £750 is what you should be thinking. Yes, you can spend less and God knows you can spend more; but this is about the level where you will get something which will do the job admirably and no one you meet will be in any position to sneer at it or you. As to the breed, let's whistle through them.

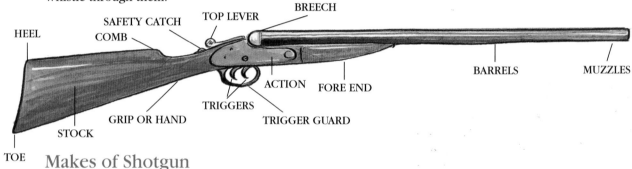

HEEL · SAFETY CATCH · COMB · TOP LEVER · BREECH · BARRELS · MUZZLES · ACTION · FORE END · TRIGGERS · TRIGGER GUARD · GRIP OR HAND · STOCK · TOE

Makes of Shotgun

British - makers of the world's finest guns since time immemorial and at the top end still superb. Perfectly reasonable to buy something old on a modest budget, but you should remember that with age and experience can come decrepitude. British origins are not a guarantee of superiority, however much of a start in life the Empire may have given. The top names - Purdey, Holland & Holland, Boss & Co need not concern us unduly. They do creep down as far as four figures from time to time, but when they do the name is, very generally speaking, the only bit that still works. Second tier names from around the town such as Harrison & Hussey, Atkin and Boswell are all quality and provide a tool of lasting satisfaction. From Birmingham, second division only geographically really, makers such as William Powell or Westley Richards are up there with the cream of the crop, while regional makers like Gallyon or Rosson from Norwich, or Chaplin from Winchester reflect a time when any respectable market town had a gun maker of quality. Nor should Scotland be overlooked MacNaughton, Dickson, Alex Henry were all fine makers. Modern gunmakers, often working under revived older names such as Churchill or Watson Bros., generally service the top end of the market and fall outside our remit except in dreams, while the contemporary makers of fine guns under their own names, such as Tony White of Shugborough or the estimable David McKay Brown of Glasgow, should be paid a visit only when the Lottery numbers have rolled in big time. Lovely. Simply lovely. If anyone can be said to have taken the zenith of British gunmaking and improved it, Davy can.

Spanish – Thirty years ago this was where every novice shooter started, unless he was a very rich novice shooter indeed. The AYA – Aguerre y Aranzabal – No.4 boxlock non-ejector twenty bore was the workhorse of the beginner's market. I don't know how many they sold, but it must have been a lot. Mine cost £72 in about 1972 and is probably still going strong somewhere. Two years later I traded it and, as I recall, £100 for a twelve bore sidelock by Laurona, and that I have still. Spanish guns were, and are, mass produced at very reasonable prices and have, as a result, almost no second hand value. Not because they are poor guns, but because there are a great many of them about and they are all working perfectly well, and a brand new one still isn't expensive. There are any number of reputable Spanish makers and most gunshops will have a few examples in stock which they will be happy to sell to you. Spanish guns tend towards the utility end of the market though and always strike me now as being a little dark and heavy, more reminiscent of the bull than the matador. Perfectly fine for all that, though.

American – For American think Browning. Or Winchester. They are the same as a matter of fact. Certainly under the skin. They make custom Brownings in Belgium, and custom and standard Winchesters in Conneticut; and now many of them are made in Japan. So how confusing is that?

What is there to say about American guns? When Browning really put his mind to it he made some lovely guns; but, and I think this is perhaps the key to the whole thing, like many Americans he put function firmly ahead of form. If a gun worked then it was a good gun. Browning's repeating shotguns are a case in point. If a gun which fired a single shot accurately and reliably was a good thing, then a five shot automatic repeater was at least four times better, right? Wrong, John Moses, wrong. Brownings and Winchesters and the Miroku brand for that matter, are all fine guns which need embarrass no one; any more than a Ford Escort. And that is not sneering, quite the reverse in fact. But not, my dears, a repeater. Why not? Well, we always used to say because you can't see whether they are loaded or unloaded; but then you can't see whether any gun is loaded or unloaded if it's shut. Actually it was just snobbery again. Bit modern; bit mechanical; bit furry dice, to be honest. Whatever. Anyway, the Government banned the five shot repeater in 1988, I think, and reduced the permitted number to three shots which is hardly enough of an ammunition advantage to count when all is said and done.

Italian – Think of the Renaissance. Think of Michelangelo's Pieta or the Sistine Chapel ceiling. Da Vinci's Mona Lisa. Think Rome and the Coliseum or Canaletto, Giotto and Carravaggio. Then think Alfa Sud and Lambrusco and Banco Ambrosiano. All that talent squandered, all that heritage debased, all that skill diluted. Well, that was a bad patch and today the Italians are enjoying something of a golden age in gunmaking where ancient skills are combining with modern technologies to make some very handsome and serviceable pieces indeed. At the top end among the bespoke makers of Gardone, there is probably no one to touch them. Even at the more manageable levels inhabited by the rest of us, no one who is buying a gun should disregard the Italian makers. Beretta are the best known, as befits the world's oldest gunmaker, and make a fine range which are particularly good in the smaller gauges and will meet the needs and resources of any aspiring sportsman. The Italians are, it must be said, more at home with the O/U than the side-by-side conformation, but given that we have already established that there is nothing to choose between the two, why should that be a worry any more?

Technical Terms

What is probably more of a worry to you, is understanding some of the technical terms that are being bandied about and getting to grips with what is important and what is just gunroom loose talk and gunshop sales patter. Consider the picture and we will run over the key points.

The barrels are at the front. Two twin tubes of steel that start life solid and then have their middles bored out to form the bore, the size of which has already been discussed. At the other end the stock or butt which can range from the finest French or more recently, the French having run out of trees, Turkish Circassian walnut to a nondescript plank. The variegated lines of black and brown in the wood is called figuring and is likely to be much commented upon where it is pronounced and where not, not.

The metal block in the middle where the two elements join is the action and this is where the mechanical gubbins is housed. Actions are, for the most part, either boxlock, which is square and box shaped or sidelock where the sides extend back somewhat in an attractive curve. The difference between the two is that the boxlock is the more pedestrian action while the sidelock is more complex inside and correspondingly more expensive to make and therefore pricier to buy. Specifically the sidelock incorporates an intercepting sear, which loosely translated is a secondary safety device, which renders the owner a safer and more loveable person to shoot with, as well as indicating that he is a richer and possibly more generous soul, which makes him a better shooting companion in any case. In theory, at least.

Underneath the action is the trigger guard containing sometimes one, sometimes two, triggers. Older guns have two triggers: one for each barrel. The single trigger is a more modern mechanism altogether and fires the barrels in sequence, usually right/left or up/down; and the really modern single selective trigger can go in any order you like if you can remember to make up your mind in time. Complex but cool, and cool always has a price.

On top of the action is the top lever which opens the gun and locks it when shut. Again some guns have a mechanism which causes the gun to spring open of its own accord when the top lever is pressed aside and which is a very snazzy and expensive feature indeed, the true value of which we shall consider in due season. Just behind and below the top lever is the safety catch. This is a crucial little knob which locks the triggers until the moment of firing is imminent. Some, most, are automatic and click into the 'SAFE' position whenever the gun is shut; others, perhaps surprisingly among modern guns, are not automatic and this should be an issue for any beginner. Get the automatic safety. It cannot be over-emphasised that where a shotgun is concerned safety should always be the default position and even an automatic safety catch should never be allowed to substitute for safe behaviour and handling. Finally there is some more wood in front of the action underneath the barrels. This is the fore-end and quite apart from holding the other two bits, stock and barrels, together it contains elements of the cocking and ejecting mechanisms. Put simply the action contains two firing pins which stick out of the face of the action and which strike the backs of the cartridges when they are belted from behind by the hammers. The hammers are driven by two springs which are cocked when the gun is closed and released when the triggers are pulled. There are two further springs which are released when the gun is fired and are activated when it is opened to mobilise the ejectors which are embedded in the breech of the barrels where the cartridges are and which automatically flip the used cartridge cases out of the gun after firing. When the cartridges have been replaced and the gun is closed all these springs are once more tensed for action and the safety catch is in 'SAFE' mode until the whole process is repeated. That's enough technology for a bit.

There is no earthly reason why you should need to know all of this in detail, you shoot and stuff just happens, right? Surely, but when you are buying a gun, it helps to have some glimmering of understanding during the sales spiel or you will give away the fact that you are a rube of the first water and will get skinned accordingly. The gun trade is like any other. Most of its inhabitants are universally honest and forthright and charming and would not take advantage of a novice even if he had 'Ignoramus' tattooed on his forehead. But like any business there are those who would take advantage of the inexperienced, so casual references to single selective triggers and auto safeties may save you a bob or two, so listen and learn.

There are other more esoteric actions too. The back action which is very old now and the round action, which is a Scots invention which is a sidelock which looks like a boxlock (an expensive gun dressed up as a cheaper version)– a concept so Presbyterian as to be almost Amish – and there are boxlocks with false sideplates (making them look more expensive than they really are, which is much more logical in my view) and pinless actions which are frightfully expensive and therefore hardly worth describing, and detachable trigger-plate actions which fall apart at the touch of a button. You may even be shown a hammer action where the two hammers are on the outside of the action, flintlock style. This is an antique and while no one will give an O/U a second thought in the field today, you will get some very strange looks should you turn up with one of these.

So what are the principal features you should be looking for when contemplating a purchase? Starting at the front.

Barrels

What is there to say about barrels? We've been through the longs and the shorts of them and we've been through the conformation debate. What is there to add? When looking at barrels from the point of view of a purchaser the key aspects are that they should be straight, strong, original and clean. Simple enough you would have thought. Yeah, like buying a secondhand car is simple enough. Barrels are steel and rust is the enemy of steel. Rust eats away at the metal and weakens it irreparably and you can't always see it at work. Where it has been at work it is also possible for the unscrupulous to disguise the fact. The barrels which you are holding nervously in your hands are two tubes joined together along their length by ribs soldered on top and bottom or either side. I think we'll stick with side-by-side speak for now otherwise this will all get needlessly complicated. If you are holding O/U barrels just turn them on their side and think laterally. The key places to look for rust are along the length of the ribs and around the fiddly bits at the thick end. If the gun has been neglected during its life then the chances are that this is where you will find the evidence. Look for any deformity, roughness or signs of abrasion. Look for gaps. Run a fingernail along and see if you feel any unevenness. Then wrap your hanky round the tubes and wipe it up and down several times slowly. Your fingers are immensely sensitive, you may be surprised to know, and you will be startled at how easy it is to detect odd bulges or dings, dents and bashes which are invisible to the naked eye. If you feel any it's bad news and you should abandon the trade. You can also hold the barrels up to the light and look at how the light reflects off the outside of the barrels. The light should reflect in a perfectly straight line. If it has ripples in it then you have a problem. You may see ripples or you may not, but either way it is a professional sort of thing to do and as we all know, in negotiations, looking as if you know what you are doing can hardly be disadvantageous.

On the flats of the barrels, underneath at the thick end, there should be a series of stamps and imprints. These are Proof Marks. Every gun sold in this country is required to undergo Proof. The gun is sent to either the London Proof House or the Birmingham Proof House, or in the case of imported guns an approved foreign Proof House, where the Proofmaster puts an unreasonably large shell through it, between one-and-a-half and two times what it might reasonably expect under normal circumstances. If the poor old gun survives the ordeal it is deemed to have passed proof and is duly stamped by the Proofmaster accordingly. Every gun, from the one you are holding at the moment to the immensely complex looking target rifle on the rack in the shop, every service rifle in the armed forces to the .50 calibre Magic Dragon on a helicopter gunship has been through proof and will bear the honourable scars to show for it. The stamps are many and various and form an interesting hobby for those who are interested in researching such things. What concerns us, and what should concern you, is that there are some stamps on the piece you are contemplating. Not, unfortunately, that the stamps themselves are any guarantee of soundness. With age and use, and abuse, barrels progressively wear out getting thinner and thinner until they are deemed 'out of proof' at which point they must be replaced. The wearing out process can, of course, be massively accelerated if some complete swine has taken barrels full of rust and dings and bashes and filth and simply shoved some emery paper down the tube and riddled it all out leaving a nice shiny inside with a wafer thin metal wall round it that will blow up at any time. No reputable gunsmith or gun dealer would dream of doing such a thing, of course; but at auctions, for example, it is possible to find guns of impeccable shininess which look as if they have never had a shot through them, that some dodgy dealer has scrubbed up for the purpose of duping the unwary. The auction houses are pretty good at spotting these and marking them 'Barrel walls marginal' which means they might blow at any minute, but the system is not perfect and when it is your hand gripping the barrels in question the phrase 'Caveat emptor' rings out loud and clear. For a beginner the best advice has to be to make a friend of your local gunsmith who has a reputation and a business to protect and then take a knowledgeable friend along with you.

Finally there is another helpful test. Back at the fat end of the barrels there are two metal projections. The more forward of these is the Hook, usefully shaped like a hook, and the rear one is the Rear Lump. Both play important roles in holding the whole shebang together, but for our purposes we want to dangle the barrels from the tip of a forefinger and flick each barrel with a fingernail, or a biro, or whatever, somewhere near the muzzles. A sound barrel will ring like a church bell, and the better the barrel the purer the sound will be. An imperfect barrel gives off a dull thud. Like all these tests, it is not perfect, but it is reassuring and when a lot of chaps are sitting about of an evening cleaning guns after a day's shooting they can dong away quite tunefully. Small pleasures.

A gun might have had its barrels sleeved. When the word 'Sleeved' appears on the flats for instance. This is a legitimate and reasonable process, but not one that should be either disguised or denied by the seller. Indeed a sleeved gun must be marked 'Sleeved' when the new sleeves are sent for proof as already described. Sleeving is where the bulk of a worn out barrel, from the chamber out, is cut off and discarded and replaced with a new tube which is tapered into the existing residual lump. It is, as I say, a reasonable and cost effective way of prolonging the life of a good gun, but a sleeved gun is not original and must not be represented as such. On close examination you should also be able to see the line of the cut about a hand's width from the breech where the new tubes have been attached.

And now we turn to the inside of the tubes. Shiny as anything, of course. No trace of rust or pitting left by rust, just clean, shiny metal. Basically, you and I just can't tell a thing from looking down the inside of a barrel. If there is a lot of rust and pitting and cobwebs and old bits of chewing gum and putty; or a cartridge stuck up it, we might think we are in the wrong sort of shop; but otherwise we are not expert enough to be out by ourselves.

What you should know and understand about the inside of the barrels is that they are not straight. Not meant to be; never intended to be. That is why you can put cartridges in one end without them falling out the other, which makes sense upon a modest degree of consideration. However it is more complicated than that. Now this may cause some eyebrow raising and it is a much debated and often heatedly debated issue, so it is as well to be equipped for it when it comes up. Choke.

Choke is the degree by which the thin end, the muzzles, are constricted relative to the fat end of the barrels, the breech. Got it? Now why does this make any difference? Back, I'm afraid to the physics thing again. Shot from a shotgun, as it's flying along at N yards per second, starts its journey as a tightly knit band of pellets just as they were packed in the cartridge. The moment at which they leave the cartridge case their little lives begin to change radically. As they leave the muzzle of the barrel the ones in the front are confronted by the resistance of the air and they begin to deform and slow down as a consequence. As they begin to slow and to veer off the straight and narrow where you were aiming, they are replaced by the next rank to whom the same things begin to happen. And so forth and so following. Until by the time the whole crowd have gone a bit of a way – let us say, for the sake of argument, forty yards – they have become a very confused bundle of pellets indeed, with some going faster or slower and some veering off hither and yon about the place. This is the 'pattern' or 'spread' and it is most frequently represented in books and instructional texts as being a circle about thirty inches wide at or about forty yards. It isn't. It is actually like a piece of weasel shit, pointy at the front where the latest rank of enthusiastic speedsters are zooming ahead of the gang, fat in the middle where the early leaders are taking a well earned, if slightly erratic break, and pointy again at the back, where the last of the reserves are still benefiting from the slipstream of those who have gone before. The whole buzzing horde being about ten feet long and two feet across its widest part and, depending on how fast and in which direction you were swinging at the time, flying spread out slightly on the skew.

Imagine, if you will, a hosepipe. You put your thumb over the end for a moment, take careful aim at the fly on the wall or the cat, and then release a burst of water. Does it end up in a neat puddle? It does not. It ends up as a stripe smeared across the wall or the cat or whatever at a bit of an angle. This is shot string. The reason shotgun patterns always look round and neatly within a circle at forty yards is because those wishing to demonstrate them have tended to take careful aim at a fixed point in the middle of a circle. As a result the pointy end of the shotstring duly arrives at the point aimed at and the fat middle and pointy back end catch up in due course – all neatly within the prescribed circle.

Sportsmen, such as you and I, are not supposed to shoot sitting targets so it is as well if we get a clear picture of what we are dealing with here. End of physics; for the time being.

The effect of choke on all this is that the more constrained the pellets are at the start of their journey, the longer they take to spread out and the more effective they are when they arrive in the vicinity of a pheasant, or as it might be, a grouse. Tight choke, Full Choke, the narrowest opening you can apply to a shotgun barrel without the force of the shot peeling it open like a banana as it passes through, means more effectiveness at longer range. Great. Let's shoot for the stars. It also means that you are trying to hit something at half that distance with a swarm of pellets about the size of a tennis ball. Not so happy. The least choke that can be applied is True Cylinder, which is no choke at all; beyond which you are holding a Blunderbuss, which is deemed unsporting. In between are Improved Cylinder, ¼ Choke; ½ Choke; ¾ Choke; all of which effectively explain themselves. The question all this begs, then, is at what range are we going to be using this gun and what choke should we apply? Consider this: most shooting in this country, game or clay targets, tends to happen between twenty yards and thirty yards. Probably less. There are spectacular shoots where game is presented between forty yards and fifty yards; and those who go there go specially equipped for the purpose. There are hundred foot towers at shooting schools from which clay targets are scarcely visible, that's thirty-three yards near enough. Most trees in our countryside are no more that fifteen yards tall and a partridge over a hedge is nearer ten yards than twenty. I have no wish to be dogmatic about this, and since many modern sporting guns have interchangeable chokes that can be screwed into the muzzles in any case, as quarry and circumstances dictate, the point is probably moot anyway. In case it is not, and if you happen to be contemplating a sporting gun of a certain age, I will for the record recommend Improved Cylinder in the first barrel and ½ Choke in the second. Or what you will.

It is an irony which I never tire of pointing out that, as a matter of fact, having an open first barrel and a tighter second is really only appropriate for shooting where your quarry is going away, as it might be in walked up shooting. Since many sportsmen today confine themselves to driven shooting, where the game in question flies towards them, getting closer as it comes, they really should have a tight first barrel for effectiveness at longer range and a more open second barrel for the later, nearer shot. This would put paid to those embarrassing moments when with first shot of a drive at a decent bird at a decent range the poor creature is merely tickled with the open barrel, and presses, flittering, onward towards the shooter in question, who proceeds to casserole it entirely, plucked, drawn and minced, with the tighter tube directly over his head. I've argued the toss with shooters about this for years and got nothing but blank stares for my efforts. But there you go. We're a conservative bunch.

As a matter of fact, if you look at the muzzles carefully, and you should, you can see quite clearly that there is more metal surrounding one barrel (the right one as you are looking at it now) than the other. In fact they should both have a reassuring depth of metal, and if they don't, leave at once; but in most cases one should be discernibly fatter than the other. That's choke, that is.

Finally, concerning the barrels – ejectors. These are the spring-loaded elements of the chamber rims at the breech end. They are activated by the firing of the gun and flip out the spent cartridge cases as the gun is opened after a shot. Very few modern guns, and relatively few older guns, are without them and they make life a good deal easier for the shooter all round. However they can be problematical and it is important that they work firmly and effectively. You can live without ejectors, but if you have them, they had better be in sound working order. They should move freely on the unattached barrels and they should be smooth edged and free of chips or cuts. As should the rest of the surrounding rim of the breeches. A word of warning; cartridge manufacture has, as has been said, improved in leaps and bounds over the past several decades. One manifestation of this has been that the brass heads of cartridges can be milled to much finer tolerances than once they were. The brass is thinner. This represents a significant manufacturing cost saving for cartridge makers who can be more competitive in their pricing towards the rest of us, which is a good thing; on the whole. The downside however is that if the rim of the breech of an older gun is worn down, a modern cartridge may drop down a couple of microns too far into the breech to be effectively struck by the firing pin from behind, resulting in a misfire, or more particularly a no-fire, which in any given day of limited opportunities, is incredibly irritating and, as importantly, largely unmendable. I have a gun, an old and trusted piece built in the 1890s, which suffers from just such a problem. I discovered it when I changed from ammunition which I regularly used, to a new and improved version. The new and improved version was milled to a narrower tolerance than the previous choice, and while it worked very handsomely when it went off, more often than not it failed to do so. I persevered for a while and eventually threw myself on the mercy of my local friendly gunsmith, suspecting that the firing pin was at fault in not striking the shell hard enough. After much examination and experimentation with different pins and cartridges, the good man identified the problem which I have since resolved by using a less advanced manufacturer's ammunition for the time being. I fear for the future though, because in the competitive ammunition market, my supplier will eventually have to catch on to the cost savings of finer milling or go under. Either way I, and my old gun, will be bereft of ammo, which will be a great shame. So take a long hard look at the ejectors on older guns. You should try before you buy in any case.

A last general comment on barrels. If you are looking at older guns within some budgetary constraints, you may very well be offered a gun with what are described as Damascus barrels. These are readily identifiable, other than in exceptional cases, by the fact that they are brown as opposed to the more normal black. They are for the most part extremely old, mostly pre-1900, pre-dating as they

Full Choke
The Casserole Effect

do the time when it became possible accurately and reliably to drill a straight hole through a solid steel tube. Damascus steel was, originally, horseshoe nails (horsemen, quite rightly, insisting on the best metal available for such a key component and being rich to boot) which was then reforged and tempered and hammered into strips. The strips were then hammered into ribbons and two, three or more ribbons were spiralled around a mandrel, being a stick of approved straightness, soldered along the seam and the ends nipped off to make a tube. The tube was then bathed in an acid mixture which gives the metal its brown hue and defines the distinct 'weave' of the layered metal which is the Damascus effect. The history and science of Damascus steel-making is examined in a number of learned tomes and the detail, fascinating and remarkable though it is, need not concern us here. However, what should concern us here is that Damascus barrelled guns should by no means be pooh-poohed by the modern shooter. Damascus steel is certainly as strong, and thought by many to be stronger, than more modern steel and, in any event, all Damascus barrels must be proofed just as new guns are. There is an element of fashion and snobbery at work here too. Around 1900 when the new 'Fluid' steel was being introduced, discriminating buyers naturally wanted the coming thing rather than the old and fusty Damascus and being easier and cheaper to manufacture the new black barrels took over the market in short order. RIP Damascus. And yet the Damascus barrels represent, if anything, a higher and more dedicated level of craftsmanship than their more modern counterparts being the last truly hand-made guns and quite beautiful to contemplate. There are probably no more than a handful of smiths alive today who could make a pair of Damascus tubes and, if they did or could, the cost has been estimated at anything up to US$100,000 per tube. Since they are generally attached to very elderly guns indeed and are beneath consideration by many modern shooters, Damascus can offer exceptional value to today's buyer and should not be overlooked. Of course, as any fool can see, I'm acutely partial to them myself. I have used a pair of Damascus barrelled sixteen bore sidelock ejectors (all terms you should understand by now) made in the 1890s in Birmingham for the past decade at every sort of game and wouldn't swap them for less than a whole lot.

Let's take a look at the other end.

The Stock and Action

What you are now holding in your hand should be the stock and action of the gun you are casting a beady buyer's eye over. Probably you are gripping it by the hand which is the narrowest part and the obvious place to hold it. If it is a side-by-side gun, then the chances are that it will have a straight hand, which is to say that the hand has no projection and the stock can be broadly described as triangular. If you are holding an O/U then the likelihood is that the hand has a more or less pronounced grip emerging from it, which may be bigger or smaller according to taste. This will be a degree of pistol grip. The most extreme version of the pistol grip is the Monte Carlo, which extends almost vertically downwards behind the trigger guard and was developed specifically for live pigeon shooting in, no surprises, Monte Carlo. Less extreme is the full pistol grip, followed by the half pistol, the Prince of Wales (no surprise who made this fashionable, again) which is a half pistol grip with the rounded end shaved flat – and a startlingly good grip too, as a matter of fact – and finally the straight hand. As usual the exceptions prove the rule and O/Us do come with straight hands and side-by-sides do come with pistol grips, though more than a half pistol would be exceptional. Why the variations in grip? Control and elegance. There is, I think, no doubt that an extended grip, up to half pistol, does add a degree of control to the shooter's use of the gun. And with control comes accuracy in the final analysis. Small wonder then that competition target shooters, for whom the last degree of accuracy on every shot makes crucial differences between winning and losing, would not be without their half and full pistol grips. Equally there is no doubt that the line of a straight handed side-by-side gun is exquisitely elegant, while the Prince of Wales grip attached to a top flight game gun of either conformation is unquestionably a thing of beauty too. Given a free choice, I'd go PoW and that's not just because I'm a die-hard fashion victim who'd rather have been Edwardian. I actually think it works. Turning to the action, be it boxlock or sidelock, there is not a lot we can tell just by looking at it, but if you think for a moment I'm taking one apart you have got another think coming. There was a fad, for which I duly fell, a few years ago for putting a sort of wing-nut affair on the actions of fine sidelocks. Well, a wing-nut is irresistible to a gun-nut and I duly unscrewed it; whereupon any number of cogs and springs leapt out all over the table and refused point blank – as springs and cogs will – to return whence they came. In the end I had to take the whole gun and a matchbox of bits back to the gunsmith and ask him to put it back together, which he happily and expensively did. I'm not falling for that again. What you can look at is the face of the action, which is the broad vertical face which rests against the back of the cartridges when the gun is shut. It should have two holes in which the ends of the firing pins will be visible. In older guns without automatically retracting firing pins they may even be protruding. This face should be smooth. As guns get older it is this face which sees the brunt of things and signs of wear will be obvious. Some marking is permissible but neither the face nor the flats below it have any excuse for extensive pitting or scratches which are signs of neglect at some time or other. A new gun should be pristine. The top lever is sprung and should be tense but not stiff and the same goes for the safety catch just behind it.

The sides of the action may be silver (silver finish) or a sort of blue-brown tint (case hardened). The former is *au naturel* while the latter has been heat treated to bring out the colours in the metal. There is nothing to choose between the two; it's an aesthetic thing.

The action is also likely to be engraved and about this there may a very great deal to consider indeed. Very expensive, or very old, guns have engraving which is done by hand. A bloke with a tiny chisel has spent many hours, more or less depending on complexity and cost, carving away to achieve the look of the engraved action. At the highest level the engraving of guns which is possible today is beyond belief, with inlays of precious metals, portraiture and scenery which leaves the onlooker breathless with admiration. Sometimes the engraving alone can take months and cost several times the price of the gun it is executed upon. Check out the books on engraving and engravers and let your mind run riot.

Meanwhile back in the gun shop we are contemplating a much less expensive version of engraving which may either have been stamped or stencilled or most recently etched with a computer-guided laser. Not that there is anything wrong with any method really, but as a buyer you should not be diverted from the essential function of the gun by the prettiness of its engraving, nor should you think that apparently elaborate engraving, essentially executed by a machine, makes a gun more valuable or efficient than its plainer cousin.

More to the point is the wood of the stock itself. I freely admit to being a complete sucker for pretty wood and can forgive a gun almost any sin if it is backed up by a really handsome stock. Good wood is not cheap however. A decent walnut blank will be four figures, and a matched pair a serious premium over that. Another rule is that no one wastes good wood on cheap guns. However, again in the second hand market, it is not uncommon to find a really old gun, once of good quality, now seriously clapped out, with a very handsome stock indeed – which some rogue has polished conker bright – to distract the unwary from the poorness of the rest of the gun and the fragility of its action. So focus on the essentials and disregard the trappings; lashed up guns are like supermodels, they look astonishing and cost the earth but when you get them home they don't work in the way you hoped they would and some of them don't work at all. We've been over the fore-end already, but it is always worth checking that its wood matches the stock and that its serial number matches both the barrels and the stock. The serial number will be behind the trigger guard on the stock, on the flats of the barrels or possibly the underside rib and on the flat side of the fore-end. It's a simple thing to check they are all the same. As novice buyers we have little enough going for us. If we can point out to the dealer that the numbers on this very smart gun he is trying to flog don't match, that will put him on the back foot for once during the conversation.

Now put the three parts together. Hold it by the hand and give it a damn good rattle. There should be no play in the gun whatsoever, and if there is, this is where you feel it. Open and close the gun a few times. It should open and close easily but not sloppily. New guns tend to tightness, naturally, but they should be firm and crisp rather than stiff. And they should certainly not 'Loosen up after a few rounds'. This sort of comment is bad news. Sleeves do not ride up with wear, supermodels do not develop a passion for ironing and guns do not loosen up with a few shots. In a new gun, in my view, stiffness is as inexcusable as looseness is in an old one. A gun either works as it is expected to, or not. Try putting a cigarette paper on the face of the breech and closing the gun. It should not shut. A good gun will shear a hair across the breech and a very good gun, as it closes, will smudge the soot left on the face of the breech by a passing oil lamp. Look closely and hard at the wood to metal fit around the action. Are there unevennesses? It is proud? Are there chips where the action has been forced into the wood? Is the chequering under your hand crisp and even or sharp and jagged where a machine's tooth has been at work or worn smooth with age and use?

Do you trust the seller?

Then put the gun back on the counter or the baize or the case and stand well back and take a good long, hard look at it. This is the crunch point. Shiny metal, drop dead wood, easy price. But does it speak to you? Even hardened competition shooters have a favourite gun. We are not talking about obsessive polishing and unseemly attraction here. Guns are not she's, as yachts and vintage Bentleys are, but, for all that, to the sportsman a shotgun is the tool that is going to be with him in the field for seasons to come, good days and bad, ready and reliable. With luck you will enjoy some astonishing highlights in its company, literally some of the happiest days of your life. And so the question is not a fanciful one. Does it speak to you? Get your cheque book out then. And don't put it away yet either.

The Gun Case

If you thought that you had spent quite enough money already, think again. There is a way to go yet. The gun, your new best friend, may have come with a case. Perhaps a handsome leather case with snappy brass corners and a shiny lock, with a key even. Or it may have a more modest canvas covered affair, stained with the oil and dust of many a day out. Then again, it may not. And a travelling case is definitely something you need. In these days of mistrust and suspicion a travelling case can act as a deterrent in and of itself, and it can disguise the nature of its contents. For all the rest of the world knows you may be a peripatetic clarinetist as you board the train or taxi.

Policemen too have been known to criticise shooters who leave obvious looking weaponry visible in cars and elsewhere. And anyway, it is always easier when transporting guns to know that they are safe from accidental knocks, from being sat on by the dog, or the kid, or having your partner's weekend case dumped unceremoniously on them in the boot of the car with disastrous effects.

So a carrying case, or as it used to be called, a motoring case is a necessity. In fact, if your gun comes without one, it is something of a boon in many ways since you are in a position to choose the type and style that suits your needs. The finest oak and lizard skin version may appeal but will set you back £1,000. Antique hide cases are charming, but unless they lock properly, are less than ideal.

Airlines, for example, who make you jump through any number of hoops these days to take your gun on a short domestic flight, will turn you down flat without a working lock on your case. So my advice, for what it's worth, is to buy one of the thoroughly modern aluminium box cases lined with foam, with a stout hasp or two on the front wherein you can stick a padlock when the need arises. Padlocks are better than integral locks because when you lose the key – as you will – you can simply replace the padlock without rendering the whole, and quite expensive at £130 odd, case redundant. You won't even feel so bad as you jemmy off the padlock on a shooting morning having left the crucial key at home. I am advised, however, by friends, that some foam paddings can give off gaseous emissions which can affect the colouring of barrels and actions. Their advice is to wrap the gun in cloth while it is in the case.

Next up is a slip or sleeve. This is a lightweight full length cover for the gun for use when carrying your piece from drive to drive or stand to stand during a shooting day and which offers modest protection from occasional knocks or the weather. Again the sheepskin lined, harness leather covered option is at the top end and the fake fur and nylon version is at the bottom of the scale. Whichever end you choose, a shoulder strap is a must, and speaking entirely personally I am mistrustful of zips, preferring a stout buckle to retain the piece within. Each to his own however.

Cleaning Kit

Then there is the cleaning kit. Old cases generally contain the remnants of a cleaning kit, usually much abused and reeking of gun oil. Cleaning kits should consist of a rod in two or three pieces which screw together with three interchangeable heads – a woolly for oiling, a jag for the attachment of cloth or folded kitchen roll for rinsing and a phosphor bronze stiff brush for vigorous scrubbing of lead and powder remnants in the barrels. You will also need some oil. Any light oil will do the trick as far as lubricating and protecting the metal of your gun is concerned, but there are any number of specialist brands available in gunshops which purport to be perfect and you might as well have one, if only to stop the rest of the family nicking yours to oil their bikes or pram wheels or drills or whatever. Whether these accoutrements come in a handsome rosewood box or a carrier bag is a matter entirely for you.

While on the subject of cleaning kit, it is worth mentioning that as with cartridges, cleaning technology has also emerged blinking from the dark and into the twenty-first century. In the olden days of black powder and clouds of smoke, gun cleaning involved the pouring of many kettlefuls of boiling water down the tubes and then scrubbing away for hours with any number of arcane and outlandish potions and brews before the job could be described as almost done. Mercifully this is no longer necessary since modern powders and propellants almost certainly leave the gun cleaner after firing than before. However, as with any sophisticated tool, a gun needs proper care in order to stay in tip-top working condition and the ritual clean after a shoot should be considered part and parcel of the day. I always insist on cleaning my own guns, even when some helpful soul offers to do it for me, not so much because I don't trust them with my belongings, as because somewhere in my Protestant soul, I feel that after my gun has performed for me all day, I am obliged to see to its well-being myself and not to deliver it into the hands of strangers. Having said which, over and above the essential cleaning kit described, there are any number of gadgets and gismos which have been developed to make the whole undertaking a complete and speedy doddle.

Principal among these is a sort of full length woolly rod affair, apparently impregnated with all things good, which requires no more than a brisk rodding up each tube to leave the interior spotless and sparkling. I'm no mathematician, but even I can see that rodding with a full length thirty inch mop is ten times better than rodding with a three inch mop on a twenty-seven inch rod. Makes sense, right? So while I am not wholly convinced about the cocktail of goodness contained therein, I rod away very happily with my fluorescent mop like mad, and save an immense amount of time and kitchen roll into the bargain. I am also keen on aerosol cleaners and oils; not least because it is a much easier way of coating all areas of the gun, and me, and the study, with a fine coating of oil or whatever, than any amount of wiping over with rags. I am also a great collector of those little bags of silica that fall out of boxes of computer peripherals or the toaster or the new wireless. They absorb moisture and I heave them immediately into the gunsafe where, I hope, they do battle with non existent humidity and deter rust in the long intervals between outings.

After a wet day I lay the gun on newspaper on my desk for at least a couple of hours before embarking on any kind of cleaning. There are water repellent sprays available too and a sound dousing with one of those seems sensible to me. I don't think putting the gun in the airing cupboard is a good idea and any form of direct heat – leaning against a radiator perhaps – is a definite no-no.

And Finally...

And before you finally get that cheque book back in your pocket, you will require some cartridges and something to carry them in. Opinions vary as to how cartridges should be carried, from 'Your sporran.' on the one hand to 'By the butler.' on the other. On one point however all commentators are agreed – the carrier bag gets no votes. Not that it isn't useful for carting about the empties after the drive; but for all round convenience and style – nil-points.

Accordingly a bag or belt is called for. Which, and what style, will depend very much on the type of shooting you are likely to undertake; and like so much else on this adventure upon which you are now embarked, you will collect and accumulate any number of varieties as you plough your own particular furrow. Be that as it may, you need something this morning and as a bare minimum a fifty round bag is a must. Belts come in twenty-fives, but a belt does not always suit everyone, and everyone needs a few shells about them and a bag of fifty, whether it is full or not, is as convenient a way as carrying cartridges as any. As with everything else thus far, it does not need to be of crocodile hide. Waterproof canvas is fine. So add it to the pile.

And a pair of earplugs, or muffs. No one used to use them. Now they are all deaf. Now everyone who has any hearing and half a brain uses them. QED.

Now we can go home. There is plenty more shopping to do later, but for the time being you have the essentials. It is time to go and do some shooting rather than all this faffing about.

But, but, but … you must be wondering if this is ever going to get to a point where you will ever get to letting this thing off. You will. Soon. Promise. But there is one last stage before this gun is finally yours as opposed to off the shelf or someone else's old one. Fitting.

4

FITTING

Terribly dull. Terribly important. Such is the excitement at having bought a gun and now being part of the whole 'Shootin' thang' that many, most even, shooters forthwith hie themselves into the field with their shiny new toy and start blazing away like mad. They don't hit very much to be sure, but – hey! – they are beginners with a new gun and doubtless it will all come together in good time. Huge, huge mistake. Costly and depressing.

You may think as you look in the mirror of a morning over the toothbrush or the razor or the fizzing restorative that your face is pretty good, all things considered. Couple of eyes, bit gooey but functional for all that, nose more or less in the middle, mouth, chin – still single-ish, cheekbones still visible; this sort of thing. And it is. It's wonderful. It's lovely.

It is also unique and its relationship with your shoulders and hands and arms is unique also. The way you hold your new gun between all of these parts is peculiar to you. How peculiar can be worked out in short order by someone who knows what he is about and the whole combination can be customised in order that your uniqueness can be reflected in your gun such that when you lift into the aim, or mount it as we experts call it to nick a term off the horsey people, the whole shebang comes together in a comfortable and consistent way that ends up pointing in the direction you want.

To the shooting school then for the nonce.

Somewhere off to the side of all the more exciting stands, the Bouncy Bunny or the Springing Teal or whatever are a row of very dull tin plates. Mounted on posts these are in the order of ten feet square and uniformly grey. They may have a miniature metal duck, much mangled, dangling from a chain nailed into the top, such that the duck, or whatever, hangs about the middle of the plate. These are pattern plates and the idea is to see if you can hit them. A ten foot plate at twenty yards? I should cocoa. You'd be surprised.

It is important when organising this phase of operations to make it quite clear what it is you are about. Most shooting schools have a pattern plate, but most schools only have one or a couple of instructors who are really expert in fitting, who will be no help if they are instructing elsewhere, and it is important to have one of them on hand to supervise this procedure, because it is going to make the difference between you being a dynamite shot or a nice chap but a bit of a duffer.

The procedure is as follows: you, the instructor and his assistant (the Lad – for all he's a million and two) take your new gun across to the bench some fifteen or twenty paces from the plate. The instructor may also be carrying a very strange gun indeed, which looks like a cross between a droid, a technical drawing and a surgical mishap. It is clearly a gun, because it has barrels, but for the rest it is made up of screws and plates and wing-nuts and bolts and is contorted like it has just escaped from the Inquisition. It is a Try-Gun and it is a 'One Size Fits All' confection that has been at the school since the Ark and can be configured to fit the Hunchback of Notre Dame. It probably was.

The first step is that the instructor takes a look at your new gun. There is much lip pursing and eyebrow raising. Don't worry about this. It means nothing. This is the instructor raising the stakes a bit. What you have bought is a perfectly sound, perfectly ordinary gun; but if he doesn't lip purse and eyebrow raise, how can he convince you that he is about to perform some sort of magic? He has a fee to earn, after all.

Then he looks at you and does a deal more frowning and pursing. If you have ever encountered a bespoke tailor, or a personal fitness trainer, you will be all too familiar with the charade. Ultimately the conclusion is reached – 'Well, I think we may be able to do something.' Forget it. You're normal.

The instructor then takes your gun and opens it and displays the empty chambers to all and sundry as if about to produce a rabbit. This is very important because what follows IS THE ONLY CIRCUMSTANCE WHEN YOU WILL EVER BE INVITED OR PERMITTED TO POINT YOUR GUN AT ANYBODY, EVER. IS THAT CLEAR?

He will then close your gun, pass it to you and invite you to point it straight between his eyes from a distance of about five feet. Mount and aim. Mount and aim. And again. Mount and aim. MmmmHmm. Once more. Mount and aim. Very good.

What the instructor is seeking is to identify how your eyes and face and hands and arms combine to give you the impression of aiming where you are looking. Most shotgun shooters shoot with both eyes open. It is standard practice and completely normal. Both eyes open gives you stereoscopic vision, a slightly different perception from each eye which are combined in the brain to give you depth and distance, and allow you to gauge range and angle and to calculate lead. Rifle shooters live in two dimensions and therefore require only one eye. Shotgun shooters live in three dimensions and use both. However, it is generally the case that one eye is marginally stronger than the other. This is the Master Eye. It usually follows handedness. A right handed person will have a right master eye, and a left handed one, left. In either case there is an inclination to push the gun, and therefore the shot, in that direction. If you are aiming at the bridge of the instructor's nose, or think you are, and he can see that, in fact, you are about to shoot his earlobe off, he can tell by what degree the gun needs to be altered to compensate for this misapprehension. A quick guide round the stock of your gun: the hand we know, it's where you hold it. From the rise above and behind the hand to the back of the stock is the comb, which ends with the heel or bump and at the bottom end of the face of the butt, is the toe. Just so you know. The comb is important because its height, or lack of it, determines at what angle your head is held when you are trying to get your master eye more or less behind the barrels. If the comb is too high, your head is so bent over that your ear is on the stock and your eyes almost one above the other which gives you a very strange sight picture indeed, and incidentally every time you pull the trigger the comb will belt you on the cheekbone; which hurts. Too low and the comb will end up under your chin, as opposed to nestling against your cheek, which will again corrupt the sight picture on the one hand, and belt you on the jaw every shot, on the other. In short, without proper fitting, you can expect to be beaten soundly by your gun every time you go out and only to hit things more by luck than judgement. Fitting is key. Fitting really works. It's about the cheapest part of the whole rigmarole thus far, and by miles the best value. And yet, many, many folk don't do it, and muddle on and wonder why they can never hit the ones on the right or whatever. If you muddle on, it is the case that you and your gun may, at some point, eventually, reach some sort of compromise whereby you contort your head and neck in such a way as to almost get one eye along the barrels, most of the time, and the gun doesn't bite you every shot. You may even, from time to time, hit something. You will certainly have a good side and a bad side and you won't even know why. You sad person.

I know you are sceptical about all this. A gun is a machine, not a Balenciaga ballgown, after all. Guns don't bite or have minds of their own, or resist the will of their owner in this cavalier way. Check it out. Now we will try a few shots against the plate.

The Lad takes a bucket of wash and diligently paints the plate. You are now actually going to get to shoot your new gun. Whoopee! The instructor pops a pair of shells into the gun and instructs you,

Inherited guns may need some adjustment

starting from a relaxed position, to mount and fire at the dangling duck. BLAM! And as the smoke clears there is a clear spattering of pellet marks bottom right, or as it might be, top left of the duck. 'And again, please.' And another spattering appears superimposed on the first.

Interesting at this point to compare the two patterns. If you are choked, as we have discussed, say Improved Cylinder in your first barrel and Half Choke in your second, then at fifteen yards you should be putting your first round within a twenty inch circle, and your second within sixteen inches. If, for example, your second shot has just hit the plate like a fist leaving a pattern you can cover with a spread hand, you should get the chokes checked also while you are here.

'Sheer fluke,' you announce loudly. Maybe, maybe not. Over the next few minutes you will fire off perhaps a box of shells, aiming at the dangly duck or perhaps aiming off a little here and there with the result that you blat the duck firmly in the bonce. The instructor may adjust the positioning of the stock in your shoulder and may move your head and hands about. This is his magic. It is not for us to know all the ins and outs. He may ask you to shoot a couple of rounds with the try-gun to confirm his judgement. And at some point he will pronounce himself satisfied and you can all retire to the office. At which juncture he will write down your measurements on a card and hand it to you. This is like a medical certificate and should be stored safely along with your passport and marriage licences, Shotgun Certificate and other such precious things.

Now it should be, or have been, the case that the fitting treatment was part of the deal with the gun-dealer. Perhaps I should have mentioned this before. Still, too late now. Not the consultation you understand, that is for your account; but any subsequent adjustments. So now what happens is that either you leave the gun with the instructor so that the school smith can have a lash at it, or you take it back to the dealer who delivers it to his tame smith to work on. Either way you have to part with your new best beloved for another week or two; but it is worth it. Really. Really. Really.

What the smith does with it is also arcane and mysterious, but interesting for all that. As far as I can work it out, the stock, sans barrels and fore-end is clamped in a vice with many and various grips and is then held in the steam from a conveniently sited kettle while being massaged by the smith with warm oils and unguents and who meanwhile also tightens up the screws from various angles to bend the wood to his will and your bizarre measurements.

He may bend it laterally ('cast on' – veering right for the left shouldered shooter and 'cast off' – veering left for the right handed shooter. Same as cricket if you are interested). He may bend it up and down, raising or lowering the comb. If you are completely skew eyed he may even bend it into a Cross-Eyed Stock which starts from one shoulder and warps across your face to the opposite eye, which is extreme, unusual and expensive. He may lop a bit off the back to shorten it, or glue a bit on to lengthen it. He should not have to do this because length is the easiest thing to get right in the first place and your dealer should not sell you a gun that is manifestly too long or too short. Inherited guns though may need a spot of variation in length.

Finally he gives the whole thing a bit of a polish with some linseed oil and sends it home to you. It is worth checking the measurements, yours and the gun's, from time to time over the years. Yours will certainly change as age and lunch and whisky take their inevitable toll. The gun too might change. Central heating can cause a gun to 'spring' its cast. As can damp and cold. Consider this: you shoot all day in sleet and drizzle; you put the gun in the boot of the car without a heater and drive home at such speed that the wind-chill in the boot is –30º C; you then remove it and lean it, in a damp sleeve – you uncaring bastard – against the radiator in the hall while you have a bath and a stiff drink to unwind. What would you do in the poor gun's place faced with such callous neglect? The least it can do is unwind a bit too.

Now we really can go shooting.

5

GETTING STARTED

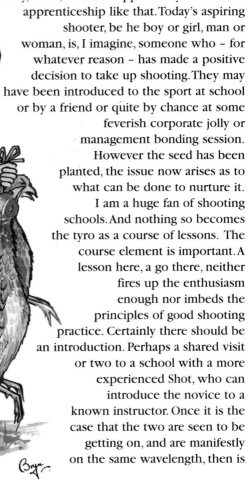

I have thought long and hard about this. There may still be a lucky few who are sent off, at a tender age, to follow the keeper and learn all the woodland ways and who cut their teeth potting pigeons and rabbits with a .410 and spend their winters in the beating line before finally being unleashed on the Boxing Day Boys' Shoot or standing beside a proud parent or an obliging godfather until their own invitations begin slipping onto the mat. Very few shooters today, I fear, have the opportunity to serve an apprenticeship like that. Today's aspiring shooter, be he boy or girl, man or woman, is, I imagine, someone who – for whatever reason – has made a positive decision to take up shooting. They may have been introduced to the sport at school or by a friend or quite by chance at some feverish corporate jolly or management bonding session. However the seed has been planted, the issue now arises as to what can be done to nurture it. I am a huge fan of shooting schools. And nothing so becomes the tyro as a course of lessons. The course element is important. A lesson here, a go there, neither fires up the enthusiasm enough nor imbeds the principles of good shooting practice. Certainly there should be an introduction. Perhaps a shared visit or two to a school with a more experienced Shot, who can introduce the novice to a known instructor. Once it is the case that the two are seen to be getting on, and are manifestly on the same wavelength, then is the time to book up a course of instruction, specifically with that instructor, designed not only to instil safety and accuracy – in that order please note – but also to consider the wider aspects of formal shooting, gunhandling and indeed to establish the most suitable type of gun for the novice to be thinking about buying.

I have travelled to shooting schools up and down the country. I haven't been to all of them by any means, but I have visited a good many and tried most of them. I have jollied and junketed and management bonded with the best of them and I have shot clays of all descriptions and variations. I have shot ZZ clays and Olympic Trench. I have shot everything from a tin can off a wall with a flintlock to a remote controlled aeroplane with a blunderbuss via psychedelic coloured exploding clays with tracer under floodlights. And I have never yet encountered an instructor who couldn't teach me something. Not necessarily something especially useful; or even something to do with my shooting; but always something.

The key to instructors is to find one you like, and trust, and stick with him, or her. I have had the good fortune to have enjoyed the services of several outstanding coaches in my career, all of whom I fell in with quite by accident and who taught me a great deal about how to shoot and shoot well, for which I am properly and profoundly grateful. Most are now retired but I still return on a regular basis to someone nonetheless to have my swing titivated and my missing deconstructed. All have told me over the years that I am an idle Shot who does the minimum necessary to perform adequately and bluffs the rest of the way with occasional grandstanding performances and periodic outrageous flukes. Which is exactly what my first school report said several decades ago. Shooting as a blueprint for life, or what?

Having attended at shooting school for a period, the new shooter will have attained a reasonable level of competence. This is a fact. Uncoordinated, cack-handed and generally feckless he may be, but the instructor will make something of him, and if there is ambition there to shoot, then the instructor will build on that until the shooter is safe and competent. What then? How do you graduate to the field? Very simple. You either buy your way in; or you earn your way in. Is this too cynical?

Shooting as a rental industry, with days and individual and occasional rights available has really only developed over the last quarter century. While the Edwardians had converted shooting from a cottage industry into a mass production undertaking where tens of thousands of birds were reared annually for the delectation of a few very rich sportsmen it was not, on the whole a very profitable undertaking. If you count social success and hob-nobbing with kings and princes and maharajahs and the like successful, then shooting on the Edwardian scale could be deemed a success. If public applause for your skill, and ranking as one of the greatest Shots of your generation is success then Lord Walsingham hit the top in both classes. However, since the whole performance cost him his fortune, his home and the family wine cellar, nurtured and built up over generations and which the shooting elite demolished in a single season, then from a financial angle the whole thing was a bit of a pudding. And this was a time when labour was the cheapest part of the job and armies of keepers were responsible for preparing the ground for a season's shooting on a single estate. 'Up goes a guinea (£1.05p), bang goes a penny (½p), down comes half a crown (12½p).' as the saying goes. Today though it is more like 'Up goes £20, bang goes 12p, down comes 50p'. And this is not the expensive end of the market. Today, what used to be considered vermin shooting, pigeons and rabbits, is deemed attractive enough for the rights to undertake it over farmland to have considerable value and for paying customers to be 'guided' in its undertaking. The time when an occasional pint with the keeper and a bottle of whisky here and there would entitle a shooter to secure a place to wander and to practice are, I am afraid, no more, in our densely populated little island.

So you can buy your way into the shooting field. It's expensive, and only gets more so as you progress, but it's possible. On the other hand, it is not particularly simple and may not be especially agreeable.

Back to first principles for a second. Part of the pleasure of shooting comes, as it does in everything, from doing it well. The other part, some would say the main part, comes from doing it in the company of friends. And buying a day's shooting, off the shelf as it were, means that you will find yourself among strangers; and heavily armed strangers at that. It may turn out that your companions are universally charming, genial, sportsmanlike and safe. If this is the case, you are many times blessed, for you will have a cheerful and agreeable day and will leave with a brace of birds and several new friends. If there is one bad apple though, the chances are that you will have a miserable day and will leave with many illusions shattered and the sense of good money having been thrown down a capacious drain.

If you are very rich, the solution is simpler, you just pay for the whole shooting day, say £4,000 or £5,000 and take along the shooting friends of your choice and acquaintance. If you are known to be giving away such largesse, you will not be short of friends, I can assure you. At the moment at which you decide to do so, you will, unless you are a very exceptional and lucky sportsman indeed, and really superbly and humungously, don't give-a-toss rich and with all the sensitivity of a flying mallet, encounter the very issues with which your more experienced friends are currently beset. The first and principal among which is safety.

We haven't addressed this huge issue in any detail yet, and this is as good a point as any. It underlies and threads through everything to do with shooting. It is the be all and end all of the sport and it is what, as often as not, makes the difference between a lifetime of happiness in the sporting field and the Seventh Pit of Hell.

I have been flippant and superficial about all sorts of things to do with shooting and sport thus far, and I undoubtedly will be so again. But on this I am deadly serious. Shotguns are lethal. The damage inflicted by a shotgun on a bird or beast at thirty or forty yards is considerable and mostly fatal. The damage a gun can cause at anything less is massive and gruesome and invariably deadly. A charge from a shotgun at close range blows a hole the size of your fist in things. A shotgun blast will have your arm or leg off in a second or leave your middle spread over a field. An instructor friend of mine always introduces the novices he teaches to this fact with a simple and effective demonstration as part of their first lesson. He makes them shoot a gallon plastic drum filled with red stained water and rags from a distance of five paces. The effect is devastating, not least on the drum. The middle of the canister simply disappears. The fountain of red water and the satisfactorily visceral smear of soaked red rags extending some ten feet beyond the point of impact make a universally hefty impression upon the pupil. A shotgun at close range, and by close I mean anything up to twenty-five yards, gives no second chances. Ever. Never ever point a gun at anything you don't mean to kill. Dead.

OK. That was the gloomy bit. Now why is this such a problem when you are offering invitations to shoot? It is a problem because you have never shot with any of these folks before. They talk a good shoot and they purport to have been doing it for donkey's years and they seem to know what they are talking about; but push has now got to shove, and you are about to put them into a team which includes yourself. Suddenly the question of whether they are really any good at this sort of thing, and more particularly, are they really safe, and I mean, and you mean, in any and all circumstances, no holds barred, under pressure, massively excited and possibly after a very jolly lunch indeed, one hundred per cent, absolutely safe? Because if they aren't, a day's shooting with birds and beaters and keepers and dogs and boozy lunches is no place to find out. It bears repeating – there are no second chances.

And they, of course, are thinking exactly the same thing. To some extent it depends on who blinks first.

Quite apart from anything else, based on your very limited experience, actually no experience, how exactly should you feel about choosing a shoot to take them on in the first place and what if the whole thing turns out to be a complete frost with no birds, a miserable and disgusting lunch, surly staff and no rebate afterwards? The potential for costly mistakes, and not just in the wallet department, is huge; the downside spectacular; the prospect terrifying. There must be an easier way – there are several.

Earning Your Way In

As with all good things, they come to those who wait. With shooting you must be prepared to play the long game. Beating has always been and remains the longest and surest way in. The beaters are the folk who, on a day of driven game shooting, are employed to walk through the covers, be they woods, crops or heather and by virtue of tapping with their sticks, waving of their flags and occasional whistles, whoops and barks, generally so discommode the game, bird or beast, to the extent that it leaves off whatever it was doing in the cover and bolts for pastures new. Which pastures, all other things being equal and taking into account weather and wind conditions, time of day, position of the sun and so forth – beating is much, much more than maundering about with a stick, you see – will involve a trajectory over, past or by the Guns who are waiting in the distance. Sidling up to likely looking characters in the pub, accosting local farmers and so forth offering to make yourself available as a beater is all very well and good, but best of all is to ask your shooting friends, who are already on the shooting side of the fence, as it were, to ask the keepers of their acquaintance on your behalf, is better still. You will still have to buy the beer when introductions are eventually effected, but an effected entry is so much better than cold calling.

There are a number of good features about beating. First among these is that you get to see the most interesting end, if not the most glamorous, of the formal shooting day. And you get paid for it. Requirements are waxed jacket and leggings, boots and hat, gloves and stick. Qualifications are the ability to get to a meeting point at or about 9.00am on the shoot morning and blind obedience to the headkeeper all day. As a beginner blind obedience to everyone might be more accurate, but a general humility and recognition that you are the new-bug is the proper approach. Most of the beaters will be beaters because they like to get out on a shoot day and because beating is the next best thing to shooting and unless it is pouring with rain or bitterly cold – where in either case you are better off than the Guns anyway – it is terrific fun. Chances are you will be put in the care and control of a more experienced exponent, as it might be Dave, or Derek or Dick or whomever and basically you stick to him like glue. As each drive proceeds the beaters make their way to one end of the cover and the Guns duly make their way to the other. The instruction to 'Line yourselves out then, ladies and gentlemen, if you please.' may be accompanied by 'Neville, can you take your spaniels down the ditch and yon end, and Jen if you can work your dog along the hedge to where Bob is stopping. Rest of you through the middle please. Quiet as you go now; not too quick and keep them sticks going.' This is the signal for the assembled company to dispose itself along the edge of the wood with Neville and Jen on the flanks and the rest of you stretched out in between. 'All ready? Off we go!' and a sharp blast of the whistle or horn which signals to the beaters to commence and to the waiting Guns that they should wake up and load up, and all is under way.

Lock yourself between Dave or Derek or Dick on the one side and the next beater on the other. Make sure you know the names of both. It is not the end of the world if you don't or if you forget, but if you are asking for help or guidance it is always an advantage to be able to call someone by name. You can always call 'Where are you on the left?' more in hope than expectation, but 'Where the bloody hell have you got to, Nigel?' is somehow more comfortable.

Nothing much happens for a while. You walk steadily, thwacking back and forth with your stick and whistling through your teeth, before someone tells you to 'Get back in line, fool, it's not a race!' or words to that effect. This wakens you to the fact that you have been lost in a little world of your own for five minutes and have neglected to notice that while you were meandering along a path Derek and Nigel were hacking their way through impenetrable Amazonian rain forest and that you are now some ten yards ahead of them. This is the great beating sin. Never get ahead of the line. By doing so you form a spearhead and birds will spill off the sides of your flying wedge and out of the edges of the drive. Beating lines must always remain straight. The angle of approach may change under the keeper's direction, as perhaps the wood or crop dog-legs this way or that or one flank may be pushed forward to adjust for wind direction or last minute Gun placements; but these are refinements which are ordered by the keeper and which should not be undertaken unilaterally by beaters generally, and especially not beginners such as you. At which point you are confronted by a huge mass of brambles. Beaters' honour dictates that you must plough straight through, hacking a path with your stick like Prince Charming storming the castle of his beloved. Five minutes of frenzied bramble slashing later and much prickled and torn and bleeding you emerge apparently alone on the other side. 'Derek? Nigel? Where are you on the left?' They are now ahead of you because they have been making good progress while you were hacking about fantasising about Princesses and dropping your hat. Catch up. Gossip in the beating line is disapproved of; but communication is important. Keep your neighbours in sight at all times where possible – being regulars they know where they are after all – and if you can't see them you can contact them by voice, but only then. And don't whine.

Having re-established yourself in the beating line things do begin to happen, and when they do everyone slows down. It is not desirable that every bird in the place departs simultaneously. This is a drive, after all, not a riot. So as the birds begin to flush, beating slows to a snail's pace and quietens to boot. The instruction is 'Just keep tapping, now!' which means you should park yourself by a convenient tree and do exactly that. Just keep tapping. Not a drum solo, but a steady rhythmic tap. In the absence of a tree, just keep tapping your boot.

This is the most interesting part of the drive. The birds are flushing and with luck you might be able to see the Guns. Perhaps they are in a valley below you or at the end of the cover or wood. If you can't see the Guns, you will certainly hear them, and you may be able to see the birds as they flush and what happens to them having done so. You will also be able to hear the commentary of the beaters, and this is a positive revelation.

'Come on. Come on. COME ON! Oh, dear God! Can none of those buggers hit anything? Who is it today, anyway? The French or the Merchant Wankers? OHHH COME ON! Who is that tosser on the end there? Is he blind or drunk? You're kidding? He's hosting? He shouldn't be allowed out by himself. Oh, look he's hit something. At last. It'll run though, pound to a penny. Whoa, there it goes. And the dog's after it, and the cartridge bag. Will he never learn? What does he do again? Well, I hope he runs pension funds better than he bloody well shoots or we'll all be up a creek. Jees! Oh, well, come on, let's tap it out now.'

And much, much more besides. Spectators in any sport are, without exception, more knowledgeable, better trained and, on their day admittedly, all round more expert than the sportsmen they are watching and beaters are no exception. But for the grace of God and a bit of money that would be them in the valley below and they would not be making anything like the complete cods that this team are making. If the team in question happen to be your friends, whom you hope one day to join out the front, beating can be a very salutary experience indeed. I recommend it.

It's not all criticism, of course. Beaters can spot a good Shot and recognise a decent team when they see one, and will point out the stars as well as the duffers. I used to beat regularly on a number of shoots as a boy and I well recall being specifically sent by the keeper on one occasion to stop on the front corner of a wood (that is to stand, tapping away, at the flushing point to 'stop' the birds legging down the hedge away from the Guns as the beaters come through) and to keep a close eye on the end Gun if I wanted to see how it was done. I did as I was told and watched as neat an exhibition of driven pheasant shooting as I suspect it is possible to see. Very smart bloke, nailing seriously high birds at all angles, fore and aft, tidy as you like, one after another. It was everything you could wish for. I also noticed when the drive was over that he, and a couple of Labradors who had sat throughout the demonstration untethered and quiet beside his peg, collected all the slain and laid them in a row beside his peg and that he had a quiet word of thanks to the keeper as he passed by during the pick up. All these things impressed me no end.

During my seasons of beating, I am bound to add, I also witnessed among the Guns basic incompetence, fundamental errors, occasional rudenesses and acts of massive and dangerous crassness that made my skin crawl and my toes curl up with embarrassment and scarcely governable fury. They still do. And, believe you me, the other beaters seldom missed them either. Well, it is hard to overlook the shot whistling about your ears drive after drive. Once can be ascribed to an honest, if unconscionable, mistake; when the entire beating line is hurling itself to the ground every time a bird takes to the air, you know that what is whirling about is not mere rumour.

And these little things find their way home to roost. The beaters make no secret of the fact, and are not slow to point out the perpetrator either. If they do not confront the guilty party directly, and I've known it happen, they will certainly drop a word in the keeper's ear, and he will mention it discreetly to the host who will make a note in his address book as he draws a red line solemnly through your telephone number. Guns you can whistle up at the drop of an invitation; good beaters are hard to find and dead ones are irreplaceable. Every Gun, experienced or not, should go beating once in a while. It reminds you that the Guns and the shooting are not the only part of the day. Beating is good for the soul, it is vigorous and healthy exercise, occasional stray lead notwithstanding, it permits you to put in your two penn'orth regarding the Guns, who may or may not be friends of yours, and you get a tenner or more at the end of it. It's hard to beat beating.

However this was not solely supposed to be a paean to beating and beaters but an explanation of how you get involved. The point is that at the end of the season there is a beaters' day where the keeper will invite the most regular and highly regarded beaters as a reward for their efforts. Traditionally the regular Guns form the beating line on this outing, though I am afraid that the tradition is more honoured in the breach. This is partially because the regular Guns are too idle to turn out, but also, I suspect, because the barracking from each side about the performance of the other would be intolerable. You may or may not be invited to the beaters' day. If you do so much the better, if not, not to worry, you will have gained invaluable insight into the shooting day and made some beating friends into the bargain, and it would be a surprise if from among them there did not emerge the chance for a spot of pigeon shooting or rabbiting or a day walking round some little shoot or other. The thing is that you are in the network and that is what we were after in the first place.

Joining a Syndicate

Lottery wins and legacies aside, this is where you are going to end up anyway. Syndicates are bunches of like minded sportsmen who combine together to make the whole thing feasible in the first place. There are several different varieties.

'Beaters will soon recognise the skill of the Guns'

The Fixed Syndicate

You sometimes see in the countryside press an advertisement that goes along the following lines:

> Shoot Lease Available – The Beechings Parva shoot, extending to some 3,000 acres (500 acres woodland) is offered for lease for a term of three years. This notable pheasant shoot comes with keeper, cottage and vehicles. Some ponds. PO Box blah blah blah.

What this means is that some large landowner has a bit of an acreage up for grabs. It may be that the previous tenant has died, moved on, gone broke, gone vegan, gone mad, gone to jail – who cares? Chances are the shoot will be taken on by a syndicate. It may be that one luckless enthusiast finds himself signing up as the responsible party on the lease, but usually he does so in the fond expectation that some of his friends are going to rally round and share the expense.

Yes, there are zillionaires who nonchalantly sign up for these things, I know, but we are not they. Even then they share the costs. If, zillionaire as you are, you invite a bunch of shooting chums round for a bit of a blitz at your pheasants and never ask them for a centime of contribution, it would be a strange thing, would it not, if they didn't invite you to have a bash at theirs in return? So six days on your own shoot, seven guests a day, forty-two invitations back. Seems fair.

So, the mates duly cough and what you have is a fixed syndicate. The skipper naturally does all the admin. and the keeper who has been accumulated with the lease, does all the work. Unless he doesn't of course, in which case the skipper has to go through the disagreeable process of firing him – if the estate owner will allow him to do so – and hire another one. And the rest of the team turn up from time to time and shoot. Unless you are the skipper, it is all very agreeable. If you are the skipper, given the amount of work and hardship and heartache you are taking on, it is often the case that the costs are divided among the team and the skipper shoots for free. It still doesn't seem like any kind of bargain, but then again, there is one born every minute, so who am I to argue? Even great landowners, if they shoot on their own estates, tend to have some form of fixed syndicate wherein can be included friends who perhaps are not in a position to invite a chap back to their own place, because there are insufficient partridges in Cadogan Square to make a day of it. So the team is invited on a subscription basis and the costs of the shooting days are thus shared. I used to beat on just such a shoot on a very grand estate, where the factor totalled up all the shooting expenses at the end of each season – keepers, birds, beaters, feed, capital inputs, pens, vehicles, rents, crop damage, divided the total by eight and then sent each of the participants' accountants a bill. The Guns never sullied their shoot days with so much as a mention of the filthy lucre. Mention of which brings us to the nub. What does it all cost? More string. When you add up the cost of a keeper and his pay, his cottage and his vehicles, birds, feed, beaters, pickers-up and so forth, shoot land rental, crops, covers, plantings and crop damage payments to farming interests and the numbers get quite eye watering quite quickly. It is hard to see how a fixed syndicate could budget much less than £40,000 per annum. The participating Guns might reasonably expect ten days sport for their money, and if there are eight of them this works out at £5,000 each for the season or £500 per day. You might get it for less; you can certainly get it for more.

The Do-It Yourself Syndicate

Under this arrangement everyone pitches in on an equal basis although not all on the same terms. For example, a landowner might make available the ground on which to shoot, free of any rental charge. The game farmer might contribute young birds with which to stock the shoot. The timber merchant provides the timber for pens and posts, and the publican throws in all the shoot lunches during the season. The seed merchant feeds the birds throughout the year, the tractor agent lends the shoot a vehicle and everyone else contributes time, energy and money such that when all is tallied up from time to time everyone has made an equal contribution. This can work out very nicely thank you and many a DIY syndicate has flourished for a good many years, and some have built up shoots from modest beginnings into very prestigious venues indeed. A shoot is very like a business in this respect (actually a shoot is very like a business in most respects, in some cases, all respects). The skipper is chairman and chief executive (these roles are sometimes split to allow a figurehead chairman to be shoehorned in for prestige purposes or because the shareholders want to fire the CEO but daren't face it, so boot him upstairs as chairman instead); the keeper is managing director. The treasurer looks after the collection of subscriptions and disbursements; the Guns are shareholders and the Beaters are subcontractors. Some businesses grow to be very big indeed. Some businesses stay small. Everyone puts in what they can and together something glorious is achieved.

Some have a huge falling out and go bust. *Sic transit gloria*.

Costs? On the basis that the DIY syndicate is seeking to undercut the fixed syndicate, or at least to provide resources on a wholesale basis, rather than at market levels, and that the season might not run to more than half a dozen days, the DIY-ers can bring the fixed costs down to probably half, not least by cutting out the keepering. They won't get so many days, but the per diem will be half the cost of the fixed syndicate, say £250 per day.

The Flying Syndicate

This is a relatively new invention but quite common now. The flying syndicate has emerged alongside the sale of shooting by the day rather than by the season or by a long lease and to understand the Flying Syndicate, we should perhaps take a look at the growth and development of commercial shooting.

It started with estates looking for ways of diversifying their revenue streams, not least to offset some of the costs of maintaining a shoot for their own purposes. Sacrifice one or two days shooting a season by palming them off on a lot of unlanded parvenus who want to play at pheasants, charge them handsomely for the privilege and trouser the moolah. The birds and the keepers were a fixed cost in any event so the marginal profitability of the exercise was pretty good. The parvenus, being the rest of us, took to it like nobody's business and the next thing anyone knew, the whole caboodle was more lucrative than most of the rest of the estate and you might as well let all the days and go and shoot somewhere else. In fact, you might quite easily give up most of the other estate businesses, flood the whole place with pheasants, let the punters in three days a week and retire on the proceeds. This is a hugely simplistic and generalised view and unfair into the bargain, but with elements and nuggets of veracity about it for all that.

When money sneaks into sport, scruples tend to get nudged towards the sidelines and ultimately kicked into touch altogether. The cost of managing ground for shooting has always been high, but there are economies of scale, which if you can harness them, may grind some economic sense out of the whole thing. Wild birds are unreliable. They don't breed properly, they wander off, they don't fly where they are supposed to and they are indistinguishable from the ones you can rear artificially. The Edwardians faked it by having their keepers nick all the wild birds' eggs, incubate them under chickens and then sneak them back into the wild birds' nests just as they were about to hatch. This was the Euston System for a full explanation of which you should read *Partridge Driving and Production* by Charles Alington (published 1904) or Wormald's *How to Increase a Stock of Partridges*.

It was then found to be easier to catch a lot of hen birds, pen them with some cocks and milk them of their eggs and incubate and hatch these artificially. After hand rearing them to an age of about six weeks they could then be released into pens in the coverts where they would grow and as they got older and braver and more inclined to fly out of the pen, would spread progressively into the woods across the estate. At which point game farmers realised that they could do all of the early part of this, catching, mating, incubating, hatching and then sell the six week olds, the poults, back to the estates as ready made birds. As a result you have an estate stuffed with pheasants or partridges – grouse cannot be reared artificially with any reliability, a feature which makes them very special as will be described in due course – which can be fed and watered until the winter, come when they are called and can be rounded up on shoot days and herded over the Guns. In other words, they are reliable. And given this reliability you can either give them to kings and princes in exchange for social promotion, as the Edwardians did, or you can sell them to rich parvenus for cash, as is done today. And the more you can deliver the greater the economies of scale and the richer the returns now as then.

All of this is fine and dandy if done in moderation. The Edwardians overdid it in their time and there are those who will still overdo it given half a chance today.

King George V recognised the fact (he could be described as the first post Edwardian, I suppose) when he commented to his son (then himself Prince of Wales, later Edward VIII) after they participated together in a big day, the biggest, at Lord Burnham's Hall Barn shoot in December 1913 when 3,937 pheasants were despatched to a far, far better place albeit via Leadenhall Market, 'Perhaps we overdid it today'.

Today there are still shoots where you can kill a thousand birds in an afternoon, if it gives you pleasure so to do and are prepared for the £30,000 bill which might reasonably follow. But you would not get much applause, I fancy.

Anyway, the position was made clear on this at the start, so we shouldn't rehash the argument again here. A thousand is probably too many, and anyway I couldn't possibly afford it, and there again one is certainly too few, especially if someone else shot it.

The point is that the artificial rearing and release of game to stock preserves upon which shooting can reliably take place, means that shooting itself becomes a tradeable commodity. There are plenty of estates today who will let shooting by the day to anyone with the requisite cash and there are plenty of brokers who will undertake, for a fee, the matching of such estates and suitably wedged up shooters and vice versa. The shooters state their requirements and the agent recommends a number of possibilities. The team make their selection and commitments are made. There always remains the possibility of upset, but when was any deal wholly certain?

Which is where the flying syndicate comes in, touching down, as it does, for a day here and a day there. Touring the country through the season for all the world like a roving house party of dukes and princes who descend for the weekend on some benighted earl in his large country house and shoot his pheasants and drink his claret before swanning off to the next one. Only these days they leave behind a handsome cheque as they depart. As you can probably guess, I am in a flying syndicate. In fact I am the skipper, although I always rather hope they will make me chairman sooner rather than later. We have been shooting together for a decade or more and undertake a modest programme each season. We do not rove nearly as much as we used to. In the early days we hurtled around the country like mad things and clocked up huge mileages in the process. But a combination of encroaching age, and more importantly encountering places which we liked so much that we wanted to visit again, means that we visit perhaps only one new shoot each season. The team, like the programme, varies modestly from season to season. There are five or six core members and then those whom we refer to as 'The Occasionals' who come for the odd day or weekend. The programme is set by about April. It is supposedly by consensus, but is largely agreed quite arbitrarily by me; if anyone mutters I suggest they might like to take over the admin. which usually shuts them up. Subscriptions are sent to the treasurer with selections of commitments. It is first up, first in. No reservations, no rebates. No pay, no play. That's it.

If you can't turn up on the day through birth, business, indisposition, hangover, illness, crisis, divorce or death, you can send someone else, or we will find a replacement for you, who may – if you are seriously lucky, and the replacement seriously sporting and generous to boot – be persuaded to part with some modest contribution towards your costs for the day, although, please note, he is under no obligation to do so. We have had to find replacements at short notice on a couple of occasions for Guns who were taken ill and we send them off at the end of the day with their benefactor's address and the suggestion that they might like to drop a line of thanks in that direction. Usually works.

However, this is where you get in. Death, disease, divorce, despair. Dead men's shoes. These are your windows of opportunity to join a syndicate.

You have done the lessons; you've practised long and hard; you've snagged a licence and bought the gun; and you have dropped every resounding hint known to man. What more can you do? Make sure that all your shooting pals, chums, mates and acquaintances are fully aware of your urgent wish to participate. If you can discreetly check their shooting dates in order that you can hold yourself in readiness against someone else's mischance so much the better; and if you let it drop that you would be inclined completely to underwrite the cost for someone, should they fall out, that alone will see you at the head of the reserve list. And then it is only a matter of time before the lightning strikes and the call comes.

Incidentally, seeking to accelerate lightning with poisons, bizarre accidents, spurious litigation, conniving seduction or bribery (unless on ludicrously generous terms) is generally considered to be bad form, and while it won't necessarily stop you being invited, unless you really have no scruples flat, it tends to take the edge off your day.

In the meantime you can save up. The cost of buying days like these is in effect the same as the cost to the fixed syndicate who are letting the day in the first place. A commercial shoot will have some economies of scale to factor in, but then they add a profit margin back on which takes you back to where you started. Then there is VAT to consider. Government ministers may no longer shoot, but it doesn't stop the Treasury getting its claws into the sport at every turn. Reckon £20 to £25 per bird for pheasants and partridges depending on where you shoot and the lavishness of the lunch and the surroundings. Shooting like this, based on a day with a bag of 200 to 250 (being the minimum anyone is likely to sell you; it's not worth incurring the fixed costs of beaters etc. for less) and eight participating Guns, will set you each back £400 (200@£20) to nearly £800 (250@£25). Budget £500 a day; but don't tell anyone I told you.

One of my team got into very hot water when his wife found out what he was spending on shooting. Like an idiot he left my letter demanding money on the breakfast table while he went to recover from the shock; and she found it and went up the wall. He has had to cut back seriously as a result. The worst part is that the letter was only asking for a twenty-five per cent deposit. If she had ever found out the true extent of the damage, I dare say there would have been murder done. It's an expensive business. Like marriage. Or divorce.

Are you ready? Oh dear me, no. Still there are a deal of things you can do in the meantime.

Clay Pigeons

I have already applauded shooting schools for their ability to teach basic gunhandling and safety skills to the novice. They can serve another function too. All practice is to the good, and practising under the watchful eye of an instructor is even better, but the modern shooting school can provide far more than one-on-one tuition.

You have been through a number of hoops. You are growing in competence and confidence. Your instructor has declared you ready for the field. Some instructors go further and are able and willing, for a fee to be sure, to put together a day for groups of like minded pupils. This is a splendid way to make the leap. If you have the confidence and trust of your instructor and are confident and have faith in him, then you will be equally comfortable with his other protégés who will make up the team. You will not stick out like a sore thumb on the one hand in the competence stakes, and at the same time you will not have to spend the day wondering if the stranger next door is about to kill you instead of the game. In addition to which, with your instructor's watchful eye on all of you during the proceedings - whether or not he is shooting with you - everyone is going to be on their best behaviour.

One step further back from this is the simulated day, which is a relatively new concept which I think is wonderful and is a heap of fun for novices and experienced Shots alike. The concept in short is this: during early lessons at the shooting school you will be confronted by single clay pigeons which travel along strictly predictable lines as and when required to do so by your instructor. As your training and skill increase these clay pigeons may vary their angle of trajectory and may turn up in pairs or even more, in order to force you quickly into decisions about which to shoot and where and so forth. Ultimately you may be confronted by a blank horizon which may at any moment be populated with any number of clay pigeons going in all directions at a variety of speeds while you do your level best to get onto terms with them. There may be a few coloured clays too which you must shoot or not shoot specifically depending on your instructor's sense of humour. Clay pigeons are great. They come in different colours and sizes and they are capable these days of doing almost everything a real bird can do except breeding. I haven't come across a Whistler or a Screamer yet, but I am confident it is only a matter of time.

Clays remain predictable though. They start from point A, and barring accidents, they fly to point B. They do not suddenly change their minds and fly at head height between you and your neighbour. Accordingly no matter how excited you and your neighbour may get you are unlikely to try and shoot one there. And that's good. And that's the key to the simulated shoot. It's very exciting and great fun and there are always lots of targets whizzing about, but they never go where it would be chronically unsafe to shoot and you can't wound them. There are rules, of course there are. No shooting behind the line; no shooting after the whistle; no mucking about; no shooting the pink ones. That's it. In addition to which, especially on a novice day, every shooter will have a minder. Ostensibly the minder's job is to load, but it is also just to add another layer of control to make sure that the novices don't lose any last vestige of self control at some crucial and dangerous point. The birds may be fake and the shoot may be simulated, but the guns are still very real. I watched a simulated shoot at a corporate jolly in the grounds of a very superior castle indeed. Everything was going swimmingly and the management consultants or whatever, were all banging away enthusiastically. They were not experienced gun handlers though. One paused to call a rude comment to his neighbour and as he did so, he accidentally put a round into the fence post in front of him. Fortunately it was wooden and old and rotten, so he blew it in half. If it had been newer the ricochet would probably have had his knees off. Instead he took a long hard look at the damage and then threw up. Apart from his minder, who was himself as green as the surrounding paddock at this point, I don't think anybody but me witnessed the incident. However usually this doesn't happen. What does happen is that the Shooters form up in a line. Much as they would on a shoot day, the 'keeper' blows a whistle just as he would on a shoot day, and then all hell breaks loose. Clays hurtle about, shooters shoot until their guns are too hot to handle – about six to eight minutes, since you ask – birds are ruthlessly poached from one another, squeaks of delight are heard, groans of frustration, barks of fury and then suddenly nothing – silence – then a distant cry of 'SNIPE!!' and two tiny orange clays whistle at angles over both ends of the line. Everybody lets off and no one comes even close. And that's simulated shooting.

But there is more. And this could be very neat indeed. Simulated shoots cost about ten per cent of the real thing. Weather and fence posts apart, there is virtually nothing to go wrong from a management angle. The folk who organise these sorts of outing – and all shooting schools will know some, if they don't do it themselves already – are skilled and experienced professionals fully able to cater for most whims and fancies. You want to get on the right side of some of your more experienced shooting buddies? This is the way. You lay on one of these jaunts during the summer. You host it. You invite your shooting friends. They see that you know what you are doing. They see that you are properly concerned with safety and sportsmanship because you lay it on with a trowel, 'It's only simulated, of course, but the guns are real and I know that you lot can be relied upon for the highest standards of behaviour and sportsmanship'... you then set to and poach everyone blind... in the nicest possible way obviously and all in a genial spirit of fun and camaraderie, and most importantly – especially if you are going to misbehave, however tastefully – hitting everything you aim at and demonstrating, demonstrating, demonstrating ...what exactly? That you are safe, first and foremost. That you recognise that you are still a beginner who has a few dues to be paid. Good. That you are a generous and organised host. Fine. That you can shoot straight. Excellent. That they can invite you back without being embarrassed in front of their friends and staff. Fantastic. That you want desperately to be invited shooting more than anything in the world, the universe and space. Sad but true, and no one is going to be fooled for a moment; but no one's perfect and, after all, you did try.

And there are worse ways to spend a day.

6

MORE SHOPPING

In common with almost every aspect of our modern lives, shooting gear is governed by fashion. unlike almost every aspect of our lives, shooting gear is largely untouched by modern fashion. This is not to say that you are obliged to turn out on a shooting morning dressed as if it was 1902, but at the same time not a lot appears to have changed.

Actually, quite a lot has changed, although the general shape has, it must be admitted, remained stalwartly the same. And the reason it has done so it because it works. The great and notorious Victorian and Edwardian shooters undertook performances that appear superhuman by today's standards, however morally questionable they may have been. When Lord Howe, Lord Ripon, Sir Harry Stonor, Lord Willoughby de Eresby and Lord Bertie Vane-Tempest together took 1,500 birds off the Golden Valley drive at Lord Nunburnholme's Warter Priory shoot using four guns and three loaders each, you can bet your bottom dollar that the rest of their kit was up to snuff too.

Boots. Boots is boots? Not these days. And not always. There is a lot to be said for shoes, as a matter of fact. A good pair of stout shoes, with well cleated rubber soles are light, comfortable and smart. They do tend to be at a disadvantage, however, in puddles. And we have more puddles around than we used to, largely as the consequence of the passage of heavy machinery about the shoot. The deep ruts caused by a few tons of modern tractor churning about the place mean that Guns very often find themselves clambering through mud and water which is well over ankle depth, so perhaps shoes are not such a good idea after all. Boots then. What is wrong with wellies? Nothing at all, everybody wears them. The modern wellie, though, has come a long way from being a simple rubber boot as we will all admit, and while rubber keeps out the water admirably, it was never very warm, tended to sweatiness and smelliness and was never especially comfortable. Quite apart from now coming in a positive palette of colours, the modern wellie is quite a different creature. Lined with neoprene for warmth or leather for comfort or sheepskin for luxury. With zips to ease you in and buckles to keep you there. With cleats and studs and uphill grip and cushioned soles and ergonomic heels the humble wellie is a thing of technology, luxury and enhanced functionality – and is priced to match. There is no question that the wellie, in its modern form, is the shooter's footwear of choice, and I would be the last to argue against it. The choice, and it is huge, is yours. There are even some Guns who have reverted back to the plain black welly, with the tops turned down *à la faux* builder look – though no modern builder would be seen dead in anything so basic, or cheap or so lacking in steel toecaps – in a sort of post modern ironic backlash, but they are only joking. I think. The only issue I have with the modern wellie is that it is now so specialised that one pair is no longer the universal answer. An average pair of wellies is now too hot for an early October partridge outing, and not warm enough for a freezing January covert shoot. So either you have to get several pairs or you have to struggle with the compromise.

Field-boots are popular today. These are sort of elaborate hiking boots with big rubber soles and

laces up to mid-calf. They are quite neat for almost all circumstances from warm autumn to the blizzards of January, and have a lot going for them. Pricey, of course, although top end wellies are hardly a snip at £200 these days, but field-boots do last with a bit of care and attention, are mostly waterproof and very comfortable once worked in. They do clog up on heavy plough, I notice, but then what doesn't?

Moving up – stockings. Not, you notice socks; but stockings. All right, woolly socks. Stockings are not just woolly socks though. There is a distinct difference, which is that a stocking is fitted. A sock, short or long, is basically a tube and it is unusual to find a sock which will stay up by itself. Hence the myth of the sock suspender which is only ever seen in theatrical farces about people losing their trousers, and hence the unhappy sight of pale expanses of ministerial shin on TV chat shows. It is not possible to consider seriously the policies of a government minister who is manifestly unable to govern his own undergarments.

Stockings should stay up by themselves. A good stocking is comfortable but loose about the foot, which allows air to circulate for comfort, hygiene and temperature control. It is snug about the ankle and heel in order that it does not chafe under boot or shoe. It should cling firmly to the calf in an orderly and upright manner and then taper into the knee. Then, and this is the killer application, you turn the top back and the very top, which folds down just to the top of the calf, is just ever so much slightly narrower still which allows the top hem to grip solidly onto the northern end of the calf muscle such that it leaves a distinct – but not cruel – mark when removed at the end of the day. That's a stocking. If it won't do all of that, it's a long sock.

You can keep a long sock up with garters, if you like, or clamp the tops under your breeches, and no one will notice, or care, or comment, but a sock it remains for all that. And when a chap who really knows his stuff, stocking wise, as you do now, sees another chap who through discrimination also recognises the virtues of a good stocking they will recognise also in one another the sort of chap who knows about such things. There are chaps, tragically, who have been introduced to proper stockings by some diligent guardian, or perhaps a generous and industriously knitting aunt, but – and mark this – without the explanation. They enjoy their stockings for a time, and when the time comes to replace them, as times will, all unknowing they replace them with socks. And forever afterwards they are complaining that things aren't what they used to be, and how standards are falling, like so many socks, and it's all the government's fault; whereas in fact it is their misunderstanding which is the cause of failure, because although good stockings are increasingly rare and expensive, they are still to be found. If you know what you are looking for. So there.

Stockings, or even socks, should, of course, be of wool. Raw wool is better than anything since it has natural waterproofing in the form of lanolin. Raw wool stockings should naturally never be washed, not at 90° with a dose of detergent anyway, not unless you want them to become bootees for the firstborn. An occasional rinse in warm water is all that is required, and then hang them over the edge of the bath on the bathmat. You can do what you like with socks, I don't care.

Stockings, or socks with their attendant garters, are the one area of clothing where you can, if you wish, be radically individualistic. Stockings in regimental, school or club colours are popular, and the occasional motto not unknown. The 17th/21st colours, blue and ivory and 'Death or Glory' is a sporting combination. A discreet gold coronet spotted on a sporting duke's calf struck me as apt. Jokes I am less comfortable with, I admit, except on Boxing Day when all bets are off. Shooting should not be all sobersides and serious, but I think Bang! Bang! Bugger!, while true, inclines to flippancy. Anyway we've all seen it now. Original jokes though are always welcome.

I freely admit that the girl I shot with whose stockings each bore the legend 'Millionaires this way ↓' on the outside of each leg and 'Billionaires this way ↑' on the inside, made me smile, and I laughed when I heard who had given them to her; but I nearly bust a gut when she told me what she gave him in return.

Next up we come to the all important trousers. Why is it that the trousers have so come to characterise the whole shooting thing? And what is wrong with them anyway? I refer, of course, to the plus-fours.

Like the stocking the plus-four has become a somewhat confused and diluted term applied generically to any trouser which ties off at or about the knee. This is quite wrong, as any good tailor will tell you. The truth is far more complex. And practical with it. The first thing to consider is function. You don't want a lot of redundant fabric flopping about uncomfortably inside your boots; therefore shooting trousers should stop at the knee. Also if the trouser does get wet with rain or from crawling about in the heather when stalking for instance, you don't want the wet making its way down the leg inside your boots anyway. Next warm and dry. Tweed is not waterproof. Good tweed has a sort of grain in the weave that causes water to run off it, as well as being full of natural oils which repel a certain amount of moisture. This means that if you choose tweed for your trousers, you should be certain that the weave will send water downwards rather the upwards, since having your trousers on upside-down rather defeats the object of the exercise.

Next the trouser should be dry where it touches and where it is wet, it doesn't touch. The waistband is dry because it is protected by the coat or jacket and where the trouser is gathered in below the knee is dry because it is protected by the roll of fabric which forms the overhang which functions like an umbrella with all the water in between running down the weft of the tweed and dropping off the roll. If the roll is too narrow or has insufficient overhang, all the accumulated dampness runs briskly off your trousers and into your boots. If the trouser itself is too narrow the damp tweed will be constantly rubbing against your legs with uncomfortable consequences. To do the job properly therefore, from about the hips down, the trousers should be broad enough to hang, when at rest, without touching the leg at any point. The plus bit of the plus four is the distance by which the roll overhangs the buckle at the knee. A plus-two therefore hangs a little below the knee, a plus-four hangs considerably below the knee, while a plus-eight plummets towards the ankle. A two-plus-two is a spurious description of what purports to be a sports car, but isn't really. Nor does the plus-four stop there. The trousers can be cut narrow or tapering towards the knee, as might be the case for walking or climbing; straight, which is the popular choice of golfers, I am advised, or fluted which means that the legs flare out as they go which is eminently suitable for shooters because it ensures that the edge of the roll, with its attendant cataracts of rainwater, is well outside even a generously capacious wellie top. Now do you see how logical and sensible and practical this all is?

Plus-eights – and very dapper too

53

Coats and jackets are additionally complex. Modern fabrics, notably Goretex and Ventile, are described as breathable, which does not mean they can be inhaled, but that they can allow moisture building up inside to get out while not letting moisture on the outside, as it might be pouring rain, get in. This means that you don't get all sweaty and damp on the inside when the action is fast and furious. This is excellent news. Modern fabrics are also very lightweight and easy and comfortable to wear. This means that the range and variety of options open to you is colossal and makes choosing a coat next to impossible. It is almost certainly impossible, rather like the footwear, to have just the one coat for all shooting occasions from partridges on a balmy autumn afternoon to hindstalking in the high corries in a January blizzard, so the first thing is to conclude in your own mind for what purpose you are buying a coat and then focus on that to the exclusion of all else.

I shoot in a suit, which limits the options considerably, and saves no end of time. If you buy a coat and trousers separately, and there is no reason why you shouldn't, it does make sense to try to get the two elements, if not to match, at least not to clash too vibrantly. In my pre-suit days I used to pick and mix jackets, trousers, waistcoats and hats until it was pointed out to me, by a good friend, that the combination of four different tweeds at once was making her dizzy when I stood in the sun.

Things to avoid when buying coats include too many zips and studs, especially around the collar and neck. This is because studs can get between your cheek and the stock of your gun as you mount it, and if it doesn't give you a sharp smack on the jaw as you fire, then it will put a nasty ding in the wood of your stock. Too many pockets are also to be avoided. Two good sized pockets on the sides should be enough for most people, although those little handwarming pockets about the tummy are good value on a frosty day. Pockets should be capable of holding a box of cartridges apiece and the flap should not be so large as to impede access. Some coats have a flap that can be buttoned up out of the way, but some people find this makes matters worse rather than better. Others complain that the button rubs the stock when the gun is under their arm in the relaxed position. Some people simply cannot be pleased. Breast pockets, though, are a complete no-no because you can catch the stock on them as you mount with disastrous effects on your accuracy if nothing else. Unless it is detachable and utterly impermeable a special pocket for the carrying of dead game should not be contemplated. You are not likely to do much long distance game carrying, for one thing, and the consequences of leaving the odd partridge in your pocket for an extended period are too awful to contemplate, even if you don't then meet it again by accident. A friend of mine had all the carpets and most of the floorboards in his house taken up looking for moribund rats one warm autumn, before he traced the stink to a forgotten partridge in the game pocket of his shooting coat hanging under the stairs.

Things essential when buying a shooting coat are warmth and comfort, obviously, and plenty of movement about the shoulders. It is vital that the coat should not impede that all important swing. I don't think it is necessary to take a gun with you when you buy a coat, but if you happen to be buying it from a shop which also sells guns, then I shouldn't hold back for a moment and borrow a gun to have a bit of a swing about with.

In the end, it is a question of what you want. One thing is for sure, as long as whatever you are wearing is of muted hue, isn't your basic broken pattern cammo (which is odd when you think about it, since that is exactly what a good tweed is, but that is just one of those things) and doesn't have 'Magnum Force!' embroidered on the back, you are going to look no different to, and no sillier than, anybody else.

On the subject of tweeds, it is always worth remembering that tweed, especially estate tweed which is unique to the estate of its origin, and fairly natty therefore as you can imagine, tends to be derived from the appearance of the ground on that estate. So a Highland tweed may have a strong purplish tint reflecting the heather on the moors, whereas a Lowland weave might be more russet like the autumn bracken beds. Tweed began life as a form of camouflage, after all. When selecting tweed therefore, and there is no fabric more suited to shooting clothing than tweed, it is worth remembering, that what renders the wearer more or less invisible on the snowy granite hillsides of the high glens with its witty combination of black and white houndstooth check with a mauve overstripe may stick out like a sore thumb on a Hampshire stubble or Norfolk plough. Having said all of which the latest scientific research suggests that all quarry species are more or less completely colour insensitive and see the world as entirely made up of shades of grey. There are always though, the sensitivities of your human companions to take into account. However, as we all know, the secret of being well dressed is to ensure that everyone else knows that they aren't.

Other clothing? Yes, is almost certainly the answer. Some anyway. Dressing for shooting is very much like dressing for any other invitation. If someone says 'Come for a drink,' you might smarten up a bit after gardening, but nothing spectacular. If they said 'Cocktails at six!' you might do more than casual. 'Kitchen supper' means spag bol, clean shirt and a decent Barolo. Dinner is jacket at least, and a modest claret. Black tie means exactly what it says, no bottle, but a bouquet and a shooting invitation. It was probably why you were invited.

Thus with shooting. 'Ambush a pigeon' is a jaunt and cords and a jacket do. 'Armed mooch about the place with a handful of shells and a dog' implies rough shooting and old pair of breeches, wellies and an old coat and cap suffice. 'Coach house at 9.00 for 9.30am. move off' means the full tweed suit, clean field-boots, cap, and tie. The tie distinguishes the formal shoot from the rough shoot and is important therefore. Anyway, you can't wear a suit without a tie or cravat. It would look silly. There are no dress down days in formal shooting. Boots whether hand made leather field boots or wellies, should always be clean. This is not vanity. Disease as we all know can be carried around the country in the mud on all our boots and shoes. It is therefore more than mere courtesy, but an essential requirement, that boots should be spotless when attending an estate. Shirt and tie are also areas where individual touches are possible. Even so, it is sensible not to go too overboard, especially as a beginner. If a salmon pink shirt with a gold lame tie is your bag, then go with it by all means; but I would recommend not missing too much if you do.

Lady guns have, quite properly, a more extensive range of wardrobe possibilities, though within the same remit of comfort, warmth and convenience. Chaps, should not, I think, wear leather – unless arriving by motorcycle, and even then it should be subdued. Girls, though, can get away with deerskin breeches, if they want. Culottes are popular. Most ladies stick with breeches and jacket like everyone else. It works for everyone. That's the point.

Accoutrements and Accessories

Hats

A hat is good. Ninety per cent of heat-loss is from the top of your head. Also birds avoid the glaring dial; so a hat is necessary. The flat cap is a safe standby, either the slightly floppy version or the straightforward wedge shape. I prefer the former because I can't keep the wedge style ones on. Shape of my dome, I suppose. Tweed, there again, is the fabric of choice but remember, as before, that you have some tweed already so don't veer too far away from existing patterns and colours.

Trilbys are popular, or even what are known as Racing Felts, as adopted by racehorse trainers at Aintree and Cheltenham – but not Ascot. Oh dear. Oh dear. Fedoras, even if not pink, are generally thought to be overdoing things and loden alpine hats with badges and brushes nailed to them make you look like a tourist. Like stockings though, the hat is a place where the individualist can shine, if

'Ladies, of course, have infinite fashion opportunities'

not too brightly, without attracting recrimination. I shot for many years in a pearl grey Homburg, which made me look like a Mississippi river boat gambler, but which was of such impeccable provenance (St Hubert de Paris) that no one dared comment. Why baseball caps, even worn the proper way round, should be completely outlawed, I have no idea. I suspect it's because they are adjustable which implies a sloppy and approximate approach to life, and sloppy and approximate approaches to life, especially your life, are not what you want from the Gun next door to you when he is contemplating potting a bird just over your head. It all comes back to safety in the end, you see.

Gloves

The purpose of the shooting glove is obviously for warmth on a cold shooting day, but also, less obviously, for better grip on a wet outing or even on a hot day (grouse in September?) where a sweaty palm can be disadvantageous and even hazardous; and for protection, perhaps on a simulated clay day, when the barrels can quickly become too hot to grip effectively or at all.

There are several schools of thought.

Mittens, fingerless gloves made of wool, or sheepskin, or even Neoprene. Makes you look a bit like Scrooge, or Madonna. I don't think they work very well, though some people swear by them.

Shooting gloves. These are ordinary gloves, but with the trigger finger missing, or in some cases with a sort of slitty Velcro affair which peels back. A fatuous compromise. It's either on or off. Flappy half fingers floating about near triggers is bad news. These are a typical present to a shooting person from non shooting people who think they will be really useful. They aren't. Some of them are quite expensive too, which makes taking them back to exchange for something better a good trade, and one which renders the 'Thank You' letter easier to carry off with a straight face.

Full gloves. Must be thinnish and fit well for sensitivity. Deerskin is excellent. Warm - a good wristband is the key here and perhaps padding on the back, possibly a silk lining. Bought by someone else is always good. If you ever find a shooting glove you really like, buy half a dozen pairs at least. Odds are you will never see them available on sale anywhere again. Immutable law of shooting - and of life come to that.

Ear Defenders

One of the reasons why shooting has a poor image among the wider public these days is the propensity of gentlemen of a certain age and disposition to go about the place shouting "What? What?" all the time. The cause of this is invariably shooting. Masturbation may or may not make you blind. Shooting will certainly make you deaf. Ear defenders were never considered feeble, or pansy or wrong. They were just never considered at all. Gentlemen of a certain age and disposition were naturally deaf as posts, and that was all there was to it. I am of an age which has seen sense at last, probably in the last decade. For some of us it was already too late. I noticed it in the car when I was driving and my passenger tried to hold a conversation, and then I noticed it on the beach when walking in a wind. I have to be on the left of people to hear them clearly if there is any competing noise, so they can talk into my right ear. The left one is, quite literally, shot to ribbons. It is the lug not directly behind the gun which suffers; so right handed left ear and vice versa. It has to do with sound waves. Whatever the science, it's a fact. So you, and anyone who accompanies you when shooting, must, must, must all wear ear defenders. Which come, as with everything else in a wide and bewildering choice of styles. Your basic plug may be of foam, or rubber or even wax. You can buy wax ear plugs from the chemist. Shooting schools usually have a case of foam plugs on the counter, and I am always inclined to pop a couple of pairs into the pocket of whatever coat I have on. Ear plugs are like aniseed balls, or biros, they should be broadcast freely about your life so that when you really need them there is always one not very far away. The basic plug is very basic indeed and simply eliminates all sound of any description. This is actually rather irritating since you have to remove at least one to undertake any sort of conversation at all which is inconvenient and tedious. Or you wear them loose which means they keep out no noise whatever and are to all intents and purposes useless. They are, however, cheap. Especially if nicked from shooting schools.

Somewhat more sophisticated plugs contain a tiny wee pinhole which has the effect of keeping out a deal of the bang, without wholly eliminating lesser sounds and these are quite satisfactory and they are modestly priced. The main complaint about plugs is that they are uncomfortable to wear because the channel of the outer ear is not uniform and ramming things into it is not a comfortable experience. The latest and most sophisticated plugs therefore are custom made from soft rubber and fit so perfectly that they are unnoticeable. This involves the making of a template which is formed by injecting what looks like toothpaste into the ears which then hardens slightly such that it retains its shape when removed and the soft rubber plug is moulded from the result. The most sophisticated version then has an electronic gismo like a hearing aid inserted so that ordinary conversation is easily feasible, while the bang is screened out completely. They are remarkable, but at £100 or more expensive. There's no price too great to keep your hearing, I (faintly) hear you say, and you are right.

As an alternative to plugs there are muffs. These are headphones which also vary across a scale of complexity from the basic plastic cups on a hairband which cover the ears and exclude most or all noise to the polywollydoodleate lobe protection units with enough circuitry in them to launch an interplanetary probe and which exclude completely any sound beyond a certain degree of harmonic, but which also enhance sounds so tiny that they would normally be beyond the range of human hearing. Batteries aren't included, obviously, and while you can't tell whether the gun in your hands has gone off or not, you can hear a mosquito breaking wind at the other end of the county. More to the point you can hear what the Guns at the other end of the line are saying about you. You think I am making fun of the serious issue of ear protection. You are right and I shouldn't. It is serious and everyone should use something, even if it's a bit of cotton wool. Otherwise a whole new generation of shooters will end up going about saying 'What? What?' and we can't have that, what?

Underthings

You may think it strange even to mention these, but as a matter of fact, and more even than that, as a matter of comfort, they are excruciatingly important. The key to the whole day's temperature control may be down to the first and most intimate layer. We are talking here about keeping out the cold. What to do on those warm October partridge days, or summer on the hill, is to shed as many garments as is possible and still have modesty maintained. Better still don't start with the 24oz estate tweed in the first place. In the raw though, weatherwise, undies are the answer. Silk first, failing which cotton, but silk is best; for vest and longjohns. I'm not kidding. Long sleeve silk vest and longjohns. If it makes you feel any better you can buy them from a ski shop and pretend you are a downhiller, which is where you will be headed if anyone catches sight of you in your *dissables*. Still, you'll be warm when they've stopped laughing. If the weather is really savage I have a heavier pair which are a silk woollen mix and are for extreme temperatures only, when you really appreciate them. Silk socks under the stockings and silk liners under the gloves too. Even I draw the line at a balaclava helmet, though I wouldn't if I were not in company, say on a hind stalking expedition in the deep midwinter.

You used to get skiing glove liners which were silk shot through with silver thread to reflect the heat. They were great. Motorcycle shops are good for these sorts of things too. Motorcyclists leave nothing to chance in the weathergear stakes, and nobody thinks any the less of them for it. At least, not to their faces.

The key part of getting the underthings right is so that we can float about all day, not only toasty warm in no more than the usual suit while the others huddle together for warmth and freeze miserably; but also because we will shoot better warm than they can cold with their frozen fingers and stiffened limbs. And while we are not in the slightest bit competitive or anything as vulgar as that, we all know that shooting well is what we are about. Warmness also means that we don't have to pile on more thermal top things which are bulky and hamper gun control which also make the cold folk shoot less well. Someone who is really very cold indeed, shivering cold, is actually a dangerous liability. Thinking blurs, coordination goes adrift and control slips. Stick them in the vehicle and get some hot drink into them. Get them home ASAP. They shouldn't be shooting anyway. All of which means getting your undies on in the right order of a morning.

Sticks

The morning mantra for a shooting day: guns; cartridges; boots; hat; stick. There is a lot else besides – wallet; car keys; map; phone; flask and Lord knows what else – but as long as you have these essentials you will be in a position to undertake the essential purpose of the day which is to shoot. Why is a stick important? Depending on the terrain it may not be. If you are shooting in the grand manner, on mown paddocks and manicured lawns a stick is by no means essential, although a shooting stick may be an agreeable adjunct to the day. If by contrast you are hiking up hill and down dale for your sport, across heavy plough or boggy marsh then a stick is invaluable as a third leg, depth tester, balancing pole or just something to lean against when it all becomes too much for your fat and breathless paper-pushing self.

Shooting sticks are not generally used much these days, since most shoots have a vehicle or series of vehicles for the Guns who are motored to within a few yards of their pegs and never have to walk more than the few yards back again at the end of each drive. Shooting sticks are now the preserve of the very elderly or those incapacitated by war wounds or gout or their 'dicky hip'. You should not use the same one for shooting as you might for racing or point-to-points. This one should be free of all the badges that festoon the social seat. This is a shooting stick.

Actually shooting is much enhanced by a seat, not least because it gives you something else to do when the birds start to move. One of the most common difficulties encountered in modern shooting, and which causes the beginner in particular to foozle, is having too long to see the birds. As you stand nervously watching the birds break out of a distant wood or cover, you are thinking all the while of the zillion things which could go wrong when the moment comes. Long before the moment has really arrived you have mounted the gun and instead of swinging naturally onto the bird you are, even as we speak, aiming carefully with your tongue peeking from the corner of your mouth which is smeared into a rictus of concentration. All of which is death to accuracy.

If you are perched on a shooting stick, however, when you observe the birds in the distance, you take a good long draw on your cigarette or cigar and contemplate life for a moment; you cast away the smoke – or if it is something truly exceptional you put it on the grass where you can find it again in a minute or two; you lever yourself to your feet and finally address the birds which are, by now, at the optimum distance; you take a bird here; a brace there; you recover the gently pluming Cohiba and subside once more into the pigskin saddle of your shooting stick as if it was the most natural thing in the world. Along the line, they are saying 'Marvellous, isn't he? Never a moment's more effort than necessary. That's the way to do it.' Those who really need the stick, the elderly and infirm, sometimes never leave it even to shoot. Be aware though that this takes a deal of real skill and should never be undertaken lightly. Somehow it never looks the same if you end up flat on your back in the grass having swallowed your cigar. Shooting sticks should be made of metal. Antique ones are made of bamboo or hickory and are delightfully attractive and quaint and so in keeping with all the other

Edwardian sillinesses which the shooting field espouses so enthusiastically. However, a foot of splintered bamboo in the fundament is neither attractive nor quaint nor, indeed, agreeable. If not quite as dangerous as a gun, a wooden shooting stick shares with its more dangerous companion the fact that it does not give second chances. Go modern, go metal. Move on.

The thumb stick has different applications. You can't sit on it for a start. What you can do is jab it firmly into the turf beside your peg and lean on it from time to time. It may be anything from an ornately carved crook with a leaping salmon curved over the handle to a simple thumb stick with a comfortable V at the top for the thumb, or a rifle *de temps en temp*. Either way it implies competence. A chap with a stick is clearly at home covering great distances in wild country. He is a stream forder, a glen marcher, a Munro bagger, fisherman (hence the salmon), deerstalker (hence the V), and sportsman. See how he leans on his stick with eyes locked on the far horizon. See how the stick nestles familiarly in the armpit as he stands relaxed and alert. They don't know you are asleep. A stick soon becomes an important piece of kit. A comfortable old friend who has been through a good deal with you. You can knock a wounded bird against a stick without a thought. A decent knife and a good stick are things which distinguish the occasional amateur from the seasoned professional. Over a long and varied sporting career, you should end up with a number of sticks.

Flasks

To flask or not to flask? Shooting is a social activity and alcohol is not banned by any means. Many shoots begin with a heartstarter at 9.00am which may be overdoing things a tad. Elevenses wouldn't be elevenses without a little something though. It will probably be provided by your host and can be almost infinite in its variety. I have enjoyed iced consommé and an agreeable Fino shooting grouse in September, and hot broth and vodka beside a covert in a blizzard in January. Sloe gin is popular because of its country and sporting connotations and home made is best. When should you haul out your own flask? And what should you put in it?

It doesn't do to have a huge flask. It makes you look like a dipsomaniac who can't make it through the morning without a snort; it is bulky to cart about and may interfere with your shooting. When the stop has been called, you can consider whether to contribute or not. If your host seems to have everything under control and has produced a basket with a wide range of goodies, then better not. It cramps his style and impinges upon his hostly turf. If, on the other hand, as it might be, soup is produced – but no snort – this is as good a moment as any. If you are a visitor though, it is advisable to check your ground with a regular Gun before pulling. 'His wife was shot by a visiting Gun last season who emptied his flask by the second drive! Hasn't allowed a drop on the place since, you know' is not what you need to hear as you are escorted off the premises. And once out, everyone gets a pull, or is offered one, so the flask must be big enough to go round.

As to contents, silver polish is bad. Sloe is fine, but doesn't last long in flasks before becoming pretty indifferent. Whisky goes with very little at elevenses and is sometimes hard to take neat. The favoured options are concoctions. Whisky Mac (whisky and ginger wine) is all right on a cold day. Rum is good too, with a drop of port and some cloves or cinnamon. Raspberry vodka or schnapps are all agreeable. Madeira or amontillado are bracing and as good on a warm day as a cold one. Liqueurs are popular. Berry Brothers' King's Mixture (ginger again) is a familiar name and Archers peach liqueur is oddly popular. Whatever rocks your boat is the answer to the question. Bear in mind though, that everyone is going to have a pull at it, and that you will undoubtedly top it up with something quite different before the season is out with potentially interesting consequences. Before you announce loudly that you like nothing better than a suck on a Policeman's Truncheon (Bailey's, curaçao, grenadine, vodka) between drives, check your audience.

Cartridge belts and bags

This is a purely functional matter. As far as bags are concerned, how many cartridges do you want with you during the day? Bags come in all sizes from twenty-five to one hundred and fifty; and in all forms from finest alligator to vinyl. If you are carrying your own shells you should have a fifty bag with you throughout the day. If you have any single drive bigger than that you are in a different league from the rest of us and will not be carrying your own gear in any case, so the whole area is no longer a worry.

A fifty bag on your shoulder and a few rounds either in a belt or in the pocket is generally speaking the answer; with a hundred bag somewhere in the vicinity for emergency refuelling. Let's think this through for a moment. An expected bag of perhaps two hundred birds between eight Guns implies twenty-five birds each. Assuming a degree of competence which permits each Gun to down, say, one in three – which is a modest average in normal shooting – indicates seventy-five rounds a Gun. So a bag of fifty and a box about the person covers it, though with abundant resources about for crises. You should always ask how much ammunition you should bring to a shoot. It's odd, asking how many birds to expect is deemed awfully poor form, but asking how many shells to pack is perfectly permissible; indeed, expected. Understatement in action. How many birds? 'Ooh, I dunno. Might round up one or two I expect, if we are lucky.' How many shells? 'I should pack five hundred if I were you.' If you are not sure for any reason pack a lot. It used to be the case that anyone running out was sent home as having shot more than he expected. That seldom happens now, but borrowing from all and sundry just makes you look ill prepared and not very competent or experienced. It is insulting to your host and his keeper too, by the way. So always pack more than you might need. Cartridges come in boxes of twenty-five, and cases of two hundred and fifty. Experienced Guns will always buy in bulk, say five thousand rounds each season, because it is cheaper and more convenient. If someone suggests a couple of boxes therefore, they may mean cases. Make sure you are sure.

You will notice that cartridges are referred to as shells, squibs, bullets, rounds, ammunition, ammo, bangs, whooshers, let-offs and much else besides. This is a British habit. Guns are shooters, bazookas, fire-sticks, smoke-poles, muskets, artillery, fist-fillers, flintlocks, widow-makers, divorce papers, and much else besides. Spouses, partners, lovers and friends of either sex, may be described as old trout, old stick, old fart, the mealticket, the alimony, the sex addict, the Amex addict, ball and chain, the cook, the staff or the kiddy wrangler. My own girlfriends, or anyone who comes with me for that matter, are known universally to my shooting friends as The Sherpa. It is just one of those things.

Back to cartridges. To belt or not to belt? This is very much a matter of convenience and choice. If you are wearing a modern jacket, chances are it will zip up. Very difficult to reach a cartridge belt. Wear the belt on the outside and you look a bit like a bandido. Anyway those jackets have big pockets for the sole purpose of taking a box of shells. Which pocket is a matter for you. You will soon find which is your natural loading hand. For interest sake, I load from the right pocket with my right hand. My friend Rick loads from his left pocket with his left hand, but then he has a self opening gun which can be opened with his right hand only, whereas I have to use my left hand to drag down the barrels and eject the empties, insert fresh rounds with the right and then use the right to lift the stock to barrels. Practice makes perfect. Or better, anyway.

And just a couple of key things to remember. Cartridges are not in and of themselves especially dangerous. Though I wouldn't want to be under a box falling from fifty floors up, mark you. They will not explode if you drop one, and I've never heard of them going off in bulk. They are generally stable and inert until they are in a gun being fired. However, they are not all the same size. They used to be colour coded by manufacturers for convenience, but that seems to have gone by the board recently. It is the case that you can, for example, slip a twenty bore cartridge into a twelve bore chamber and it will slip halfway down the barrel. You look at it and think 'Hmm, thought I'd loaded that.' and stick a twelve bore shell in behind it. THIS IS A HORRIBLY DANGEROUS SITUATION. If you let off now the best you can hope for is a barrel which splits along its length as the twenty bore cartridge is forced out of the end. That's the good news, when the twenty bore shell fails to explode after being hit in the arse by a twelve bore charge at a range of six inches. If it does explode, and it is only luck if it doesn't, you may very well be kissing your left hand goodbye. Before you dismiss this as being just nonsense and no one is that stupid, know that this is one of the commonest causes of all shooting and shotgun related accidents in this country. And by the bye, the same thing happens if you drop a twenty-eight bore shell down a sixteen bore. Think on't. It is a salutary thing to visit the Proof House in either London or Birmingham and take a long hard look at the consequences. Not pretty.

The moral of the story is never mix different shells. I know you wouldn't, you are not stupid; but with twelves and twenties being the popular gauges these days, there are a lot of both sizes around, often in the same household. Always start the day with empty pockets and only ever use one bag for one sort of shell. I have never seen this happen. No one I know has ever seen this happen. These are good habits nonetheless and will ensure that you never see this happen either.

Cars

The issue of a shooting car is certainly a vexed one. Arriving in a brand spanking Range Rover driven by your loader is unquestionably one way to do things, and makes a certain impression, but as a novice it gives you rather a lot to live up to and the impression may blur somewhat round the edges as the result. There is rarely a need for personal transport on most shoots and nothing is more ludicrous than a team of Guns all careering about the shoot in their individual wagons like so many pilgrims charging across a prairie. If you have a 4x4, by all means ask your host whether it would be helpful if you bring it. He may be relying on you to ferry any number of people and their dogs about and have his fingers firmly crossed that you will bring it. It may be the only reason you were invited in the first place. So if you are not prepared to chauffeur Guns, beaters, pickers-up and dogs who may, in no particular order, variously be muddy, wet or micturitional now is the time to think about it. You should also be confident that you can take the machine wherever you may be required to go. Nothing so undermines the early impression of the 4x4 owner as manifest incompetence over anything tougher than a kerb. Getting bogged down in the first gateway is no way to make friends and influence people. Nor is whining when you sideswipe the fence and take out most of the paintwork down the side. Or even when one of the other Guns does it for you. 'Never lend anything you are not prepared to give away' applies not only to horses, wives and guns, but also to smart 4x4s.

The car shouldn't be too smart in the first place. The best are Land Rovers that are at least twenty years old and have Bakelite steering wheels and the spare tyre on the bonnet for putting dead pheasants in. And they should be green. Even the blue ones are thought to be a bit of a pose, while any other colour is just silly. Failing a vintage Land Rover, the Range Rover is probably the only real substitute, for all it is now a Ford. All other makes are welcome, of course, though in inverse proportion to their level of plushness. A brand new BMW X5, for instance, will generally attract less enthusiasm than, say, a ten year old Suzuki jeep, unless you skid it straight across the farmyard and into the back of a tractor on arrival.

On the whole it is probably better to avoid the whole area by pitching up in a stripped down two-seater with a ground clearance of half an inch and scrounging lifts off other people. Unless you happen to have an Aston Martin DB6 V8 Shooting Brake that is.

'The issue of a shooting car is certainly a vexed one'

Licences

Anything else before we set off? Yes. More law. First up, where your gun goes, your Shotgun Certificate goes too. I think that this is a perfectly ridiculous rule. I don't like carrying my Certificate about the place for the specific reason that it legitimates the holder. Doctor the photo (and in my case, who wouldn't?) and you can legitimately buy guns and ammunition until the Certificate is cancelled. The more Certificates are carted about, the more they are lost. And if the bloke in the High Street with the gun case is about to turn over the Post Office, would he really be wearing bungalow check tweed plus-fours, canary yellow stockings and a silly hat?

You also require a Game Licence and this is available on demand at the Post Office and costs £6 or £4 after 1 November and lasts until 31 July. All game, pheasant, partridge, grouse, black game, ptarmigan, woodcock, snipe – anything, in fact, that you are likely to encounter as your principal quarry on a shooting day requires a Game Licence. It is utterly pointless and I dare say that there are some people who actually shoot without one, despite it being quite illegal to do so. And shooting without one can invalidate your insurance. So there.

Put it this way, if I was a policeman and met you in the middle of a shooting day, as perhaps you left the pub after luncheon, and despite the fact that you are not driving and you have your Shotgun Certificate with you, and your gun is locked in the boot of your car, if you couldn't produce a Game Licence, I could still arrest you, if I wanted to. They should be abolished, like the Dog Licence; but they haven't yet, so you still need one. Having one entitles you to see everybody else's, which can be good for a laugh, if somewhat alarming, and you will always have the moral high ground if challenged. If you don't shoot grouse or early season partridges get the cheap £4 version and gyp the Treasury out of £2. Do not expect Game Licences at all Post Offices. Do not expect anyone to know what you are talking about even at large Post Offices. It can be a slow and tortuous business. Ask shooting friends where they get theirs. Most will probably look utterly blank; but one or two of the less criminal types might have the answer.

7

PIGEON SHOOTING

Listen. There are any number of hoops left for you to jump through before anybody invites you up to the castle for a day's proper shooting. I warned you that this was going to be a long haul and I meant it. We are playing the long game here. You may be able to avoid some and short circuit others; in which case good for you. But it may very well be the case that by the time you reach this point it is summer in any case, which means that we are in the midst of the closed season for game in any event. Shooting has seasons, right? By law. Birds and beasts must be given a little time to themselves to breed, to relax, to grow strong and sporting for the delectation and delight of the sportsperson when the season comes round. As a quick and dirty rule: Grouse shooting starts in August – although no one takes it seriously until September. Partridges start in September – but experienced Guns don't start till October because they are still chasing grouse; and pheasants start in October, but we don't shoot them until November because we are focusing on the partridges; except by accident. And you can't shoot any game on Sundays.

Pigeons, on the other hand, are vermin. It seems rather hard on the pigeon who is an agreeable soul, but who does have a habit of both eating and breeding prodigiously and has, as the consequence of these oversights, become very unpopular with farmers. Pigeons eat seed when it is sown, green shoots as soon as they emerge and will go over a grown plant like a ticket puncher on acid. The damage is colossal, the cost outrageous and the war therefore unremitting.

Pigeons are traditionally flighted into their roosts, which is to say they are shot as they are looking for somewhere to kip for the night, in February and March. This is partly because it still gets dark early and shooters don't have to stay up too late to have a crack at the pigeons; and also to give game shooters, whose other sports have all had the plug pulled on them on 1 February, something to do with themselves until they have calmed down a bit. Then the pigeons start breeding. There is a point of view, which I have some sympathy for, that shooting pigeons during their breeding season is somehow a bit off. Poor form. Leaving orphaned squabs to die in the nest and so forth. It is a bit grim, I agree.

Having said which, they have had quite long enough to themselves by July and anyway, the number that you and I are going to shoot is unlikely to orphan many squabs, if not fewer. Anyway, you are champing at the bit, and I owe you a day out.

How to go pigeon shooting? As usual, you can buy it. There are plenty of small ads in the *Shooting Gazette* (please note the promised plug, Editor) offering guided days out with experienced pigeon shooters. I haven't done it, to be honest, so I can't comment on them, but I can see no reason why they shouldn't be everything they purport to be, and in the absence of anything else, why not? Otherwise you can ingratiate yourself with farmers of your acquaintance by filling them with beer and whisky and offering to exterminate their pests for them. If you take this route, though, you had better be prepared to make a diligent effort to keep your promise, or like any failed service offering, you will soon find yourself kicked out for a better provider. Or you can find a friend with a few acres, including a wood or two, and ask, beg, plead to be allowed to try to ambush a pigeon or three. This is your best bet.

At this time of year the best and most effective way to ambush pigeon is over decoys. Another trip to the gun-shop will equip you with several of these. They come in all forms and a bewildering variety of shapes, sizes and cost. Everyone agrees that the best decoy is a dead pigeon. A live pigeon would be better, actually, but is illegal in this country. So there are loads of bits of tackle for making dead pigeons look alive which vary from a fork which goes under its head as it lies on the ground, to a cradle which holds the dead bird with its wings outstretched on the end of the cane and wobbles in the breeze, to a sort of electric carousel affair which makes two dead pigeons chase each other round in endless circles which professional pigeoneers swear by, but which costs serious money and requires to be powered by a small car battery, all of which seems a lot to lug about when you just want to have a day out and ambush a pigeon or three. Still, your budget and your time are your own, so suit yourself. A couple of packets of thin, grey, plastic, sort of half pigeon shells which balance on little sticks and which don't cost the earth will, I imagine, meet your needs. Armed with these and a bag of cartridges, the gun and a proper pocket knife, you should be set for the day.

Now I am not proposing that this is a huge campaign. If you are contemplating a career as a pest controller, or a professional pigeon guide, then there are more than enough books on the subject to amuse and divert and advise you. I am looking upon this as a step on the way to making a competent sort of a shooter. A shooter, incidentally, who aspires to become, in due season, a Gun. This is not an attempt at a record; this is an attempt on a pigeon. There is an important difference.

The first thing to do is to look at the site of the possible campaign. You may have more or less land to work with depending on which friend you got round. Indeed the friend may have done a bit of reconnaissance and be able to help you out with a clue or hint. Which is all to the good, because I am no expert in this area. What I do know is that pigeons are creatures of habit and that they tend to progress from point A to point B along flight lines. Accordingly you want to plonk yourself down somewhere in the midst of your country and have a spy of the flight lines. It is always helpful under the circumstances, if the pigeons are assaulting a field or crop in some numbers. This gives us a clue which it is hard to overlook. Assuming then that you can see two or three pigeons gathered together somewhere in the vicinity, and there usually are, it is a sound idea to watch them for a while to see where they are congregating from and where they are departing to. These are the flight lines.

I'm not going to go through all of this step by step. I have spent years pursuing pigeons under similar circumstances and have never been able to make head nor tail of what they were up to. I have been beaten, hands up, down and sideways, by pigeons singly and in flocks who have only ever laughed at my feeble attempts to outwit them like this. I have had a couple of serious red letter days, but how the circumstances differed from the rest I couldn't begin to tell you. On the other hand I seldom come back with nothing, so I can't be doing everything wrong.

In principal therefore, if not in fact, you take gun, cartridges, decoys, knife and a folding stool is useful too, to a point on the edge of the field where the pigeons are congregated. Generally speaking, and I am happy to be corrected, pigeons will gather at a point somewhat upwind of the action, and after a good look about will swoop downwind to the point of activity, turn back into the wind and land. I think. If the birds are in the middle of the field therefore you want to be parked in the hedge on the upwind side of them, so you can intercept them as they float by. If they are on the edge of the field, as it might be under the lee of the wood you just want to be as close as possible. Decision made it is time to heft yourself into the desired position.

I have not suggested yards and yards of camouflage netting, you notice, but I did specify a decent knife. The pros will tell you that camouflage is next to Godliness and they are probably right. At the very least you should have a drab jacket and trousers and a broad hat. Your bright pink face is the biggest giveaway of all. And your fluorescent shirt will be no help. So make a bit of an effort. Nor have I urged you to buy an elaborate hide with poles and strings and cart it about with you. It should be the case though that with a good knife you can gather or cut a few decent canes which, combined with a fallen branch or two and a bit of leafy finery, should provide something of a screen. Bear in mind that you are either in a ditch bottom or sconced in the edge of a wood. Oh, be creative. Then take your decoys and park them about twenty yards out from the hide, facing the wind, more or less and roughly in a horseshoe shape. Then retire to your hide and await developments. Which if you have followed diligently everything I have suggested, will probably never arrive. Still, it was a nice day out.

But suppose something does happen? Let's imagine we are parked in the bottom of the wood. The birdies were feeding where the decoys now are until you turned up, whereupon they all pushed off into the wood on the opposite side of the field for the time being. Now one of them is making his way back. This could be it. Then again it could not. He pulls away in a broad circle and vanishes from sight way behind you. However another is en route across the crop in front of you. This one is making a bee-line for the decoys. Don't whatever you do look at him. Keep your eyes down and sit immensely still and count to twenty. Then look up, and you will see a startled pigeon some sixty yards away sit on his tail and bugger off back the way he came. If you are fortunate however this performance will be repeated from time to time, and if you keep your head down and count to thirty or forty, when next you look up or through your leafy hide, you will see a pigeon about thirty yards off and twenty yards up with his wings set, just about beginning to wonder whether all those guys on the ground aren't sitting just a little bit too still for comfort. At which moment you mount your gun, just like you did all those times during all those lessons across all those weeks and months at the shooting school, and promptly discharge your ounce of lead into the airspace only very recently vacated by your target.

Pigeons, despite being shootable every single day of the year, are amongst the least shootable of all the quarry we shall consider. They are wily and cautious, they can see for miles, fly like jets, turn on a sixpence and be gone in a trice. Getting within range is only the beginning of the problem.

Even as you are realising this however, the bird which earlier vanished behind you, has just emerged over your head is turning to drop into the decoys. Just as he is poised in the turn your shot turns him head over heels and dumps him unceremoniously on the ground in the middle of the decoy pattern. YEEEEEEHAAAAAAAGH! You got one. That's it. You are now officially a hunter-gatherer. Well hunter, anyway. And before we go gathering there are one or two things to consider, if you don't mind.

Was it a safe shot? Here you are alone in the middle of nowhere shooting a pigeon, how can it not be a safe shot? Did you consider the lane along the edge of the field? And the cyclist passing by? You did not. Did you consider the tractor driver on the far side of the crop? You did not. Did you consider where the spent shot might land? You did not.

No, it was not a dangerous shot. But it might have been and the only person who was in a position to determine whether it was or not, failed to do so. You just killed a pigeon. Fortunately you intended to. No second chances. Ever. Always check. With time it becomes instinctive. Always checking. All the time. Where are beaters, flankers, stops? Where are neighbours, neighbour's dogs, wives, girlfriends? Where is the trailer parked in relation to me? Would I see a car if it passed behind that hedge? How far away is that rambler across the field? Now collect the trophy. Check that there isn't another coming first. Then lay the gun down. Wrong! Then empty the gun and lay it down. Now leave the hide and go to the pigeon. Lying among the stubble stems, a trickle of blood from his beak, wide-eyed, with the gloss beginning to mist across his dark eye, the pink tint of his breast and his white collar flashes plain against the grey and blue. Dead. By your shot. By your gun. By your hand.

Pick him up by the neck and consider him for a moment. Then lay him breast down among the decoys with his chin on a stalk. There's no decoy like a dead bird. And there will be another one along in a minute.

Back into the hide, reload your piece and look for the next one, which may or may not turn up. Pigeons, in addition to being greedy, productive, speedy, agile and highly aware, are not stupid and it does not take them very long to work out that the dozen or so of their brethren apparently enjoying lunch don't actually seem to be moving about much and seem to be eating beside a determinedly dangerous bush. This being the case they will very often push off elsewhere. Actually there is no real certainty why they change their minds all of a sudden, any more than there is any understanding for why, from time to time, they don't. Archie Coats was a professional pigeon shooter. Probably the first in this country. Certainly the first anybody recognised. He shot 550 pigeons one day almost forty years ago. John Ransford pipped his score a few years later. In the last decade Andrew Atkinson pushed to record almost to 600 to his own gun in a single session, only to be beaten by George Digweed, a World Champion shooter and remarkable all round Shot, who went well over the 600 mark. While sportsmen, naturally, decline to discuss figures in terms of records and scores, a remarkable feature on all of these occasions was the comment made by all of those involved that they could see no reason why the pigeons were so universally committed to a single spot, when it must have been obvious that it was inhabited by a very dangerous bush indeed. How can pigeons be so bright for the most part and then be seized by kamikazi hysteria every now and again? It's one of the great mysteries.

Still, your pigeons may pile in, in which case good luck to you and your little bag of ammunition, or they may up sticks and push off. If they push off, it is decision time. If you can see perfectly well that they are now following a different, but discernible flight line down the opposite hedge, you might as well gather up your gear and re-establish yourself underneath it and start again. Assuming, that is, that they are still on ground where you have permission to shoot; boundaries and permissions are a mystery to quarry of all kinds. You have to be rather more careful. Trespass and poaching are quick ways to a short shooting career at the best of times. If you should stray inadvertently onto the property of the Fluffy Bunny and Poorly Hedgehog Rehabilitation Sanctuary and Vegan Sandal Knitting Collective, and many a rough looking acre may well be one such, and start waving guns about you will have a very short and, I dare say, somewhat public, career climax indeed.

Alternatively you can stay where you are and hope that either the pigeons will have a collective memory lapse and come back or that one or two stalwarts will still come to visit you from time to time. Keep one eye on the wind. Your decoys should be, loosely, facing the wind. If the breeze has veered about, as it often does, it may explain why the pigeons have changed their outlook on the broader front. It may also have left your decoy pattern looking singularly unrealistic and signally dangerous and unpromising to passing birds. So fiddle with your decoys for a bit and then sit where you are and indulge in a spot of quiet and restful contemplation. It's a beautiful day. You are sitting in an agreeable ditch or hedge bottom with a gun and a sense of slightly diffused purpose. You can see tractors or, as it might be, combines chugging about in the distance. If you sit still enough and long enough you will be surprised what may be encountered. You may see any amount of wildlife. You may see one of the Vegans from the other side of the road nip behind the hedge for a surreptitious smoke and a beef sandwich. You may even shoot another pigeon. On the other and you can pack up your gear and go home and do the crossword. The choice is yours.

While we are on the subject of pigeons, we might as well address the other form of popular pigeon shooting, which is flighting at the back end of the shooting season. As a beater and a shooter you may very well get involved in this as the roost shooting can involve many dozens, hundreds even, of shooters over huge areas. The purpose of the roost shoot, quite apart from giving a goodly number of people a jolly outing, is to thin out the pigeon population a bit and break up the flocks before the breeding season starts in earnest.

Accordingly a number of farms and estates across an area will coordinate their efforts in this regard and estate managers, farmers and keepers will alert those of their acquaintance whom they wish to be involved. Plans will be hatched over pints here and there and the basis of the whole thing is that every likely looking wood in the vicinity should be occupied by a suitable number of shooters on the evening of the exercise, the principle being to keep the pigeons moving about until they get the point. 'Do you park yourself in the bottom end of the plantation below the viaduct on Tuesday. Derek will be at t'other end, you know Derek and Nigel of course from beating, and Nigel will be in the Christmas trees opposite. We'll start after lunch and knock off when the light goes. OK?'

So, come Tuesday, you duly pitch up in the prescribed place with gun, bag of bullets and plenty of warm clothes, especially gloves, scarf and hat. Not only for warmth but because in a grey and largely leafless landscape, pale hands and face stick out a mile. It is as well then to wear gloves and a big hat and to wrap your scarf at least round some of your moon-like dial. Derek and Nigel are in the process of disembarking from another car and appear to be taking the whole thing rather more seriously than you. For a start they are in camouflage battledress, complete with stripey facepaint and hats full of twigs. They appear to have brought enough ammunition for a modest war. They also have what look like entrenching tools, some very businesslike torches, a folding stool and a thermos each. These boys have done it before. Greetings exchanged, positioning is agreed. You and Derek in the plantation and Nigel in the Christmas trees. Rendezvous back at the vehicles in three hours unless there is still heavy action.

This may all sound unduly militaristic. Indeed it may seem unduly militaristic; but when you are trying to organise several dozen armed personnel across a considerable acreage of varied terrain in failing light for what is a not altogether social pursuit, things get a bit this way and militarism tends to work rather better than more easy going and approximate democracy.

Acutely conscious of the fact that you seem to be taking it less seriously than you should, you wander up to your designated end of the plantation. The question is where are you going to sconce yourself? The answer is to take a long hard look about as you walk. The plantation is a longish strip and you are supposed to be covering a block which is some two hundred yards across its front and twice that in length. If you are lucky you may see a pigeon or two floating about the place and even pitching in among the trees as you walk. This is a boon, since it will give you some idea of the birds' preferred landing area. There are no hard and fast rules that I can share with you on this sort of thing. At least there may be, but I don't know what they might be. However, observation of sundry roost shootings suggests that while you can see a good deal of what is going on about the place from the edge of the wood, the birds are more likely to be looking at the middle of the wood as a roost for the night. So while you can see more at the edge, you can do less about it. If you sit in the middle of the wood, you can't see anything, but if you do see something, there is a chance of getting usefully involved. It's not a great choice, I admit, but there it is. Keep an eye out as you walk for empty cartridge cases. It may just be the case that Derek or Nigel has been here before and they may have left some signs of past successes. Broadcasting empty cartridge cases about the countryside is not generally approved of these days and rightly so, but two or three cases left under a tree where a shooter has made a significant bag may not be mere carelessness, but a signal to the alert that this was a good spot last week. If, for example, you should find such a little cartridge cairn just behind a tree on the edge of a small clearing within the plantation, where perhaps three or four trees have been felled or damaged by a storm or some such, this may just be a very likely spot indeed. Within the heart of the plantation, bit of open sky to see things, bit of cover below. Or there would be if you had an entrenching tool. Oh well, there are some trimmings lying about on the floor which, if heaved together in a loose lattice between trunks, will give you a screen which, if you had brought a folding stool, you might have sat very comfortably behind. Hey ho. We live and learn.

On squatting behind your twiggy screen you can now gaze enraptured towards a watery afternoon sky with your face shining like a beacon for every pigeon in the county to see. Use that scarf and pull your hat well down and squint skywards. Nothing happens. It takes about ten minutes before you decide that moving is the obvious answer. Do try to resist the urge. It generally isn't much help, when all is said and done. Patience usually works better. A shot from down the strip suggests that Derek is getting under way and soon another in the distance means Nigel has made a start too. Why is it that you are the only one who has got the dud patch? At which point a solitary pigeon wafts across the gap in front of you and vanishes over your head. Massively alert now, pulse racing and adrenalin pumping you scour the sky. Nothing happens. Then another bird pops across your front and shies wildly as you leap up and pull the trigger. Then it flies off. This teaches us a number of things all at once. One: you are better disguised than you might be. That one didn't see you until you jumped up at least. Two: there are no guarantees from which direction birds will come. Three: pigeons are tricky birds to shoot.

The birds are starting to move. The afternoon is wearing on and they are looking for a place to spend the night. Every time they see a promising roost however some bugger starts shooting at them. Another drifts across the opening. This time you don't jump up but merely swing through him while crouched and he tumbles into the trees opposite. You are on the scoreboard at last. You may be inclined to zoom out and gather this bird forthwith, and I don't blame you for a moment. One bird firmly in the bag is worth any number floating about above and there will be something to show for all the noise. It is easier to be confident now, and confidence always boosts accuracy. Roost shooting is tricky though and averages can go all to pot in a moment. Still, by keeping your eyes open and picking your opportunities and concentrating you begin to make a bit of a bag, though by the sound of the banging and crashing from the others it is going to be a very modest score compared to theirs. You will certainly miss more than you hit, but as long as you hit a few, you have no complaints. As the light fades the birds seem to be coming more frequently. Could it be that they are conscious of running out of options and are becoming desperate? Maybe. That was the point, was it not? You begin to worry about the cartridge situation. At this rate - damn, was that a right and left, by any chance? - you are not going to be in business much longer. There is not long remaining before you are supposed to be back at the RV in any case.

Then, quite abruptly, it is dark. A couple of minutes ago it was dull. Now, it is dark. And you have to pick up yet. Have you been counting your birds? Er! You should. It's not always easy, whether pigeon shooting, or any game shooting, always to remember exactly what the score is. One tends to go 'One, two, three, a few, some, several, a lot,' but as a sportsman one really should know. In a situation like a roost shoot, unless it is absolutely frenzied, which it isn't often, after all, one solution is to make two little piles of empty cases, one for hits and one for not. All right, one little pile and one big pile; but you get the point. Then you can count up the little pile and go looking for those birds. It's not foolproof, but it helps. Five minutes mooching about convinces you that the torches Nigel and Derek had were a good idea too. You have a splendid nine in the bag, for all you have only a handful of shells left in the bag which holds fifty and was full, quite full, fullish, full when you started. Five to one is not bad, for a beginner. Collect birds, empties, bag and gun and return to RV.

Back at the vehicles a few minutes later Derek has laid out his contribution as he nurses a cup of tea against the boot of the car. As you add your row to the two of his, he thrusts a warming mug into your hand and congratulates you. 'Nigel has been banging away like a mad thing' he says 'though I don't suppose he hit anything as usual. Hopeless shot, Nigel is. He keeps 'em stirred up right enough though.' Nigel, when he emerges from the gloom has indeed been banging away like a mad thing, but when he comes to add his tally to those laid out in the headlights he can only manage half a dozen. As he explains about the tricky crosswind and the lack of short horizon and the false economy of cheap cartridges, Derek's conspiratorial wink speaks volumes.

Then home, tea, and a promise to meet later for a pint with some of the others and a debrief with the keeper who likes to record the bags from the different woods and copses for his analysis and the estate books. And perhaps a mention of some decoying in the summer if you are interested...?

And that, my friend, is roost shooting for you.

8

PHEASANT SHOOTING

Can it really be that we are here at last? Only a few short months and several thousands of pounds ago we were just starting out in this great adventure and yet here we are looking at an actual invitation. And what, pray, does it say? It says:

'Dear Novice,

We are shooting at Pheasanty Towers on Friday and Saturday the 4th/5th December and since we know that you have to work for a living we thought you might like to join us for a bang on Saturday. It's a nice shoot and we have taken a few days off them for a number of seasons now, so we can invite you and they won't mind. In fact we've got a couple of beginners on the day, clients, but quite reasonable for all that, so the host is laying on some loaders for us. Would you like one? You'll have to tip him, of course.

We are not expecting the full works so a bagful of bangs should do the trick. Why don't you come up Friday night for dinner? We shall all be staying at the Feathers in the village. Come on the train, if you like, but you'll have to get a taxi to the pub because none of us will be in any condition to pick you up.

Do come. It will be a blast.

Love

Roger and Liz NewBestFriends'

Now you know that the NBFs are serious shooters and you know that this is just one of several weekends that they undertake, partly business and partly purely social. You also know that the social shoots are far more serious than the business ones. You have been dropping hints forever to the NBFs. The fact that they have heard your hints is good. The fact that they are inviting you to a non-serious business oriented day, may look, at first blush, a bit of a put down – but just think it through before jumping to any conclusions. As a business oriented day including clients, including you, who gets to be an honorary client for the day, the cost is borne by the NBFs' business. Your invitation is not coming straight out of their pocket therefore. It is still expensive, it is just not as expensive as the invitations they give to their serious shooting friends. Then again their serious shooting friends all invite them back to equally serious outings, whereas you invited them to your simulated shoot in the summer. Also the fact that it is not considered a wholly serious day takes some of the performance pressure off you. The Friday might have been in at the deep end in a line of seasoned killers happy with nothing but the highest and fastest birds the estate possesses. You would have been like a fish in a tree.

According to the invitation though, there will be other duffers there too, a fact of which the host is aware, because he is providing loaders for them. These are not actually loaders, but minders. They may be local keepers who are not themselves shooting on the day; they may be instructors from the local shooting school, or anyone who knows how to shoot and is happy to turn out to guide a novice through the rigours of the day and avoid disaster. The host being aware of this tells us something else, along with the comment 'not the full works'.

You have heard the NBFs talk of Pheasanty Towers before. It is an old shooting estate and fully capable of testing the best with its birds, or so the NBFs have said and they should know. They have also said that they like it because with its variety of drives and considerable commercial professionalism, the keeper and the host can match the drives to the capacity of the Guns such that they will neither be over- nor under-stretched. The NBFs said in the summer that they had taken all sorts of teams to the Towers and never been more than a handful of birds over or under the mark. This is fine commercial shoot management, and probably why the NBFs choose to entertain there. The hot Shots will have a day of the tricky shooting on the Friday, and then the beginners can have a go on the less challenging drives on the Saturday. The host knows all these facts in advance and plans his manoeuvres accordingly. The 'bagful of shells' means 100 rounds, because neither of the NBFs ever carry less, they said. You are looking at a day of 175 – 200 pheasants depending on how duff the clients really are, and how inclined, or otherwise, the NBFs, or their other guests, are to help themselves on what will be easy shooting for them. You can tell that it is not a completely serious outing by the emphasis on the party on Friday night after the serious shooting.

Still, they've asked you, and that is the main thing. Breakthrough! Although the season begins in August with the grouse, pheasants are where the modern shooter is likely to get his baptism of fire, so despite it being out of order, as it were, this is where we shall begin.

Always respond immediately and irrevocably. Only death or something approximating to it is a viable excuse for dropping out of a day's shooting. Hosts, keepers, beaters, Guns, pickers-up have all to be arranged for the same day. Think in terms of organising dinner for fifty. Never drop a prior invitation because a better one turns up. Ever. It is astonishingly rude and you will always get caught out. There was a Gun who was notorious for it. One season he was invited for a modest day and accepted. Then he was invited for a bigger day, so cancelled the first and wrote himself in. He shrugged off that one for a better outing and shirked that for one better still. He recanted on half a dozen invitations from hosts up and down the country, with various vague explanations and excuses until he was at last booked in for a super colossal day that was unlikely to be bettered. When he turned up all his previous hosts were waiting for him to announce that the shoot was cancelled. Then all the hosts went out to lunch together. My, how they laughed.

By train or car, plane or coach, the transport is a matter for you. What though will you need to pack? Gun, cartridges, boots, hat, stick – the mantra. Licences, wallet, ear defenders, gloves, gun sleeve, cleaning kit. If you are going on the Friday night you will have to pack your shooting clothes as well – jacket, breeches, stockings, shirt, tie, silks (it's December remember), maybe a scarf. It's beginning to look like a car job considering the heap on the hall floor.

Couple of tips here. Always try to go the night before, unless the shoot is on your doorstep. We are talking winter here. My team and I used to perform the most prodigious journeys at ludicrous hours of the morning to get to far away shooting venues. We once all arrived at a farmyard at 8.45am in dinner jackets and long dresses (the girls were in the long dresses) having driven directly from a ball in London. We changed as the beaters watched. They were not impressed and probably rightly so. We gave up this foolishness after burning up the A1 one late December in six cars in line astern. We had to turn right off the dual carriageway by pulling off the fast lane into a slip and across the other carriageway. It was a bright and sunny morning. We were nearly there but we were pressing on. We were the first cars on it that morning. It was sheer black ice. Six cars in line astern just off the fast lane of the Northbound A1, about to slide either into the central reservation or into the fast lane of the Southbound A1 or each other. It was a moment which stays in the memory. Since we were early there was little Southbound traffic. The first three cars gunned straight across without anything coming. The fourth slid to a halt sideways on the slip with five's bumper within inches of the driver's door. Six took advantage of another gap in the traffic and just kept going round them. Since then we always try to get within a few miles of the shoot on the night before, even though the consequences on a shoot morning of staying the previous night in a pub can be severe. Trains are not the most reliable of things these days, but as a matter of fact, they are more reliable than cars. They do not however take you to where you want to go, but to somewhere in the vicinity. Standing tweedily outside a station at 8.30am on a shoot morning looking for a cab is a frustrating experience. In order to take advantage of the train system, a degree of forward planning cab-wise must be undertaken if you are not to be cut off at the knees at the last step. Otherwise trains are good. You can have breakfast and read the paper while others are pounding up the motorways. You can do 125mph – occasionally – while the rest of the Guns are looking fretfully in their rear view mirrors. On the way home you can drink. Indeed, you can drink all day on the shoot too if that is your wish, and not worry about the journey home. Trains have many advantages. Sitting in public in plus-fours and stockings nursing a brace of recently deceased pheasants however is not one of them. Some discretion is required.

You sort out the transport. I'll take you through the day.

You may have noticed that you have, until this point, been referred to as a shooter. This is what you were. You shoot; you are a shooter. On a formal driven day you are a Gun. As distinct from a beater or a loader or a picker-up or a keeper or the headkeeper or the captain or the host. If you show any talent for the whole enterprise, you may be referred to as a Shot. Formal days call for major organisation and organisation calls for clear delineation of roles. It saves confusion and time and everyone knows to which group they belong.

All are assembled at the farm or house or assembly point at the appointed hour. No one is late. There may be fifty folk involved in a shooting day. The one who is late keeps the other forty-nine waiting. The mobile phone, so often a curse, is a boon here. You may be sitting in traffic or at the station or in a ditch, but you can call the host and alert him to the fact. If you are only seconds away and scratching up his gravel at that very moment, all well and good. If you are a few minutes away, a beater can be deputed to await your arrival and gather you up. If you are totally disabled for whatever reason, he can redispose his plans accordingly. Information is power.

You will also have noticed that hosts and Guns and keepers and bodies generally are 'he'. This is not simply sexism run riot and Bufton Tuftonery of the worst and most choleric sort. It is the case that most Guns and hosts and keepers are men, and they must be referred to as something and 'he' is one solution. Many ladies shoot. More and more are doing so; and they shoot very well indeed. Many host days and some have lovely estates on which they do so and there are lady keepers up and down the country also. The modern shooting field is not an especially sexist place. There are those who will seek to put down the ladies in every walk of life, mainly because of their own insecurities and the fact that they have a winkle the size of a peanut. We disregard them and scorn them utterly. Safety and courtesy are the only issues in the shooting field. Gender is an irrelevance and all are, or ought to be, welcome. Sex is a separate issue which will be addressed later; for the time being consider all references to 'he' to apply equally happily to 'she' unless in the context it might be illegal.

It is 9.15am and all are assembled, booted and spurred. The Guns have put together their various pieces and gathered up cartridge bags and slips and hats. There has been a certain amount of 'Hello' - ing and 'You're looking pretty ropy this morning' -ing and now the captain calls the day to order. Strictly speaking the host is the estate owner and the captain is the bloke who has organised the

Friday Night

Saturday Morning

Guns. Hosts and captains can be the same person, but not, obviously, always.

'Guns please!' gathers the crew. Introductions first for those who don't already know one another. Unless you are a genius at this sort of thing you won't get all the names first time. Do what you can, is the only advice. The other Guns look frightfully efficient and relaxed, but don't worry because you know that at least two others are beginners too, but are making a decent fist of looking efficient for the time being. The beaters are clambering into a trailer and several serious looking folk are sitting in 4x4s with great numbers of Labradors, retrievers and spaniels misting up the rear windows. These are the pickers-up.

Introductions concluded the next order of the day is the draw. Roger NBF sets out the regime. 'We are numbering eight Guns, but we will only draw seven; numbering from the right. We'll move up two after each drive. Liz and I are going to share number eight throughout the day so we can watch the rest of you make fools of yourselves.' This may, or may not, make any sense to you. Loosely translated it means that there will be eight Guns in the line at each drive. The NBFs are reserving their place on the left flank of the line throughout. The flank Guns generally expect less shooting than the middle of the line, so this is a generous gesture on the part of the NBFs. They both shoot, as you know, so they are going to share this position, taking perhaps alternate drives to shoot. The rest of you will move up two numbers at each drive so that you circulate throughout the day. This also means that the NBFs get to shoot next to more of their guests, which is congenial, while the rest will have the same neighbours throughout the day.

Roger then offers a fistful of cards to the assembled company each of whom takes one. There are many and various ways of allocating the peg numbers. Some captains have a little wallet containing numbered slivers of silver or ivory. Some will give you a glass of sloe gin where the number appears on the bottom of the glass. Others use playing cards and some have a capful of screwed up scraps of paper. Roger, bless him, is using game cards which are the size of a folded postcard and contain a list of all the Gun's names, a schedule of the drives and columns for the head of game shot with totals at the foot. Normally game cards are distributed at the end of the day by the host or keeper, but these contain useful information since you have already forgotten everybody's name. Roger is clearly an experienced and sophisticated captain. Your card also contains the number '3' indicating that you will be third from the right on the first drive, fifth on the second and so forth. Roger NBF now describes the format of the day.

'The plan is' he says, 'to do four drives before lunch and two after. We will take elevenses mid-morning. We are shooting pheasants, although there will be a few partridges about and you are welcome to those as well. No ground game whatever if you please, and since we are in the middle of prime hunting country, for Heaven's sake no one shoot a fox. There may be a woodcock or two and you can shoot them if it pleases you. Please don't shoot pigeons before the pheasants have started to move. The last drive before lunch is especially complex and early pots at pigeons may screw it up completely. We may need a walking Gun on a couple of drives, but Mr King, the headkeeper, who is off setting out the stops for the first drive and who you will meet later, will give them their instructions as and when he needs them. There will be pickers-up behind the line on all drives and stops dotted about the place throughout the day, so keep an eye out for them. We will be back here for lunch so that you need only take what you need for the morning.

All right then? Any questions?'

It all seems very comprehensive to you, but one of the others has a question.

'What about whistles, Skipper?'

'Aha! Quite right.' says Roger, 'Always forget something. King has a horn with him. Two blasts to start, one to finish. Have a good day. By the way we are asked not to pick up empty cases, but to gather them and leave them on the peg. We will be travelling in that commodious wagon there. Now these three nervous looking bodies are loaders for those of you who are using one. Let's meet them.'

What does all of that mean, exactly? Six drives is normal for the time of year. The light is gone by 3.30pm and while you can fit in eight or even more, if you are quick, in September, six is standard for a December pheasant shoot. A break for drinks after two drives is comfortable. Ground game is hares and rabbits. Very few shoots now permit ground game. For one thing hare populations have declined alarmingly in some parts of the country, though they are abundant elsewhere. More to the point on a commercial shoot such as this one where not all the Guns are known to the host, either well or perhaps at all, ground game is not shot because of the obvious safety implications. Pheasants and partridges can at least be expected to be airborne and although there is always danger on a shoot, there are fewer risks in the air than on the ground. Hares and rabbits dashing through the line are at ankle height and the risks associated with them are correspondingly higher. On the whole a total embargo is better for everybody's peace of mind. Also hares take a deal of shooting and a wounded hare is an awful sight and a worse sound and deeply upsetting. Best left to the pros. Foxes definitely ditto. Woodcock are a marginal call. This very pretty little bird is much prized, not only for its eating qualities but also for its characteristic zig-zagging flight (which makes it a bugger to shoot). Some sentimental shoot owners won't have them shot because the woodcock is only an occasional visitor to this country; others, more pragmatically, know that some Guns get very overexcited by woodcock, whose erratic flight often includes low jinks at head height, and for safety reasons err on the side of caution.

The pigeon issue is sound. Complex drives take a fair time to reach their critical point, which leaves the Guns at the front with time on their hands. Pigeons, being wilder and flightier than the average pheasant, see what is going on much earlier and bail out accordingly. If the Guns at the front are getting bored and start blazing away at these early pigeons (and if one does, then they all will) a carefully controlled drive can go all to pot in no time. It may anyway; but if the Guns haven't let off a shot, they can't be blamed for contributing to the disaster.

Walking Guns are sometimes co-opted into the beating line to cover birds which break out of the flanks of the drive and which would otherwise be lost to the bag. It is usually the role of the flank Guns, say numbers 1 and 8, to fulfil this role since as already observed they are likely to have a leaner drive in any event. Being a walking Gun is generally a good thing, because you get to overhear the beaters' commentary on the Guns, and you may well get a deal of shooting if you are lucky.

Stops and pickers-up – and their attendant dogs – have a habit of turning up where you least expect them and when you least expect them to be there. Pickers-up you can count and should in any case be far enough from the Guns to be safe; but best not to test it by shooting at them. Stops are usually parked on the edges of woods and in hedges, you will have to spot them as you go, but to be on the safe side – and where else do we want to be? – don't go shooting at likely looking bushes and hedges.

It is useful to know that the Guns will be back at their vehicles for lunch. Ammunition is the key consideration, but also things like a change of shoes (if lunch should be indoors) and additional clothing (a scarf or waistcoat, should the afternoon turn cold) can also be picked up as circumstances require. Empty cartridge cases should always be picked up after each drive. The present instruction is an interesting modern development, which permits a beater to collect the empties after each drive. The number of empties beside each peg will be relayed to the keeper, who will know who has been in the shooting and can gauge as the day progresses the quality of the Guns by the reports on the walkie-talkies from the game cart on the one hand and the cartridge gatherer on the other. This will permit him to judge his last drive to a nicety.

The whistle question is important and if not explained by the captain as a matter of course then someone should always ask. Early shooting can mess up complex drives as with the pigeon issue, while shooting after the end of a drive is a terrible sin. Why? Safety again. During the drive everyone is focussed on the Guns and will make sure that they are in a safe place, or as safe as they can reasonably make themselves. After the drive is concluded stops, beaters and pickers-up - especially the latter - will move out of position to fulfil their allotted tasks and make their way hither and yon secure in the knowledge that the Guns are now unloaded and out of commission for the time being. Shooting after the whistle breaches this important trust. In addition to which, on a closely managed commercial shoot, the keeper may have a very good reason for stopping the drive before all the birds have flushed over the Guns, like they have shot quite enough already. Shooting after the whistle or horn, not only shatters trust, undermines shoot discipline and is an affront to the keeper's authority, but also blows his careful management of the day to the four winds, or will do if you should hit something. I can think of only two valid reasons for a shot after the horn. One is to shoot a wounded bird out of a tree, and the other is to let off a cartridge which has misfired. You should ask the captain for permission to fire on either occasion, or you may be in for an only slightly unjustified bollocking.

The Loaders

Loaders load. It is a specialised job, involving two or more guns and a deal of footwork and co-ordination. It only concerns a very select few Guns these days. The chap you are about to meet is a minder, who has been recruited for the day to look after a beginner like yourself and to make sure that you don't shoot yourself in the foot, either socially or, God forbid, literally.

There is no knowing, as has been said, what nature of chap your loader is likely to be, other than that he will know what he is about. That's his job. The next minute or two therefore can be quite tricky, a bit like the school dance or picking the sides for footy. Here are three novice Guns and there are three experienced loaders. Who picks whom? I'm not sure that there is any accepted form for this and in the end it is just a pick and mix job; unless the captain has done some homework. Roger NBF has definitely done this before.

The three novices are the two NBF clients and you. One client is French and the second American. You are you. 'Jean Claude,' says Roger, 'ici Michel. Michel parle très bien le Français, à un bureau en Paris et un château formidable prêt à St Emilion.' Michael is, in fact, a successful wine merchant who certainly speaks fluent French and may very well pick up some useful contacts off Jean Claude. The French is a nice touch.

Roger turns to the American. 'Danny meet Jack. Jack's retired now - right Jack? - but he used to be a stringer for NBC news in London. Danny is a scribbler too, Jack.' Jack was indeed a stringer for NBC; he is also a successful novelist. Your turn.

'Novice, this is Chris. He coaches at the shooting school just down the road here, so there is an outside chance of you hitting something during the course of the day'.

Roger NBF has *definitely* done this sort of thing before. It is a good example though of shooting as a many layered thing. This is a corporate entertainment outing for the NBFs' business. In order for it to be a success everyone must be safe in order that everyone can be comfortable since that is the environment where business can be successfully done. The NBFs clearly understand that and have gone to some lengths to find loaders who will not only see to it that their charges don't do anything untoward but who will be at ease with their wards and make them easy with their loaders and both sides may get more than a day out from the experience.

Once loaders were servants; albeit in that rather curious manner that butlers and valets are servants too, and yet aren't really. It says much for the democratisation of shooting that they are not now, for the most part, servants at all. And definitely should not be treated as such, unless you want to make a complete fool of yourself. There is a very posh shoot - castle, battlements, moat, Earl and all, where the earl and his younger brother, who is only an honourable after all, regularly turn out as loaders for shooting guests. Sometimes they own up, sometimes they don't. One American guest was introduced to his loader as Earl and happily called him Earl all morning. At lunchtime he earnestly pointed out to the captain that as a Democrat he was very concerned that Earl should join the Guns for lunch in the castle. 'I expect he will,' came the reply 'it's his castle, after all.' Which was naughty really, but irresistible.

The Drives

The talk in the wagon is of weather, prospects and re-introductions. Never miss a chance to confirm who people are and tick the faces off against names on the game card. Make quite sure that you have the names of numbers 2 and 4, who will be your neighbours throughout the day, firmly in mind. If, for example, a shot bird is hurtling towards them (always a possibility and quite dangerous) you want to be able to shout something more than 'Er... I say...'. Introduce your loader too. Do not be surprised that neither of the other novices is next to you. Roger NBF has quite properly and discreetly fixed the draw to avoid this happening. Where there are novices in a line of Guns, they create a gap through which a certain volume of birds will escape from each drive. They will not be as accurate or as quick as more experienced Guns. Three novices in a row makes for a big gap. By splitting them up the captain has ensured that his top Shots are in a position to stop these gaps where possible. This is not an invitation to some guests to poach the novices blind, but to be on hand to take advantage of moments where the novice is unready and, where possible, to kill cleanly birds which the novice has wounded. This is both proper and sporting. In your case too, the NBFs, who are thinking of involving you a bit more next season perhaps, will be looking for reports from two of their top Shots on your performance during the day. Not that you should worry about that.

The Guns debus at the first stand. The frosty air is crisp and your breath floats away on a little breeze. This is it.

Across a grass field are the line of pegs, each with a numbered card in the cleft at the top; each angled towards the wood that crests the hill at the edge of the field beyond the hedge. Some keepers no longer point their pegs in the direction from which the birds are expected, which is a pity, because it is useful for the Guns to be facing in the right direction.

You have your gun in its sleeve and Chris has accumulated your cartridge bag. Together you walk across stiff grass to peg 3. The moment has arrived to determine how this relationship is going to work. You should take the lead in this, even if only to ask your loader how things are going to work. The issues are these: where will the loader stand; will he actually load for you or would you rather load for yourself; do you want him to actually coach you as you shoot (he is an instructor, after all) or to let you do your damnedest on your own?

You decide to load for yourself for the time being, but you would welcome his input in the accuracy department, which being the case he will probably want to stand directly behind your shooting (right?) shoulder. Unship the gun and lay the sleeve on the grass beside the peg. Open the gun and put it in the crook of your elbow. Chris has the cartridge bag so help yourself to a few handfuls of shells and stick them in your loading pocket. Apply ear defenders and gloves and anything else you need at this juncture. You might even try a practice swing or three to settle your jacket and loosen your shoulders.

Check your neighbours are at their pegs. Rory, on your right at number 2, is a known killer and gives you a broad smile and a thumbs up. Greg, on the left, is reported to shoot three days a week in the season and has a very sharp looking O/U resting on his shoulder.

Turning round you can see three teams of retrievers and their handlers some two hundred yards behind the line against the far hedge of the field. There should be four. 'The fourth team is further back on the other side of the hedge' says Chris, which is a point in your favour, because he has spotted you spotting them. 'Good. Can you see any stops?' He scans the hedges which run away from the wood in the distance. 'I can see one on the corner of the wood and there's another working a dog up the ditch on the right.' You spot them both.

And that is the conversation for the time being. You should not talk in the line. A murmured comment perhaps, but not chatter. There is time for talk between drives. The horn drifts down the wind.

A glance down the tubes –you never know – and two shells in. Close the gun, butt to barrels. Do it barrels to butt and the barrels end up pointing somewhere other than at the ground. Always butt to barrels. If something should occur, all you blow a hole in is the ground. Three ways to now hold the loaded gun: in the crook of your elbow, by the grip, on (not over) the shoulder, triggers upside and muzzles skyward or at the high port, by the grip with the stock against your hip and the barrels at forty-five degrees up and away to your front. The way not to hold a loaded gun is anything else.

Any minute. Any minute now.

The beater working up the hedge on your right puts out a cock pheasant with a deal of squawking and the line tenses and several guns are jerked off shoulders, yours included. The cock flies low and fast into the wood at the top of the slope. He's going to be disappointed when he gets there. A couple of pigeons are floating towards the Guns. Too high to be in range. On the left Greg swings up his gun, and for a moment you wonder if he's going to breach the team orders and have a crack, but he lowers it. Grinning. He's just having a bit of a practice swing.

Then a bird erupts over the wood. A hen pheasant. She climbs, wings beating, towards the right of the line and it seems that she may swing wide, but she sets her wings and begins to glide down towards the American, Danny, who is at number 1. You can't help but feel a pang of sympathy. First bird of the day and he's clearly going to have to start proceedings. The gun comes up. Bang! Nothing. Bang! And the hen clearly flinches as she flies and a tail feather floats. Bang! And she folds up and bounces on the grass. Rory flips out the empty case. It is permissible and proper to tidy up neighbours' wounded birds, but it doesn't do to do it so often or so obviously as to make them feel uncomfortable.

'Coming left.' You have been watching too long and Chris' quiet comment alerts you to the fact that more birds are moving including a pair that are moving towards you and Greg. There is a hen well up and a lower cock. The cock is just like the clays you have been practising at the shooting school. The hen is definitely not. They are going to pass between the pegs. You decide to focus on the cock. Quite apart from anything else he looks the bigger target. The safety catch comes off as you mount focusing every ounce of energy on his beak. Pull through, blot out and Bang! Bang! The cock is dead in the air. You were vaguely aware of the second bang and the hen bird is down too. That must have been Greg dealing with the taller of the two. 'Well, done,' says Chris. 'Give the next one a bit more, though and you'll be spot on. More coming.'

Indeed there are. Quite suddenly the air seems to be filled with birds, some high, others lower. Chances are the lower birds are partridges, whose tendency is to fly in groups quite low. Their faster wing beat makes them look quicker than they are and their habit of appearing suddenly over a hedge together and then scattering over the Guns is their principal defence mechanism. Pheasants fly faster and higher, which is theirs.

How do you determine which bird is whose? Whose head is it flying over? Whose head is it most nearly flying over? If you imagine a solid wall bisecting the gap between you and each of your neighbours, the channel between the two walls is your polite area of activity. Your safe arcs of fire may be greater, indeed, should be greater, but this is where politeness dictates you participate. Only depart from it if your neighbour is unloaded and you have nothing else in your airspace or to address a wounded bird.

Another pheasant is almost upon you. The gun goes up, but the shot is definitely too late. 'Way behind!'

'Way,' comments Chris. 'Here's another.'

This time there is no mistake and a hen bumps on the grass beside the earlier cock.

Up and down the line there is the clatter of shooting. You see Jean Claude on number 5 beyond Greg miss with his first barrel and then absolutely connect with his second at a pheasant leaving a cloud of feathers hanging in the air. The full choke casserole effect. Still, at least he got it. On the other side Rory takes a partridge in front of him and a second behind from a little bunch that went directly over him which looks very impressive.

As number 3, almost in the centre of the line, you are in the thick of things this drive and have little time to watch the performance of others. Some birds you kill and others you miss. There was one that you definitely hit, but which didn't fall and neither of your neighbours were free to do anything about it at the time. There was one huge opportunity of a right and left when you missed the first of two cock birds with your first barrel but killed the second. Thinking too much about the right and left and not concentrating on the bird. And more besides.

Two long blasts of a horn decrees that the first drive is over. Well. Well. Well. That was just marvellous. Your first proper pheasant drive and you haven't disgraced yourself, or shot anything but the pheasants you intended. Five down and that irritating wounded hen. You say as much to Chris. 'The picker-up directly behind us saw that one. I think she sent a dog for it already.' You both look back to where the pickers-up are working steadily forward towards the line from their position at the rear. A woman in a headscarf catches your eye and holds aloft a hen pheasant and points towards you indicating that it is yours. Raise your cap in acknowledgement. Between the two of you the five other birds are picked from the grass. Three cocks and two hens. Look long and hard at the first of the cocks. He is your first pheasant. As you hold him a beater approaches. 'Take those for you, Sir?' Take a last look, and hand him over without regret. There are five more drives to come. A quick point, always manage wounded birds first. Indeed wounded birds which fall nearby, within a few steps, should be dealt with forthwith, even during the drive. You can reasonably ask Chris to do it. Confronted by a wounded bird, discard your gun – unloaded – first, then grab the bird and holding it in one hand by its wings, give it a sound belt on the back of the head with your stick, or your clasp knife. Never hit a bird with your gun or your gun with a bird and don't whirl birds about by the neck. The inevitable, when it happens, is gruesome and scarcely properly respectful to the birds. If all else fails, hold the bird real tight, but real tight, by the neck until someone arrives and takes it off you.

'Guns this way, please!' suggests it is time to go. Gather together your empty shells as requested, take a last look at the site of your first formal shooting, and move on.

We could go through the whole day, drive by drive and shot by shot. It would not however be particularly useful, even if it was interesting. Instead let us content ourselves with a moment's consideration of other aspects of the day. You will recall that the NBFs mentioned that they were going to share their peg. This being the case they each had the chance to spend three drives mooching up and down the line and spending a drive each with their three principal guests. The two clients, Jean Claude and Danny; and you. There will have been time before, after, even during, the drives to make sure that each guest was having a satisfactorily happy time, getting some shooting and connecting from time to time. A raised eyebrow at the loaders would be enough to elicit a full report from them on the guest's performance without a word being exchanged. That is the way of things and there will be a fuller review afterwards. All that is required for the time being is confirmation that emergency action is not required. This is good business as well as being a good host.

Then there was the third drive, when you were number 7 (number 8 being dropped, you recall) when you were asked to walk instead of stand. Come to think of it, that was directly after Roger had stood with you the previous drive. There's a coincidence. Mr King, the headkeeper (headkeepers are always Mr) put you on the inside edge of the dog-leg wood with instructions to kill any pheasants coming back across the angle. As it happened quite a few did and as they all followed exactly the same line and as Chris told you very specifically after you missed the first one to put your shot a yard further forward and about a foot down for the next one, and as you did as you were told, you didn't miss the second, or any of the next seven which followed, including the stonking right and left at the end which left you feeling what can only be described as pleased as punch, especially when one of the old beaters leant on his stick at the end and commented that 'Tha' wor pre'ty sho'tin, naw error.' Praise doesn't come higher than that. There was also a moment on this drive where the cry went up from the beaters 'Woodcock! Woodcock right!' Before you had any chance to react sensibly a tiny brown blur came zipping through the trees in the corner of your peripheral vision. Up, down, in front, behind. You had the safety off and were swinging around to get some sort of bead on the thing when Chris said something and by the time your brain had processed that and everything else the woodcock was gone. What he said was actually 'No!' The sharp negative registered in your brain just in time to stop you in mid swing. After the drive you ask him why he said it. He tells you. 'He was moving fast and jinking like fury. You were off balance because he was basically behind you and you hadn't moved your feet at all. To get onto him at all you would have swung over the beaters' heads and if you had got a shot off at him behind you, there was a beater about thirty yards behind the line getting a thorn out of a spaniel. It wasn't a safe shot.' You can accept the theory. You felt off balance at the time. You hadn't even registered the beater who was out of line. Not knowing he was there would not have been much of an excuse. A word of thanks is called for. This is why loaders like Chris are so valuable.

The last drive before lunch was a big killing drive. Very often it is the biggest of the day. Partly this is because the birds will be dried off after any overnight rain, will have fed, and be in good trim for a serious burst of flying. Partly because the host wants a good first half closer to send the Guns happy and excited into lunch with three-quarters of the bag under their belts so that if they can't hit a thing all afternoon following too much claret, the day still won't end in disaster.

Posted at number 2 for this drive, you were content to watch Greg on your left at number 3 and the other experienced Gun at number 5 beyond JC get well engaged with some seriously high pheasants. JC was blazing cheerfully away between them, but from further along the line it was clear that two shoots were taking place at wholly different elevations as the hot Shots sent bird after bird arcing to the ground a good fifty paces behind the line. It was exhibition stuff, and while they didn't have anybody helping to load, they seemed so quick. Greg, in particular, was using a self-opener; and loading from his left coat pocket. Whenever his hand emerged from his pocket it held three cartridges. He would load two and grip the third between the fingers of his left hand as he shot. As each little flurry of pheasants came to him he would invariably take two birds in quick succession and then a third from the same bunch with the quickly loaded spare. Very snappy stuff. He must have killed fifteen on that stand alone.

At elevenses, after the second drive, there was soup with vodka or sherry or both and baby sausage rolls from thermos flasks. The flask issue didn't arise because you had left it in the car, and after all the worry too. Lunch in the house was splendid and there were plenty of rosy cheeks on the first drive, where at number 4 you were not quite as bright as you had been on, for example, the third drive. Despite holding your own, there were several double misses and a number of wounded birds which couldn't be explained by the growing afternoon chill.

You did recover some ground at the last, even stealing a cock from behind Rory which he missed with both barrels, so you weren't the only one slightly off the pace. This is referred to as 'Wiping his eye', though why it should be, I can't imagine.

The End of the Day

Savouring the thought of a cup of tea and some fruitcake as the team foregathers once more back at the house several important thoughts occur at once. First thank the beaters. They have worked a sight harder than you and you have benefited from their efforts. A grateful Gun is all too rare and the Gun who pops his head round the door of the game larder or the barn and says a personal goodbye and thank you will find the quality of his shooting throughout the day has magically improved in subsequent reports.

Next what about Mr King the headkeeper, and what about the loader Chris? Some sort of tip is rumoured to be required, but what sort of size and what is the procedure. The modern loader or minder may have agreed a price for his services with the host or the captain in advance of the day. If this is the case, the sum will have been communicated to you in advance and you will have it ready in your wallet. If the number has not been whispered to you, the answer is £40. Or so I am advised. On a big day with serious loading going on, it is generally considered that £50 is more the spot, but for your purposes two £20 notes is the solution. Strangely, or perhaps not so strangely this being a modern development, there is no ceremony or ritual to be gone through with Chris. You shake him warmly by the hand, you thank him profusely for his help and support, he congratulates you on your shooting and tells you what a pleasure the day has been. Then you hand over the cash, which he pockets without a glance. Farewells aside the relationship between the two of you is now concluded.

Mr King, the headkeeper, is a different kettle of fish altogether. There is a deal of debate about tipping keepers and it sways back and forth. The widely held view is that keepers should be tipped £10 per hundred head in the bag. This is not unreasonable, and as a novice in this game, with little experience to bring to bear on the day's performance, you might well stick to this convenient rule of thumb.

More experienced Guns, however, take a different view. Modern commercial shooting being what it is, a competent keeper, on a sizeable estate where perhaps 10,000 birds are put in the woods before the season, should be able to round up a couple of hundred head without difficulty. Truth to tell, the skill lies perhaps in keeping the bag within sight of two hundred head, especially at the beginning of the season. The management of the day is what should be rewarded, rather than the numbers. Did the birds fly well over the Guns and were they spread across the line or were numbers 4 and 5 the only spots worth having? Were there birds on all the drives?

You know for a fact that the last drive before lunch was a biggy, but then again you still had some shooting on number 2 as well; and you had just had a cracking drive as walking Gun anyway. You know that you were not shooting well in the afternoon, but you also noted that the bag at lunch was 154 pheasants and the final bag was 205. So Mr King had his three quarters by lunch and then managed the afternoon to spot on target. There was no great whooping and wailing from the beating line, and when you walked with the beaters they were quiet and efficient and polite, without wild dogs or rancorous yellings. Nor were you harried from pillar to post throughout. Indeed there was a full hour and a half for lunch, when you think about it. Put short, Mr King managed things to a T.

On the scale of things £10 for a successful day, without incident or interruption. Another £10 for managing the bag and the spread of shooting so that all the Guns got a fair opportunity at birds which challenged a varied team. And beyond that, you personally had one great drive which will stick in your memory for seasons to come. That alone is worth another £10.

Now for the how of it. First Mr King's tip should be three £10 notes. It doesn't do to mix up denominations. It looks as though you have either thought about it too much or not enough. When you leave for a shooting day, you should have plenty of money and plenty of different notes, such that you can make up the required tips without looking as if you have just emptied the ashtray in the car. Brand new notes are perfect, but difficult to procure now. Somehow the crispness added to the moment. You may be lucky and scrounge new notes from a cashpoint machine; it's worth a try anyway. The tip should be folded and concealed in the palm of your right hand. As the Guns mill about before tea, Mr King moves between them with eight brace (pairs) of pheasants on his left arm. As you stand beside the open boot of your car, he hoves up beside you with a 'Brace for you, Sir?' This is your moment. The speech goes something like this:

'Thank you, Mr King. Just pop them in there if you would.'
'Very good, Sir'
'Marvellous day, Mr King, thank you very much indeed.'
'Very happy you enjoyed it, Sir. I thought the birds did well.'
'Indeed they did. Well up and nicely spread out. A deal too good for me anyway.'
(All laugh heartily)
'Well, Sir, I gather you had a few. You had a nice walk, anyway.'
(Loosely translated this means 'It was reported to me that you were safe enough to walk and shoot at the same time and that you made it the length of the wood with only a single woodcockian moment of terror for my staff, and shot well enough following emergency tuition.')
'Didn't I just? I shan't forget that in a hurry. Thank you very much.'

At which point you shove out your paw which Mr King shakes firmly and somewhere during which the folded notes transfer from your palm to his with a magical sleight of hand. And are counted even as they zoom into his pocket.
'Well,' you say, 'I hope I shall come again, perhaps?'
This is a key question and relates very much to the transaction which has just taken place.
'I hope so too, Sir. I'm sure you will.' (Just as well you tucked in that extra tenner.)
'You never know, Sir, perhaps you will.' (Marginal call, the others have all gone overboard tip-wise.)
'I don't know how many days are being let next season.' (This crew are never getting within one hundred miles of this place again, if I have anything to do with it.)
'I don't know if any days are being let next season.' (This crew are never getting within one hundred miles of this place again, if the host has anything to do with it.)

Perhaps I'm just paranoid. I don't think I am. Perhaps they are all out to get me. They probably are now.

Put it this way: a very senior keeper indeed was handing out the birds after a big day on his ground. He was a man of fierce pride, and known never to brook fools. The day had been nigh on perfect, although the Guns had not performed as well as the birds by any means. One of the Guns,

A crispy handshake

whose performance had been noticeably modest, took his birds and dumped them unceremoniously in the boot of his car, mumbled his thanks and shook the great man's hand. The keeper never even looked down. He grabbed the Gun's wrist and pressed the tip straight back into his palm. 'If that' he said quietly, though several other Guns heard it, 'is your idea of gratitude, I'll settle for respect!' Then he walked away. Scary, isn't it?

I know of a Gun too, who attended a very poor shoot as a guest. I was there and it was grim. The birds were thin and undernourished and did not fly. The coverts were bare and unkempt. As a shoot it was scarcely worth the name. The keeper was certainly not doing his job properly. When the keeper came for his tip, the Gun shook the man's hand without a word, but instead of the usual discreet transfer, the Gun kept hold of the keeper's right hand and held aloft in his left, in plain view in front of the man's face, a single, scruffy, £5 note. He took it too.

It's all a bit of a minefield. No wonder a tenner a hundred has become the rule.

There are a number of variations on this theme. If you are on a big estate, where there are teams of keepers and underkeepers and beatkeepers, it is generally the case that the headkeeper is tipped and that all the tips are then pooled and shared among the keeping staff in agreed ratios, either on the day or across the whole season. If you are a guest on a day on a beat where there is a beatkeeper, but the headkeeper collects the tips, it is as well to check this point with the host or the captain. If you have enjoyed your day, you should single out the beatkeeper in question, and thank him personally, and you should applaud him to the headkeeper too, so that it is clearly understood that you know who has contributed to the day.

If you are on a small estate, where the bag is correspondingly smaller, you should recognise that the keeper has probably worked harder to achieve your bag than his grander neighbour would have to. Similarly, where an estate rears and releases no birds, but relies on wild game for sport, the keeper again will have to work harder still. Under such circumstances, a tip, perhaps well out of proportion to the bag, is appropriate. A good keeper works damned hard for a very modest wage. If you throw in the risks he takes in confronting poachers or antis or the like, and the fact that his home is very often tied in with his job, such that he is at risk as much from the agricultural cycle or Lloyds fraud or stock market collapses as the estate owner, it is fortunate that there are still men and women prepared to do the job at all.

You will have only a few chances during a season to reward their efforts. Don't blow it. And when you get home, don't forget a prompt, effusive and deeply sincere 'Thank You' letter on proper paper and in proper ink. Thank the NBFs, of course, and ask them to pass on your thanks to the host and the keeper as well and compliment all and sundry. A quick note of thanks to the host directly shows that you really have got some manners and you really, really want to come again. Which is all to the good.

That is the pheasant shooting experience, more or less. Not everything to be sure, but enough to be going along with. For the time being you should take yourself home and clean your gun and fill in your Game Book with the story of the day. Did anyone tell you to buy a Game Book to keep your shooting journal in? They should have done.

Unless someone mentions the ducks…

9

DUCK SHOOTING

It may very well be the case following, say, a day at the pheasants, more probably on a private shoot than a commercial one, that a chap, or chaps, especially if they are staying the night, may be asked after the conclusion of formalities at the end of the day, whether they feel up to 'A slap at the ducks?'. Now this may seem an innocuous question on the surface, but it begs an awful lot of very serious questions indeed.

First up there is the question of what is meant by 'the ducks'. Fowl come in many and various different forms and while pursuing some of them can be tremendous fun, this is not always invariably the case and the discerning sportsman will want to make quite sure he is batting on the right wicket before agreeing to the escapade.

Bad Ducks

The worst of all ducks are those who are, even now, paddling amiably back and forth across the farmyard pond. They may indeed be wild ducks. Or they may once have been wild ducks, who having spied a likely looking pond while whistling past on a howling gale, dropped in to find that not only was it as likely a pond as you could shake a stick at, but that some kind individual was feeding it to boot. And so they stayed. But that was years ago and now unless there is a bucket of old spuds heaved into the shallows every morning without fail, they will make their way, pit-pat-waddle-pat, in line astern to the keeper's door and quack with increasing indignation until someone brings them their breakfast. These are very bad ducks indeed. They will never willingly leave this place even if men and dogs wade in among them with raucous cries and questing noses, yea, even unto thunderflashes. They will do no more than lollop out of the water for a brief low level circuit of the vicinity before sploshing back down once more from whence they came. And if you are, as a household Gun, set back some twenty odd yards from said pond when said ducks are eventually bodily launched from the water by halloing beaters who have whipped the pond to a foam and should you, under all the circumstances, duly execute such a duck as it swings round and about your hat, then shame on you. If this is what is meant by a 'Slap at the ducks' then the best thing that a sporting chap can do is to make his excuses and leave.

Less Bad Ducks

On the other hand it may be the case that your host has dug out some ponds in a couple of isolated copses at the foot of the farm and has floated a few duck on them for the purpose of providing the wherewithal for just such an exercise. Mallard, for it is a certainty that mallard are what you are about to confront, are good breeders and a hardy sort of bird even if they do give the impression of being a bit simple. Bought in as hatchlings and released in such an environment they do retain a degree of wildness and wariness as long as they are not over-pampered by the keeper. Fed from time to time, neither too regularly nor too well, they will stick to their pond as a place but not necessarily adopt it as home at all costs and are therefore a generally more sporting bird.

There is a deal of skill though, even here, in presenting a proper target rather than a cloud of mallard wheeling forlornly about waiting either for a landing slot back on the pond or a shot from below which will render the landing issue academic. This is basically a drive, just as the pheasants earlier were a drive, and should be addressed as such. The Guns may be set out behind the wood housing the ponds or, in the case of some very glamorous shooting estates, disposed about the lake – across the bridge for example, or beside the falls, while the birds are driven from the higher end of the lake to the lower. It must be said that, as far as the quality of the birds is concerned, a good deal can be overlooked when you are standing on a Vanbrugh bridge over a Capability Brown lake watching the sun dropping slowly behind the Palladian façade of some socking great house wherein lies a distant decanter with your name on it writ large. Anyway, given the scale of such lakes the duck have very often started a fair way away and may very well be very sporting indeed by the time they get to you.

On a diversionary note, when shooting duck off ornamental lakes it is always as well to ascertain whether anything is likely to be coming that is really desperately rare and exotic, and if so what it might look like. It is, in my view, wholly unreasonable to send a whole raft of duck hurtling down a lake over Guns and then raise a fuss about the extermination of your precious pair of Arctic Glacier Bantams, but then different people take these things in different ways. I well remember setting off one morning with Uncle Philip, of myth and legend, to do in some of the Canada geese which were infesting the lake at that time and, as Canadas will, breeding prodigiously and puddling the perimeters and generally making a right nuisance of themselves. There were many Guns and we were dropped out of the back of the Land Rover beside suitable bushes and trees and fence-posts just as an autumnal dawn was creeping over the distant horizon. As I was being dropped out Uncle Philip added a rider to his instructions. 'The keepers tell me' he said, 'that there are a couple of Egyptians floating about somewhere. Don't shoot them, for Heaven's sake, they are incredibly rare. Good luck!' Good luck indeed. I spent the next hour crouched in a miserable huddle of indecision, certain only that if I shot anything at all it would come down complete with pyramids and a plague of boils. On the other hand I had to let off the gun at some point or I would scarcely be doing anything constructive concerning the Canadas. It was a real dilemma. I fired off a few shots into what I was fairly certain was thin air, although the prospect of an Egyptian suddenly inhabiting it at short notice was never far from my thoughts, and only slightly redeemed my position by polishing off what was very obviously a wounded something that staggered to the shot of my nearest neighbour and which I managed to clout comprehensively shortly before it landed almost at my feet. Anyhow, end of diversion and back to the meat.

Whatever the circumstances in which you find yourself engaged in a duck drive, be it humble or grand, the procedure is invariably the same. The Guns will have their individual locations explained in detail before setting off, there may even be pegs or butts for the purpose, and will line out in their indicated dispositions as quietly as possible. Quiet is very important as, with wary birds, there is very often only one chance of such a drive and when the birds have left they are gone. So you do not want to be the one responsible for setting off events before anyone else is ready. So quiet. Once all the Guns are in position, the keeper and beaters will begin and the birds will shortly begin to flush. Duck, once flushed, are unpredictable and while it may be the case that the bulk of the birds will follow a particular route, there is no guarantee that all will do so, so it behoves all Guns to be ready at all times. It is sensible to start the drive with one or two spare cartridges between the fingers of the left hand so as to speed reloading for it is not unusual to get three or four shots in quick succession with, perhaps nothing before or after and it is sensible to make the best of them. It is also sensible to be aware that the preferred path of mallard in particular, but also teal, is a wide circle. You need eyes in the back of your head therefore, because while the birds are unlikely to circle more than once, perhaps understandably given the circumstances, it is certainly likely that they will creep up on you after their initial departure as they seek to sneak back to their familiar surroundings. These 'second wavers' are very often at extreme range and dropping one, or two, apparently from nowhere in sight, beside your neighbouring Gun delivers very considerable satisfaction.

As mentioned earlier this is a last drive exercise rather than a foray after wildfowl, but it can be agreeable for all that.

Really Quite Good Ducks

This is where the whole thing begins to get quite serious and represents an outing almost in its own right. Indeed it is best to consider it in exactly that light and to accept the invitation or not accordingly. What is involved here is spending the next several hours, depending on the time of year, hunched in a hide beside a pond on some corner of the estate, waiting for the arrival of wild duck. These are not reared or released – although some may be ex-release birds from previous seasons or indeed neighbouring estates – but to all intents and purposes are thoroughly wild birds with all that that implies. The form is that the Guns, perhaps four or five, probably less rather than more, will dispose themselves around the pond where duck are known to feed and where, indeed, food may be provided for their encouragement and await the arrival of the fowl with the dusk.

There may be a few decoys, even, strung across the pond, further to encourage the incomers. Guns will usually occupy a hide of reeds or wattles with perhaps a bale or an oil can as a seat. The reasons why you should consider this as a wholly separate invitation are more or less the same as you would apply to the invitation to any shoot, formal or informal: Who else is shooting? Are they reliable sorts? Congenial? Safe? The answer to the latter question is magnified in the circumstances because this type of shooting is largely undertaken in near pitch darkness and at targets that are dropping into the pond – or scrambling off it again – in either case passing by your head as they go. The question is therefore whether you are going to be comfortable knowing that your companions are going to be trying to shoot these birds from the other side of the pond at something certainly less than a safe distance? Any difficulty with the answer and my advice is to head for the decanter. It may kill you in the end, but probably not this evening, and there is no joy in shooting duck, however exciting, if the excitement derives in no small part from the knowledge that if you don't get every single duck on the way down, it is odds on that one of your companions will get you on the way up. If therefore during the course of the day one of your fellow Guns has pointed out to you his neighbour who has been clouting low birds between the beaters or swinging through the line and who is now agreeing enthusiastically to the duck slap, mutter something about enough fun being enough for one day and retire at once.

You should also consider the nature of your host. Flighting of duck such as is being proposed takes place in and after dusk. I don't know what your wildfowl recognition is like in the dark, but with all candour I would say that they all look like wine bottles to me, assuming I catch any real sight of them at all. For the most part you are unlikely to be troubled by anything other than mallard or teal, but if you are shooting in and about the park and your host is likely to have any kind of misgivings about the occasional Mandarin or other ornamentals then better to settle for the sideboard now, rather than under a cloud later.

While we have decanters in mind, it is also worth remembering, assuming that the expedition under contemplation is in the back end of the year or beyond, rather than on some balmy autumn evening, that once the sun has dropped below the horizon the temperature will plummet accordingly – indeed unless it is going to do so, there is little point in starting out anyway and while we are only going to be out for perhaps an hour or so in full darkness, that can be an uncomfortable time if you are not equipped with the necessary cold weather gear. Scarf, gloves, boots. Perhaps an extra sweater or a thicker jacket. Given the chance you should retire to the house and re-equip almost from scratch, as a matter of fact. Thick pully and coat, gloves, scarf and a broad hat – nothing puts off an incoming duck so certainly than to see one moon reflecting gently at it from the smooth water of a welcoming pond and another leering at it from some bush on the nearby bank. For all mallard may seem simple, they are not that stupid. Warm stockings and boots, even waders unless there is a reliable dog on hand – although wading in strange ponds in the dark is not recommended and if there isn't a dog, then your waders will be taken as volunteering you as retriever, which is worth thinking about. A torch is good and a flask of tea or better or both together won't come amiss. You may also want to consider changing guns and cartridges for such an expedition. You are legally bound to use non toxic shot these days for duck and if you haven't got any you are out of the picture from the off. Few of the new cartridges perform as well as lead, despite the manufacturers' claims and anyway duck tend to carry a deal more shot than pheasants and partridges and may be addressed at longer ranges so a handful of 1⅛ths oz No.5 bismuth or tungsten in the pocket will do as well as anything, and I dare say, you may not want to put those through your best twenty bore. No reason why you shouldn't of course, no logical reason, but you may not want to anyway.

So a complete review of the company, the gear and the options and we're still up for it. And so you should be. Anyone generous enough to ask deserves to be accepted, a bit like marriage, unless there's a real danger to life and limb lurking in the undergrowth. Just like marriage, actually.

Having once sconced yourself in the hide indicated the first thing to do is to identify where the other Guns and pickers-up (if any) are located. If you are uncertain, at all, now is the time to sing out. Don't be embarrassed; safety first. Always. It should, as a matter of fact, still be light enough to see your companions clearly, but if in doubt hail. Then make a careful note of where they are in relation to the skyline. Once the light has all but gone, the trees etched against the sky will be about all you can make out and you will have to work backwards from there to where the other hides are. The surrounding wood and the water will just be a black mass. Set out your stall and try to sit looking, as it were, across the wind. Duck tend to land upwind so you should have a clear sightline in this direction, but in a light breeze especially, there is no guarantee, so it is best to keep your options open.

Then it is sit and wait time. Keep your head down. There is every chance you will hear duck long before you see them, and it is equally unlikely that you will ever see them before they see you, so your hearing is the principal sense on which reliance should be placed. Turn the volume on your muffs up.

When you hear the first quack, keep staring resolutely at your boots and hold your water. When you hear the whistle of wings directly overhead or, indeed, nearer still, is the moment to cautiously raise the eyes and then, and only then, to spot the birds. Or try to. The chances are that the birds will see you, or one of your compatriots, at the same instant and what follows can, as a consequence, be somewhat confused. Basically what should happen is that as you raise your head a leash of several mallard or, as it might be, a spring of teal are just in the process of setting their wings for a landing on the pond. At this juncture you and the other Guns pop up from your hides on the bank and neatly take a brace apiece with consequent satisfactory sploshes as birds fall into the water.

What actually transpires is that just at the moment that you are leaping up like the proverbial coiled spring, your neighbour – either because his excitement has got the better of him, or because his eyesight is better than yours or because he is shooting at some quite different birds who have arrived, neither seen nor heard by you, from the other direction – discharges his piece with a roar and a great gout of flame. Accordingly the birds on which you had been focussing abruptly change direction and with much mad quacking and a flurry of wing beats begin to evacuate the area. A process only accelerated when they catch a glimpse of you and you of them, and to add to the confusion you let off in their general direction with more noise and flame. The flame thing, incidentally, is important. Especially for the novice. A shotgun discharged in daylight emits no flame. It can be unnerving therefore in the dark, when you realise for the first time that actually there is a good yard of explosion when you pull the trigger. I well recall the first time I saw this in action and fully expected to find that I had exploded my gun altogether, before I realised that a) I hadn't; and b) it was unlikely, even given the crew I was shooting with that evening, that we had all exploded our guns simultaneously. However, back to the pond. With the ducks departed and eyes re-adjusted to the gloom, and assuming some modest success on someone's part, there emerges the question of whether to pick-up or not to pick-up. Probably this will have been agreed in advance. If there are still fowl moving about then the general rule is not. If there is a wounded bird within sight or reach then, obviously, it should be retrieved with all despatch and finished. If there is a cripple moving about on the water too, a dog should be sent without delay or it will dive and be lost. Failing which a Gun with a safe angle should send another shot after it to finish the job. Ducks which give the appearance of being definitively dead should however be closely marked for later collection.

Meanwhile it is back to the 'heads down' ready position. More quacks indicate further ducks and in due season the whole riotous undertaking is repeated with more or less success. And so it continues for as long as duck are dropping in or there is sufficient light to see and shoot safely or until the chill gets the better of everybody.

With luck and fair conditions this sort of outing can be a very satisfactory end to an already splendid day and a bag of half a dozen mallard and a few brace of teal adds no end to the satisfaction felt when you do finally get your hands on that decanter.

Very Good Ducks Indeed

This is what happens very occasionally in a chap's life, unless he is blessed with spectacularly generous friends who are themselves blessed with spectacular resources. As you wind up the formalities after a day at the pheasants courtesy of your already saintly benefactor, your host considers the sky and sniffs the wind and remarks to his keeper something along the lines of 'Mmm, that wind's filling from the east, if I'm any judge. I shouldn't wonder if there were not a few duck about the marsh. We might take a look, do you think?' To which the response which we are all hoping for is 'I don't doubt they'll be in tonight, Sir, if some of the gentlemen would care to.' Because the gentlemen would very much care to, given half a chance, the gentlemen knowing full well that there is every prospect of a blistering flight on the horizon.

So it is back to the house for all the changes already described, except on this occasion we are not looking for a handful of shells in the pocket but a spare, expensive and non toxic bagful. The estate is bordered from one side by the sea and on its perimeter just inside the sea wall are several acres of splashes and reedbeds which are permitted to flood and which are periodically fed to attract passing ducks who move back and forth to the estuary beyond. At this time of year there may be hundreds of wildfowl moving about, especially in hard weather which provokes them not only to seek out fresh food supplies but also seems to encourage them to circulate for its own sake. So with a rising tide urging the birds off the estuary itself backed by a mounting breeze pushing a cold front inland there is every chance that we are about to be in for a blinder.

Hides are set out among the reedbeds and we are shown to them by the keeper splashing through occasional shallows as we go. The hides are commodious, even extending to hooks on which to hang gear clear of the water, a sack for empty cartridges and a tethered five gallon drum half filled with sand as a seat. Even as we arrive there are birds moving about on the gathering gale. The keeper very properly points out the direction of neighbouring Guns. Such is the extent of the marsh that we are unlikely to interfere much with one another's shooting but it is always helpful to know where others are. With a confirmation that he will return with retrievers in a couple of hours he splashes off into the gathering gloom and we are left to our own devices.

Almost before we are settled a pair of mallard come planing in from behind and are off again before the gun is even up. More alertness is called for if we are to take full advantage of this opportunity. A small pack of teal buzz in directly in front. They appear all unconcerned until they spot the movement of the gun and then they simply change down a couple of gears and scream skywards, as teal will. Unlike the simulated target at the shooting school however they are not slowing and while one drops to shot, it is one well behind the one we are aiming for. The second shot at a tailend Charlie has less effect.

However there is always another chance around the corner and as teal, mallard, wigeon, shoveller and gadwall wheel, dive and climb on the wind about the marsh there is plenty of shooting and one begins to wonder if the bag of cartridges will be enough after all. And running out of ammunition on a duck flight is almost unheard of. However, just as we are getting down to the last handful, the keeper emerges from the gloom with a couple of Labradors and asks for the score. Which is a) not as many as it should be given the opportunities; b) not as dead as it should be; c) not as certain as it should be; d) not as identified as it should be and e) not as well marked as it should be. All of which being the case the dogs nonetheless retrieve several mallard, some teal, a couple of shoveller and one thing which looks like a gadwall but isn't, and seems to be a crossbreed of some description. Knowing how many empties are in the sack, it is not a great score, but then again, it's not something we do every day.

Wildfowling

None of this has anything to do with wildfowling by the way. Wildfowling is something quite different, although it is rumoured to involve ducks or geese or both. Wildfowling involves driving probably into the middle of the back of beyond, almost certainly in the middle of the night. This is followed by a route march further into the middle of nowhere and invariably beside the sea. Indeed the route march takes place where the sea only recently was and will be again in a few hours. This all happens in the pitch dark in the wee small hours of the morning, and, if possible, in a howling gale and into the teeth of some nasty sleet. After the route march you are required to dig your own grave and lie in it for several hours during which time dawn will break and sundry ducky, or as it might be, goosey sounding birds will variously tweet, quack, whistle and honk their way past, over and round you at great speed and greater distances. It is almost certainly the case that most of these are protected species. I know that shelduck are and I know that Brent geese are. For some reason these are the only two species of wildfowl that I am really confident of recognising, probably because they are utterly common in my particular part of the world, the Brents especially almost reaching plague proportions. This is one reason why I don't go wildfowling. A pound would get you a penny that I would bag one of each and be arrested before I could get off the marsh.

After several hours lying in your grave, you are alerted to a change in circumstances by water trickling over the edge. This means that the tide has come in and now you have to repeat the route march in double quick time or you will be cut off by the returning sea and will be drowned.

Staggering back across the estuary mud and sand ahead of an advancing tide is a battle waiting to be lost so as a last resort the true wildfowler will unlash the barrel of his unfeasibly large gun and stand in the tide race using it as a snorkel until the floodwaters once again subside. Since the huge guns beloved of wildfowlers all have thirty-six inch barrels, this is known amongst the hardened wildfowlers – and there are no soft wildfowlers, let me tell you – as 'Going the last yard'.

The only good thing which can be said of this purest form of shooting is that if, and it is a big if, you make it home or back to dry land anyway, you are entitled to stumble into the nearest hotel, pub, café or camper van and consume the biggest and greasiest fried breakfast that the kitchens can throw at you through the steaming fug. By the time you have finished, it is time to go out again for the evening flight.

Wildfowlers are recognisable by their enormous size, partially made up of huge fry ups and partly by the umpteen layers of flannel and rubber clothing and their uniformly muddy appearance. Wildfowlers just love mud and are never happier than when playing in it. They also have waders which they wear rolled down, giving them the air of slightly dishevelled khaki musketeers and they use huge guns, double eight bores or single four bores with great hammers and gaping muzzles which, if they were ever let off, would drive the wildfowler straight into his beloved mud like a six inch nail into butter. Wildfowlers eschew all forms of shooting other than wildfowling as being completely pansy and they are probably right. They also deplore any bag larger than that which can be carried in one hand for several miles across thigh deep mud ahead of a quickly rising tide, which is why actually shooting anything is a concern that is well down the wildfowlers' list of priorities – somewhere below getting home alive and avoiding frostbite.

Sir Peter Scott, the renowned naturalist, was a great wildfowler in his youth. You have to really love wildfowl to go through all of this to get on terms with one. Even this level of frozen madness is roundly and soundly pooh-poohed by puntgunners, who are to wildfowlers what wildfowlers are to the rest of us.

Puntgunning

In order to be a puntgunner, you need, naturally enough, a punt. There is no more connection between what we are talking about here and the punts that chinless boaterheads shove up and down the river through our great university towns while casting yearning looks at shy girls with downcast maidenly eyes and hidden appetites, than there is between a Piper Cherokee and the Battleship Galactica. For a start gunning punts are pointy, not square. They have fore and aft decking. They have a sail. For choice you should build it yourself. And they have the biggest gun you ever saw short of a Royal Navy destroyer. Check out Sir Ralph Payne-Gallwey in the Badminton Library series if you want instructions on how to build a punt, twenty-one feet long, three-and-a-half feet wide and six inches deep; colour grey; with a cannon on the front. It's little more than a heavily, hugely, armed canoe.

The cannon will weigh in at one hundred plus pounds, be ten feet long and have a bore about three inches across. To load it, you put 4oz or 5oz of good black gunpowder down the front, followed by 16oz of assorted shot. Then you attach it to the front of the canoe. Pointing forwards, obviously.

Punting at sea, at sea for Heaven's sake, should be undertaken by the light of dawn on a flooding tide, which gives you about one go a month which should be more than enough for anybody, although you can probably fit in two or three dawn raids on consecutive days when the tide is at or about dawn. Obviously you can punt up and down lakes, Broads, meres, dykes, Fens and canals to your heart's content. Inland fowling is for wussy types though. Real men go to sea. Through ice.

In the dark the punter and his mate paddle and row out to where the fowl are overnighting on the sand and mudbars of the estuary. There they lurk. Having identified a goodly paddling of fowl in a convenient spot, the fowlers lie low in the punt and handpaddle their way towards the target. The object of the exercise is to get to within fifty odd yards. Nine times out of ten something goes amiss and the shot is abandoned. Either the duck spot them and decamp; or another gunner puts in an appearance and parks himself in the firing line. Or a group of naturists come scampering down the beach for a morning swim. Anything can happen. But on the tenth time, the fowlers get within range and line up the great cannon, and as the fowl jump '**BBBWWWAAAOOOMMM!!!**' One can only imagine the consequences of such a discharge. But Sir Ralph is there with the answer from his diary of January 1881 when in a few days fowling in severe weather he bagged 565 assorted fowl including shots of fifty-six and forty-seven at wigeon. He doesn't describe ramming the sandbar backwards at great speed with his hat on fire, which is what might reasonably be expected to happen.

When the smoke clears the fowlers paddle in to collect the slain and finish off any wounded with a shoulder gun; and then it is up with the folding mast and Hey! Ho! For home and another well earned wildfowling breakfast.

The exploits of these people are astonishing, even for Victorians, but no less startling are the stories of the Fen shooters around the Wash and the Broadsmen from Norfolk who were very far from being nobby types and hunted for the markets and for meat. Sir Ralph may have had his swivel guns made to his own design by Messrs. Holland & Holland, but the Fen tigers were using a bit of downpipe loaded with gravel for their outings. There are books galore on the subject of wildfowling ancient and modern. If the idea appeals to you then I commend them to you.

In the days when wildfowl were more plentiful and less protected puntgunning was a great sport and a subsistence living. Today it remains great sport and is a marvellously eccentric thing to do. Since the number of experienced puntgunners can probably be counted on the fingers of one hand, you are never likely to do it or to see it done. It is worth describing even so.

On an important point of law, it is now illegal to shoot ducks and geese with lead shot. Waterfowl spend a lot of time shovelling up mud from the bottom of ponds in order to filter out gravel and grit which they retain in their gizzards for the purpose of grinding up weed and plant material as an aid to digestion. In doing so fowl have been found to swallow spent lead shot which, being lead, eventually poisons them. For this reason the use of lead shot over wetlands and in pursuit of ducks was banned. Fishing weights of lead were similarly outlawed. Substitutes have been developed by cartridge manufacturers including tungsten, tin, steel, molybdenum and bismuth. They are all significantly more expensive than lead – four times the price. And they all have ballistic distinctions from lead too, into which debate we will not dive for the time being. The upshot however is that you must use one of these substitutes for all ducking and fowling. The moral therefore is always to travel with a couple of boxes of your favoured substitute in your luggage so that you are prepared, and if you are confronted by a brace of shootable duck, during, for example, a pheasant drive, raise your hat and let them pass unmolested. Unless that is, you see them coming in good time and have a pair of bismuth shells in a back pocket. In which case do a masterfully quick change and belt the pair of them.

Let's go grouse shooting.

10

GROUSE SHOOTING

What compares to grouse shooting? Lafite '85? Being marooned on a desert island with Cameron Diaz or Brad Pitt – according to taste and inclination? Grouse shooting beats both. A bottle of Lafite is gone in half a dozen glasses, and Cameron and Brad may not age well and are reputed to be prone to chronic mood swings anyway. Grouse shooting is always perfect and is just as perfect again tomorrow.

What is it about grouse? For one thing the red grouse, as opposed to the black grouse which is a wholly different kettle of grouse, alarmingly rare now and while unnervingly beautiful, quite gormless and by no means as sporting as the red, live in wild country and fly like bandits. The red grouse is a thoroughly wild bird.

These days that alone makes grouse special. The pheasant is a common bird all over England and lowland Scotland too. All over Britain, in fact. Reared and released in huge numbers, the pheasant is the backbone of modern game shooting, but the fact remains that the pheasant is to all intents and purposes a domesticated fowl. Partridges are no better. Once the wild English partridge was not only the mainstay of English sport but formed a large part of the English rural diet too. Changes in agriculture and neglect, I am afraid, by sportsmen have brought the English partridge close to disaster. To compound its troubles the poor old English partridge has to compete with its imported French (or Redlegged) cousin who has been imported as being easier to rear and easier to keep – and incidentally, easier to shoot. Reared partridges are common too. But your grouse bird is truly wild. They can't be reared in captivity. Every now and again someone says that they can, but nothing ever seems to come of it. They live on the shoots of young heather and they nest on the ground. Their environment is harsh, their predators numerous, their diet meagre and they have a brain the size of a pea which means that if there is any way in which they can contribute to their own misfortune they will grab it with both hands. In addition to which grouse have a delicate constitution and are prone to disease. Balanced against which is the fact that they live in fantastically breathtaking countryside in Scotland and the north of England and go like dingbats.

No one really took much notice of grouse until Queen Victoria bought Balmoral and insisted that everyone spend the summer in Scotland. Then someone noticed that the wee birds were good eating, well grown by August and supremely challenging targets. Here was something worth coming to Scotland for. Even the Prince of Wales thought it worth staying with the parents, if he could shoot a few grouse. Grouse shooting promptly became frightfully glamorous and exclusive.

Today grouse shooting is not exclusive; but it is frightfully expensive. Truly horrifyingly expensive. When all the odds and ends, travel, hotels and tips are factored in, you are looking at numbers in the order of £100 per brace of birds in the bag. A hundred brace day on a driving moor, then, if you can get one, racks up a bill of £10,000. Between eight Guns that is £1,250 per head. If you go for a week, with, say three days shooting, the price per day may even out a little lower. The total however goes ever upward. Grouse are not for the faint walleted.

There are quite practical reasons, glamour and excitement apart, why grouse are so gruellingly expensive. You need a lot of heather to keep a grouse in grub. The first step therefore is to buy a big moor. The bigger the better. Moors don't come on the market too regularly so potential buyers have to be prepared to bid up for a decent bit of ground. Around the world there are a remarkable number of extraordinarily rich folk who think the world of grouse and you must be prepared to outbid them for openers. You must also be prepared to outbid interest groups who would buy moors for reasons other than grouse. The RSPB (Royal Society for the Protection of Birds) is a case in point. I could go off on a major tangent about the RSPB, but this is not the place. Suffice it to say, that they are very well funded and are quite likely to be in the bidding for one reason or another and shooting grouse is not one of them.

Then, in order to keep the heather in good fettle you will have to put in, or improve, the drainage and that will almost certainly involve improving the roads, if any, or building them if not. The house, if there is one, and the keeper's cottage or keepers' cottages will doubtless need some improvements too. About the only thing you can do with a grouse moor that brings in any money, as opposed to consuming it in bucket loads, is put sheep on it. Sheep however have the effect of degrading the heather and they are guilty, inadvertently, of spreading disease among grouse via the ticks and bugs they carry without necessarily harming themselves. It is a toss up whether it is better to own a moor which consumes a terrific lot of money but which produces a goodly number of grouse, or a moor and some sheep which costs less but produces very few birds. It all depends how much you like grouse - as opposed to money.

In addition to which grouse populations tend to be cyclical anyway, with periodic population crashes due to disease. There is a whole science devoted to understanding grouse, and there are robust debates on what the causes of these cycles might be. Weather conditions and overpopulation of sheep or grouse are generally agreed to be the principal contributors. The final irony of the grouse is that it is possible to have too many of them. More than a few grouse left on a moor to their own devices will cross infect each other with everything going, principally a gruesome worm, and promptly die in droves. This is one of the great inconsistencies about grouse that those who don't shoot or who don't like grouse to be shot can never totally grasp. There is no such thing as leaving a 'A jolly good breeding stock of birds'. I am no expert, but I know that a few over the odds at Christmas and they all die by Easter. Keep after them hard right to the end of the season and the chances are that there will be more grouse next year than ever. It seems improbable but if you want the science ask the Game Conservancy Trust. Owning a moor is a vocation, not a hobby, like being a grouse keeper is a life not a job. On top of which you have to set fire to your moor from time to time. Heather sprouts, grows old and dies. Grouse only eat young heather shoots. So in order to maintain a nicely developing pattern of heather growth you have to systematically burn off the older areas of heather in order to encourage new growth for the grouse. Burning moorland is a dodgy business, best left to experts who are now constrained by laws anyway, to stop them burning up their assets and livelihoods and themselves, to a small window of opportunity. If it's not raining.

If there are not too many birds, or too few, overwintered on the moor, and if the burning season is a success and the breeding season not overshadowed by rain or sudden cold snaps or disease or a sudden population crash for reasons as yet unrecognised and if predators have not run riot through the chicks, then you may be in for a season of grouse shooting and that, dear friend and novice sportsman, is why grouse shooting costs so much. Every bird shot must subsidise the three years out of five when shooting fails to cover its costs and pay for the fixed costs of money and of maintenance and keepering for the full five year cycle. And that is just to break even.

'Grouse shooting is not for the faint walleted'

There are three principal ways to shoot grouse, each progressively more expensive and each progressively more difficult. It is arguable which is the best fun. I don't want to harp on about money, but this is supposed to be a help to the novice so suffice it to say that walking up is probably the cheapest method. You may be charged by the bird or by the day, but either way don't expect much change from £200 per Gun for a day. 'Dogging' will involve fewer Guns, involves dogs and handlers and may accumulate the same bag. You should expect therefore to pay the same price as a walking up team, either per bird or per day. Driven grouse shooting starts at £75 per brace of birds and a bag of perhaps fifty brace between eight Guns and it is just uphill from there. Don't be surprised if there is a queue regardless of price. Mere money will not get you to the head of it. I don't know what does, because no one I know has got any.

It used to be the case that if you were fit and enthusiastic and broke you could walk parts of the moor which were inaccessible to those less fit and enthusiastic and rich enough to shoot the easy ground. Sportspersons would seem to be fitter and more enthusiastic today than ever. Or perhaps I am just more broke.

'Dogging' and 'Walking up'

Three chaps, Guns, in a lay-by in the middle of nowhere, 9.00am, middle of September; probably in Scotland. Not all grouse shooting takes place in Scotland, indeed, the best grouse moors are probably in the North of England – North Yorkshire, Cumbria, Northumberland, Lancashire. In fact, they are so good that they are mainly driving moors, which is why the enthusiastic novice may well find himself in Scotland where the range of moors is greater and there is a wider variety of sport.

So three chaps in a lay-by. For me breeches, stockings and short hiking boots with waterproof gaiters. Angus always wears a kilt and his army boots. You wear what you want. Flannel shirts all round and either a tweed jacket or a good pullover and a waterproof. I am a jacket sort of person and keep a jersey in my gamebag. Angus, by contrast, ties his sweater round his middle and keeps a light waterproof in his. We both have caps and cartridge belts. I have six leather loops for carrying birds by the neck buckled to the back of mine. Angus has a small pair of binoculars in a case locked to his. Gamebags are useful under these conditions. A canvas or hessian satchel with a flap, two compartments and a string front. In my life the pully goes in the front; lunch goes in one compartment and game in the other. A broad shoulder strap over the left shoulder where it won't interfere with the stock as I mount. A thumbstick in the left hand. You are the third Gun and must dispose yourself accordingly. I would venture that you might be overdoing things in a kilt. This is a modest sort of outing and is therefore informal in terms of attire. The weather forecast predicts fine, but you can never overlook the occasional shower in Scotland. Having said that it is summer and we will have professionals with us, so that even if the weather does close in we are not expecting any extreme conditions. One can afford to be relatively relaxed in September in a way that you certainly can't in a Highland winter. Wet is one thing, cold is another. We also have lunch; the piece. Two buns with cold meat. No salad; it gets soggy. Slice of cheddar. Lump of fruit cake. Two apples. No drink. There are burns and trickles all over the hill, cold and fresh. That's it.

Two 4x4s pull up. Three folk jump out. For the sake of argument they are Davy, the keeper in a suit and fore and aft hat. Michael and Jean who are a husband and wife team of dog handlers. This day has been set up by a sporting agent through the factor of the estate. Davy, Michael and Jean have worked together for several seasons now. Michael and Jean bring their dogs here for the season and work them to Guns combining a working holiday on the moors with developing and bringing on their dogs which they breed and work for a living. If there is a driven day on the moor they may pick-up or either one can load for guests as required. Davy has a beat on the estate. While the headkeeper has overall control of the grouse shooting Davy manages one beat on the driving moor and is responsible for periodic days like ours on the periphery. Since none of us has met before there is a round of introductions to begin with. Davy's first suggestion is that he might remove his tie. 'Ye never 'naw,' he says, 'some guests always need ye t'look the part. So it a'ways starts on.' In his estate tweed suit, boots and gaiters, the tie is the only element of his gear that is other than purely functional. The others are dressed much as we are. Boots, breeks, gaiters, jersey and waterproof. We follow the two vehicles off the road and a little way through a meadow under the lee of a steep hill. This time as we disembark Michael and Jean decant four pointers from their truck while Davy adds a Labrador to the throng that is presently milling about. 'Gentlemen,' he says 'Ye'll see the moor we shall be working yonder.' He points with his stick towards a patch of purple heather that runs along the ridge between the hill under which we are presently gathered to another of similar scale some three or four miles distant. It looks a very long way off. 'We'll make our way steadily up the hill to come to the moor at the far end first, given the way the wind is lying. Then we can work back along the ridge and down the flank across the saddle. Then we can work steadily down through the day, so that we can finish just round this shoulder and only drop down to be back here.'

It sounds like a lot of work.

Actually Davy is being quite kind. By starting here we can walk the full length of the ridge climbing progressively as we go, gaining height all the time, so that we arrive at the right end of the moor to be able to work the dogs. Then we will spend the bulk of the day working the moor and losing height, such that we end up on the nearer end and will have a short downhill walk back to where we presently are. There is never any avoiding the first climb, but it will be less painful on the angle than yomping straight up the face. There are moors where a Range Rover can drive you directly to your butt, or to your point of departure for a walk. So I've heard.

This is better for the soul. 'If you'd like to get your guns then, gentlemen. Off we go.'

Davy and his dog lead, three guests in the middle, handlers behind with the dogs. Lean, short haired pointers. They might be English Pointers, German Shorthaired Pointers; they might be Vislas or Weimeraners, or English or even Irish Setters. The key thing is that they hunt and point; find by scent where birds are sitting and then freeze before the birds are disturbed.

The Guns are carrying their guns in the sleeves. This is where a light canvas or nylon sleeve is a boon. A big sheepskin and leather affair is fine for standing at a covert shoot, or protecting a gun from the rigours of the motor car, but where you may have to carry your gun for several miles and then carry the sleeve for several more, lightness and the ability to be rolled up and tucked in the game bag are central.

Just how central becomes apparent after walking for the first couple of miles. The modern, sedentary, screen gazing, indoor existence is no preparation for the rigours of affordable grouse shooting. Even those diligent visits to the gym, with which we delude ourselves concerning our fitness, are insufficient preparation for an undertaking such as this. If you run every day with a half marathon at weekends and reckon five or ten miles should be sprinted; then maybe you will not suffer like the rest of us. If you are SAS trained, cross country ski for fun and think that an aqua lung is for cissies, then skip ahead. If, on the other hand, your idea of a fun evening is a glass of wine, some funky pasta and a jig on the dance floor before bedtime, you are going to be in trouble. If you fall into the beer or three, some nuts, a curry and a video category then you are going to be in Hell right about now; while the steak and kidney pud, bottle of decent claret, steam pudding and a good cigar crew shouldn't even apply. I have seen urban sportsmen beaten to a pulp before we even reached the moor.

If you have any doubts about fitness, try this simple test. Find a down escalator, as it might be in a shopping centre or office building – not Holborn on the Central Line, but something comparatively modest – and run up it. If you make it, chances are you will survive grouse shooting. If you don't, either pay the big money and be driven to your moor of choice, or stick to the pheasants. This is not a joke.

Just how much not a joke you will probably be discovering right about now. We have been walking for an hour and while Angus pounds on regardless, being an SAS trained marathon running masochist – hence the kilt – I am certainly seeing the world through a red mist of pain and with any luck you are too. Sensitive keepers, familiar with the failings of fat neo grouse-shooters from the soft south, will stop frequently to point out features of interest on the hill opposite, as it might be bracken or a bush, or simply to admire the view – mostly bracken and bushes – such that thee and me can get enough breath to survive this important period. Then quite suddenly it doesn't seem so bad after all. This is second wind, and is a Godsend. Either that or the keeper has slowed the pace to the extent that while we shall have no time to shoot the moor on arrival, we shall at least make it without a coronary. The last half an hour, incidentally, is invariably the worst; characterised, as it is, by the steepest climb and endless false horizons which fall away one after another to show that you are not there yet.

The upshot is that after a couple of hours of walking we are assembled on the ridge and can sit for a minute and contemplate both the truly spectacular views and the relentless pounding of our hearts. Never neglect the views. Quite apart from their soul lifting and awe inspiring abilities, which are considerable, grouse are fickle creatures and this point may very well be the highlight of your day. Make the most of it.

Beyond the ridge the heather sweeps down and round back towards the hill where we left the vehicles which are still visible, speck-like in the distance. Davy outlines the plan. With the wind now more or less in our faces we can work the dogs back along the top of the bowl in the first beat. Then we can walk back through the heather on a narrow front shooting as we come and dog back the final third of the moor in the final beat of the day which will leave us almost at the foot of the far hill with only a short hike round and down to the cars. Three swathes may not seem like a lot, but there is a big acreage of heather to cover and three should be quite enough for our purposes. The early mist has now burned off and the sun is beginning to warm us up. There is even a debate as to whether we should dump some surplus gear here to save carrying it. The bowl is quite steep though and by the time we return to this end of the moor we shall be several hundred feet below this peak. No one fancies the climb when they could be having a rest, so with spare gear stowed in the game bags, it is time to load up, unleash the dogs and set to.

Walking in heather with a gun is something of an art in itself. The best way is to keep your stick in the uphill hand and to lean slightly into the hill. The gun meanwhile should be on your shoulder, or at the high port with the butt on your hip. Always, of course, with the safety catch on and fingers away from triggers. Remember that there are dogs to your front and folk to either side of you, not least uphill. Should you slip, always try to fall into the hill keeping those muzzles well up to the vertical. If you do take a spill, and everyone does from time to time, always open the gun afterwards, remove the cartridges and check the barrels are clear before proceeding. Even if you have kept the muzzles clear of the heather at all times, still do this. It helps to settle you after the adrenalin rush of a fall, and – just as importantly – it is a signal to others that you recognise that you have just undergone an 'At Risk' moment, but that you are a collected and responsible and safe Gun nonetheless and you would be very grateful if the subject was not raised again. And if you get into the habit of gathering yourself together and checking the muzzles every time you fall over then you may be assured that no more will be said. If the keeper or one of your neighbours in the line were to say, 'I should check your barrels, if I were you' it has less to do with the fact that you may have heather sprouting in your muzzles, than it does with the fact that you apparently don't care that you do; which makes you unsafe, and them nervous.

There is also the loaded question of what to shoot. The answer is grouse, and to be honest, the likelihood of seeing anything else at this elevation is remote. If you haven't seen a grouse before, and you haven't, the impression is of a brown and white rocket which gargles as it flies. Your red grouse is only reddish, somewhat like a henna-ed partridge if that is any help to you. The underside of the wings and tail are paler, and they have fluffy white spats on their ankles. They also have red eyeliner. Take a look at the label on the Scotch bottle. If it has just leapt off a pointer's nose, out of heather, on a grouse moor and is going away at high speed, and gargling, it is probably a grouse. You will probably hear grouse before you see one. The call of the grouse is distinctive and does wonders for the spirits of Guns labouring up a mountainside. It is traditionally represented as 'Go Back! Go Back! RRrrrrrrrrrr!!!!' This last rolling gargle is what you tend to get when they burst out of the heather under your feet or as the consequence of having a pointer's nose up their paler parts.

You might see a hare or two in the high tops. These are mountain hares and broadly similar to the brown hare of the lowlands. They are shootable, but since the last thing you want to do is lug a great hare about all day, don't shoot one. By the time you are half way up the hill the logic of this position will be unassailable.

Dogging with pointers or setters is not a complex procedure but, as with all shooting, it requires a degree of discipline and a deal of trust between dogs, handlers and Guns.

We adjust ourselves more or less into a line. We are three Guns, two handlers and the keeper. We want a Gun at the top of the line and a Gun at the foot, with the third somewhere in between. The handlers will usually work one pair of dogs at once to keep them fresh and give each pair a break from time to time. The handler of the working pair will be broadly in the centre of the line, near to where the keeper will govern proceedings. The second handler and the spare dogs will walk in the line probably below the centre. The roles are something like this: the dogs will lollop about back and forth under the guidance of their handler seeking to wind or scent the birds as they sit motionless in the heather hoping that we will all amble by without noticing them. From time to time a dog will catch wind of one or more birds lying just ahead of where we presently are, at which point the dog in question will freeze solid as a rock, traditionally with one paw raised pointing to where the birds are sconced, hence the term pointer.

At this juncture the other dog or dogs will be restrained for the time being and the attention of the party alerted to the dog on point. The nearest Gun or Guns and the dog's handler will then close up in formation on the dog which will be encouraged to make further headway with caution or 'Lay on' which it will duly do by moving slowly and stealthily forward step by step until the grouse, one, several or more, finally lose their collective nerve and burst forth from their hiding places and zoom off at top speed as fast as their wings will carry them. At which point the Gun or Guns will neatly pot one or more grouse each as the birds depart. That is the theory. Key elements to remember are to shoot the grouse and not the dog. This may seem obvious, but there is much that can go wrong and this is a tense and exciting moment and tense and exciting moments are where disasters often occur. For example, a Gun might, while moving into position on a dog which is pointing, step on another grouse, which takes off with a strangled squawk almost from under his feet sending him flailing backwards into the heather, which sets off the birds under the dog's nose, which causes the dog in question suddenly to bound forward in a temporary and entirely understandable lapse of its iron self control, causing its handler to shout 'STOP! STAY! YEBUGGER! BRUTUS! STAY! STOP! LEAVEIT! COMEHERE!" or something very similar, while guns start going off on all sides. The summary of the situation is that

Perplexed Pointer

there are now grouse flying in all directions, dogs bounding about, handlers yelling, one Gun taking a shot or two at birds which have just broken unexpectedly past his nose, one Gun trying to get a bead on rapidly departing grouse, one Gun flat on his back in the heather thinking he has just stepped on a mine, the keeper's retriever hearing shots and assuming she can now get in on the act at last and a keeper wondering who has just shot what and why and whether he wouldn't be better off with an office job himself instead of shepherding a lot of soft southern jessies about the hill. It is very important therefore that everyone 'Keeps the heid,' when the *moment critique* occurs.

Under which circumstances the following happens. The pointer comes on point. The second dog, dogs usually being worked in pairs, is restrained - a quiet word or whistle or a hand signal at which he simply sits obediently in the heather - admire that training, why don't you? - the two nearest Guns lay aside their sticks and carefully approach the pointer, one a little above the dog, the other a tad below, as far as possible not from behind. With the Guns in position the handler signals to the dog to push on, which he duly does, a step at a time until the covey bursts from the heather. Half a dozen grouse hurtle away dead ahead across the heather. The dog never flinches. Each Gun, waiting until the birds have reached a properly sporting distance, then takes a right and left dropping four grouse into the heather thirty odd yards ahead. Both quickly reload, because the young birds in a covey very often break first and the dog is still advancing slowly when sure enough another brace of birds erupt and with one neatly judged shot from each Gun - both having instinctively recognised which bird was the more sporting for the other - another brace drop into the heather. The Guns reload again but the dog has lost interest for the time being indicating that this is it for the covey and everyone - not least the keeper - relaxes.

On the basis that things have gone somewhere between the disaster scenario and the text book version, take a deep breath and savour the moment. OK, so we did not get six for six; but we also didn't shoot the dog, the handler or each other. Perhaps there weren't even six to shoot at, but so what? There were one or two and we haven't come far, after all. We are on the scoreboard at any rate, and with the grouse rather than anything else. Life is good right now.

Don't go galloping across the heather to fetch the birds. Where grouse is, grouse may yet be. Retrieve your stick. Adjust the game bag on your shoulder. Tighten the pullover round your middle. Wipe the smile off your dial. Bet you can't. Take a long hard look at where those birds fell into the heather up ahead.

This may be a good moment to change the places of the Guns, most particularly in order to put someone who has not yet shot into the middle in order to maximise their chance of a shot. We may agree to change every hour or every shot or at random, but politeness dictates that each Gun should have an equal opportunity and the one in the middle is likely to get more than most.

Having gathered ourselves together once more we can proceed. Nothing eventuates for the next thirty yards, and so we arrive without incident at the point where there should be several dead birds lying in the heather. All heather looks very much alike. That is why it is so important to look long and hard at where your birds fall. It was about here. Aha! Two steps up the hill are a few feathers and there is a grouse, which means that the second should be 'Here!' or 'There!'. One is still missing and Davy's old Lab finally gets her oar into the game and after a degree of snuffling about does a bit of pointing of her own before pouncing on a clump and emerging with a not very dead grouse and returning with it to her boss. He knocks it on the head with his stick and stows it in his game bag. Three picked. On we go.

And so the first pass of the bowl proceeds. We walk steadily but not fast, allowing the dogs time to work the ground effectively, watching as they quarter back and forth, back and forth, never getting too far ahead of the line, looking back at regular intervals to Michael or, as it might be Jean for guidance or just to make sure they haven't gone off by themselves. Every now and again there has been a point, and the two nearest Guns have closed in, and there has been a shot or two with more or less effect. Each of the Guns has had a shot and everybody has scored. Not all the grouse have been pointed. Several times birds have been disturbed by the walkers before the dogs had time to point them, noticeably just before the dogs were changed about. This is unsurprising. As the dogs work, their ability to scent effectively becomes progressively dulled by the continuous work and it is important to give them regular breaks. Several of the birds thus flushed were nonetheless shot and collected. There is no rule in dogging that all grouse must be flushed by the dogs. It is crucial though to be aware of where the dogs are at any given time, since if the dogs are working ahead of you when you flush a grouse at your feet the bird may fly over the dog at some point, and to shoot at it there would be disastrous. Despite the sun on your back and the fresh air in your lungs and the fact that the heart attack which you thought was imminent only a couple of hours ago seems to have receded, and the grouse in the bag, you cannot relax completely. Keep an eye on the dogs. Remember to keep in line. Stay alert and try not to daydream. These few rules apart, it's a walk in the park

Having completed the first beat, it is time for a rest and lunch.

Lord, can there be a better way to spend forty minutes? Leaning against a warm stone on the edge of a Scottish hillside, guns propped - unloaded in case you were wondering, which you shouldn't be by now - on the gamebags, dogs lying comfortably in the heather, the sun shining and the shadows of clouds rippling across the purple below. A bap, a piece of cheese, a few brace of grouse in the bag and more to come. As you watch the ravens, soaring in the thermals, there is a sense of having worked hard for your sport and the satisfaction of things having gone right and having been done right. Yes, it is all very old fashioned, what with the dos and don'ts and the rituals and the rigmarole, but, as you know now, there is a purpose behind all the fiddly bits and sense in the whole regime. There is not a snowball's chance of your being here for any other reason than to shoot grouse, and once here, the only proper thing to do is to grouse shoot. These are fundamental rules the logic of which is inescapable from where you are presently sitting. A setter plants her head in your lap as your cap slips over your eyes for a moment. The sun is warm, the surroundings are unspeakably peaceful and quiet and comfortable. 'Aye,' says Davy, 'time we were about it again.'

The beat back will be slightly different. Since our backs are against the wind now, the dogs will not be able to scent the grouse far enough ahead for a proper point to be established. If the wind is in the right quarter, it is sometimes possible to point back and forth across the wind and make use of the dogs in both directions. We could climb back to the top of the ridge and go back to where we started and dropping down once more repeat the first beat on different ground. Time and energy being what they are however, the form is that we shall walk the second beat back, flushing the birds as we go, and then dog back the final sweep.

In effect we shall be 'walking up' the grouse. This is a common way of shooting grouse and while more uncertain than using pointers, is thoroughly agreeable for all that. The dogs can hunt, but they will be unlikely to wind birds before they flush. Accordingly we line out much as before, ten or fifteen yards apart to cover new ground and once in line we begin to walk slowly through the heather. The pointers are being kept back by Jean and Michael to save their energy for the last beat of the day, so Davy gives his Labrador her head and she is moving steadily ahead of him in the centre of the line. Since you are at the top of the line, the Lab is not working in front of you. This is therefore one of the few times when it is permissible to carry your gun 'at the trail', that is gripped from above around the action and carried horizontally, muzzles forward, at hip height. If there were either people or dogs ahead, this would be a mortal sin, but since there are neither it is both permissible and comfortable. It also does not require much adjustment should birds flush and you want to mount quickly.

Which, indeed, they do and you do. A quick glance to confirm that Davy's dog has not got unnoticed between you and the birds – there is more time than you think, even though the grouse are flying downwind – drop the stick and 'Bish! Bosh!' a brace into the heather. A right and left. Hell, you are getting a bit good at this. Reload quickly because where one is, more may be; and with a close look at the heather where the birds fell, take a step and away goes an old bird behind you angling down the hill. You must have walked right over him. You try to swivel but the hill catches you off balance and only a deal of teetering actually keeps you upright. Not that it matters because it passes directly behind Angus who spins, gun neatly vertical the while, and drops it thirty-five yards out. We now have a brace of birds ahead and a singleton down behind. The line stops while Davy sends the Lab for the singelton. As she gallops back she disturbs yet another bird. Three guns come up, but quite rightly none are discharged. Two reasons; first and most important there is a dog working in the vicinity. Second, the bird got up some fifteen to twenty yards back. By the time it is a safe distance from the dog it will be forty yards off; too far for a reasonable shot. Leave it be. The Lab soon finds Angus' bird and returns it to Davy. Now we all move forward, you especially focusing intently on the clump where your birds fell. And indeed, there they are, side by side in the heather. Into the game bag and onwards once more. Since all the Guns have an equal chance of treading on a grouse when walking up there is no need to vary the line after each shot. It is worth knowing however that grouse are much more likely to run up hill than down, so it is never a disadvantage to be at the top of the line when walking up. It may require an extra climb first thing, but it nearly always pays off.

It is also not inconceivable when walking up grouse, if you are at the very top, to see a ptarmigan. I don't suppose that one Gun in a dozen has shot a ptarmigan or even seen one. They live way above the tree line and they are the grouse's somewhat simple country cousin. I dare say I do them an injustice, they're not that simple; it is just that they so seldom see people, let alone Guns, that they have a very limited fear of us. They also have astonishing camouflage and as you walk through the mossy scree along the ridge, your first impression is of rocks rolling under their own steam. Then several rocks detach themselves from the hill and fly in a short arc to land behind you. These are ptarmigan. Lighter in plumage than the red grouse, and pure white in winter dress, they are rather sweet birds with their naïve sense of security as you hove into view. If the terrain is seriously steep the little snowbirds may give Angus down below a sportingly high shot as they circle round you. From where you are, shooting one will be a relatively simple affair. If you see ptarmigan though, you will know that you have earned your sport today.

Yes, I have shot one. I see from my gamebook that I recorded that I doubt I shall shoot another. I don't have the heart for the climb, let alone shooting cute little snowbirds. Back to the moor. And we have almost come to the end of the second beat when we encounter another covey which break every which way from under the line. We must have walked almost into the middle of them. This time you make the turn without incident and drop one bird behind you. Another is shot in front. Both are picked and the second beat is complete.

A pause for a drink at the burn that runs down the hill between the rocks and then it is time to complete the last beat of the day. It has clouded up somewhat and there may be rain on the way. Scent doesn't work well in rain and while you can walk up grouse in the wet, the damp takes the edge off the whole escapade big time. At this height too, the clouds can come in as thick as fog in no time flat, and not even a man as local and experienced as Davy would want to go far under those conditions.

It is always worth remembering that conditions can change on the hill very quickly and very dramatically indeed. Sometimes this is bad. I was once walking up grouse in the high tops when the clouds came in from nowhere. We stopped at once and foregathered in a corrie and ate the remains of our pieces. It was a job to see our hands in front of our faces and no one, not even the two gillies with us, was going anywhere for the time being. Then it came on to rain. Sitting in the hills in September is not the end of the world. Sitting wet in the hills begins to get miserable quite quickly and a couple of the party were without wet weather gear and they began to chill. It was all looking increasingly bleak when the clouds lifted as quickly as they arrived and all was well.

Sometimes changing conditions are really rather good. I took a girlfriend stalking once. She had not been to Scotland before and was not at all sure about stalking from the off. We arrived at the lodge at night in the pouring rain. We stood about in more drizzle next morning for a bit while the stalker 'Ummed' and 'Ahhed' and then determined that we might as well take a walk for our efforts. We tramped through the rain, up hill, for a couple of hours. Eventually we sat, damp, depressed and exhausted, in the usual state of high altitude disrepair, in the lee of some rocks somewhere. You couldn't see twenty feet. She was one cheesed off lady. I could feel this affair slipping away with every drip from the rim of her hat.

Stalkers, keepers, gillies; is it luck half the time or do they set these things up deliberately? Even as we sat steaming gently and catching our breath a shaft of sunlight pierced the cloud as sharp and defined as if you could reach out and catch it in your hand. As we watched, it spread and spread until our little world was filled with golden light. Then as if a magician had whipped a hanky off a jar, the mist vanished and there below us was the glen in all its glory and the loch sparkling away in the distance with a rainbow over it. The poor girl was so gobsmacked by the sight that she just sat and stared. Not only was there Scotland all sparkly and damp and in glorious technicolour, but we were also surrounded by deer.

So time for the last beat of the day. Setters and pointers and grouse and Guns. A re-run of the first beat, except that you are not the novice of this morning. So rather than repeat a description of the beat, let us consider instead what we have learned during the course of the day.

We have learned that walking up hills is no stroll and that the right gear and just a tad of training saves a deal of pain. We have learned to love our stick all of a sudden too. Grouse can sit for a long time without moving but when they move, they move very quickly and there is no guarantee which direction they will go. Where one grouse is, several more may be also. Grouse like walking up hill. Pointers point and retrievers retrieve, although there is no hard and fast rule about this. Always check the barrels, not only after a slip, but generally. Never shoot over a dog. Walking, warm sun, a bap and a dog can be a soporific combination. Keepers do not understand the concept of a snooze. Conditions can change quickly and dangerously on the hill. Never rush to retrieve a grouse and always reload immediately. Ptarmigan live high up and are pretty rather than sporting, though it is a hell of a climb just to find that out. Grouse shooting is great. All of which musings bring us all to the end of our day on the hill for the time being. The birds are laid out on the grass, while gunslips and pullovers are retrieved from the bottom of gamebags along with the squashed remains of fruit cake which is a welcome snackerel, it being teatime. Thirteen-and-a-half brace in all, twenty-seven grouse. Hearty congratulations all round. Guns in slips. Check once more that it is empty. When you pick up a gun: check. When you put down a gun: check. When you get it out: check. When you put it away: check. If someone gives it to you or if you give it to someone: check it again.

Another diversion. Chap I know was hosting a day and someone took a dangerous shot, nearly topped a beater. Chap was absolutely furious and tore strips off the miscreant in full view of everyone. Lots of apologies and embarrassment. Chap says the rest of the morning is cancelled; they'll take an early lunch and review the afternoon. Shoves his gun in a sleeve in a frightful paddy, slings it into the car and storms off. Even the beaters are feeling a bit sorry for everyone. Over lunch the miscreant creeps off. Chap says he'll allow the other Guns the afternoon drives. Lines them out. Unships his gun and checks it. Loaded. No one else saw. But me. No one can expect to be completely lucky three times in the same day.

With the birds stowed once more, we amble down and round the hill to the vehicles. Uphill may be harder work than down, but down can be death to guns. If the gun is hung over your shoulder in its sleeve, and you stumble, you can sit on it and break the stock or bend the barrels. Carry the gun on your shoulder, or, being sleeved, at the trail. This is safer for the gun.

Back at the vehicles the thorny issue arises of how everyone is to be rewarded. Walking and dogging fall slightly outside the general scheme of things and there is no established tipping tariff. If this has been a rented day – which is likely – then the fees of Michael and Jean and Davy, will have been included in the price and tips might be considered redundant. Gestures are important however. There are three Guns and three staff. In my view, Guns on a day such as this should equip themselves with a wad of £10 notes and a bottle of malt whisky. We shot twenty-seven grouse, and I venture that two £10 notes from each Gun will be appropriate. It is probably best to agree this in advance with the other Guns and then stick the lot into the palm of the skipper, organising or senior Gun and let him do the actual handover, otherwise the whole thing becomes an absurdly formal pantomime. We'll make Angus do it. So the senior Gun shakes Davy warmly by the hand and the notes pass. He may quietly say to Davy that he should see Michael and Jean right for a drink also, at which Davy will nod firmly, though whether he ever will is a mystery we are not vouchsafed. What we have left however is three bottles. Three Guns, three bottles, three staff. If Angus and I give one each to the handlers with a warm thank you for their efforts and a word of appreciation for their diligence and the brilliance of their dogs, this leaves you, as the novice, to thank the keeper. He's got a brace of birds for you anyway. Small estates may leave you with the whole bag, but grouse being one of the few gamebirds still having real market value, generally a brace each is the rule. Shake his hand, thank him for delivering your first grouse and a memorable day, hand him the malt. He may be a teetotal son of the manse, but it is the thought which counts after all. If it has been a successful and agreeable day and if there has been geniality and friendliness between all and sundry, do not be surprised, when he hears that you shot your first grouse, if he 'bloods' you.

Blooding is a strange ritual. It is actually not really a ritual at all. More a gesture. If you tell a keeper or a stalker that the grouse or the deer, for whose recent demise you were responsible, was your first of that species, it is not unusual for him to take a blob of blood from the carcass and smear it on your cheek. That's it. The whole deal. Squealing and rubbing at the smear with a hanky is not the approved response. It is a serious moment. It goes right back to the premise from which we departed at the beginning of this book. You, we, all of us undertake these activities for sport and for our own satisfaction. At the end of a successful day we are happy, elated, content. We feel strangely alive and fulfilled. It has taken the death of an animal, a wild thing and free, perhaps more than one, to bring us to this pass and that should never be overlooked. Their blood is on our hands and on our heads. The smear is a literal manifestation of that blood. It signifies neither the vanity of victory, nor any existential theorising, it means that you did the deed and you wear the blood as proof that you did. You can wash the blood off later, but the mark remains.

I don't know of anyone having been blooded by a pheasant keeper on a lowland shoot; perhaps they are not as superstitious as their Highland brethren. It's part of the day anyhow.

Driven Grouse

I suppose we had better consider driven grouse. I certainly wish I could. Let us dream of being zillionaires; and supremely well connected zillionaires at that. Let us dream of driven grouse.

It must be said that driven grouse shooting is regarded by most shooting folk as the ultimate sport where shotguns are concerned and the point where skill and excitement ultimately collide.

We know it's expensive. We even know why it is so expensive. But why is it so exciting? Two reasons, I suppose. First, grouse fly like Cruise missiles; which is to say that they fly very fast and hug the contours of the ground. They skim the heather at top speed, dipping and jinking like so many tiny jump jets which makes them very hard to shoot and harder still to shoot well. The truly stratospheric amounts of money involved add a patina of glitz into the bargain. Secondly, this low level tactical ability makes grouse shooting quite dangerous, not only for the grouse, but for everyone else involved too.

You recall that ground game is mostly banned on commercial shoots because of the danger of Guns blazing away from time to time at ankle height? Well, ground game is big and slow compared to grouse, and grouse shooting largely takes place at or about head height. The Guns who shoot grouse regularly are recognised as being among the most proficient, reliable, level headed and safe Guns around. Just to be included in a party shooting driven grouse is therefore a badge of considerable importance. It is one thing to be a steady pheasant Shot or a tidy partridge Gun. An invitation to shoot driven grouse – even if accompanied by a hefty invoice – is still a signal that you have passed every shooting test, social and practical, with flying colours. People still get shot though, and not only by zillionaire parvenus either, all of which makes for a very exciting day indeed. The best driven grouse shooting, by which is meant the most prolific moors, is situated in the north of England. Wemmergill, Bolton Abbey, Blubberhouses, Broomhead, Littledale – names to conjure with.

The format for the day is very much the same as for any other formal driven shoot. Guns assemble at a house somewhere in the vicinity of the moor which is to be driven and there are introductions all round. The beaters will probably start somewhere else entirely. This is not social segregation, mark you, but a reflection of the scale of the drives and the acreage which is involved in the whole undertaking. Pickers-up will also be floating about somewhere near the Gun end of the proceedings. The pickers-up tend to be a bit special on a big grouse day too. Best dogs and best handlers. Not only is picking-up on the moors good training for competitive dogs in the summer when there is little other work about for them, but the conditions are more clement than winter days and there is the chance to see top Guns in action. Invitations to pick-up on notable moors are almost as sought after amongst doggy people as invitations to shoot among the Guns.

The Guns are dressed much the same as ever, only less so. Lightweight suits or sleeveless jackets are the order of the day, and short boots with light stockings. Sunglasses are often a help; not least in the context of an off shot. There are several brands of reinforced shades on the market and they are good value when you consider what your eyesight is worth. It need not even be a poor shot. When shooting into the heather, pellets have been known to ricochet off stones and pebbles. Not that it makes anyone feel better that it was an accident rather than an error. Especially if it was your shot; or your eye.

On a top day, each Gun will also have a loader. The loaders too are in a different league from our previous experience. They are not here to mind their Guns, but to load and manage the spare gun for each shooter in order to maximise firepower. You will have heard of guns coming in pairs; this is why. A top Shot will have his guns made in matching pairs or even garnitures (threes); each a replica of the other. The makers of best guns pride themselves on being able to render each gun of a pair indistinguishable from the other, beyond the discreet '1' or '2' engraved about the metalwork. Hence the user is equally accurate, and fast, with either – think Johnny Ringo; or the Sundance Kid.

So there are perhaps eight teams of two. The Guns draw for numbers and embussed in a wagon, or more probably a fleet of Range Rovers, they decamp to the butts followed by another fleet of pickers-up. A brief journey, perhaps up a winding track and the wagons park up. Across swathes of purple heather may be seen a series of hummocks. These are the butts. Butts come in all shapes and sizes. Some are built up, some are sunken. Some are wooden and some are stone. Some are as commodious as a Cornish teashop and some are like a shellhole at Mons. This being a grand day, the butts are naturally frightfully smart – a drystone interior wall with peat turves banked in the front and along the top and a good gravel floor. There may be ten or more butts in a row to allow for wind direction and the complexities of driving grouse in different conditions. The ground under the further butts rises distinctly such that the Guns and loaders in the top butts can see into all the butts lower down while being largely invisible to those below them. The Guns and loaders dispose themselves among the butts in accordance with their allotted numbers. The guns are unsleeved and the cartridge bags conveniently placed – for the loader. The Gun may have a few shells in his pocket for emergencies, but on the whole, loading is the preserve of the loader and shooting is the function of the Gun. Usually the loader will sling a cartridge bag around his neck with a spare within reach. Some loaders use specialised equipment for speed loading such as the Gannochy (a sort of board with fifty shells in clips brass outward) or a cartridge dispenser which issues a pair of rounds at the touch of a button, but this is a trifle overdoing things and smacks of professionalism.

The loader loads the number 1 gun and passes it to his boss; then he loads the number 2 gun and holds it on his shoulder. He keeps two cartridges between the fingers of one hand. He stands slightly behind his Gun's right shoulder.

Do you really want a description of the Loading Waltz?

For the record then (to avoid there being too many Guns and guns, guns are number 1 and number 2, you are the boss, and the loader is loader. Everyone is right handed, too), thus:
Boss shoots twice with number 1 – Blatt! Blatt! Loader holds number 2 at the vertical by the grip in his right hand. Safety catch ON.

Boss holds number 1 by the grip in his right hand and brings it back to the vertical beside his right shoulder, slipping ON the safety catch as he does so.

Boss extends left hand across his body, beyond number 1.

Loader lowers number 2 to slap the fore-end into the Boss's outstretched left palm and at the same time grips number 1 by the fore-end in his left hand lifting it free from Boss's right hand.

'The loaders too are in a different league'

Boss tugs number 2 free of loader's right hand, transfers his right hand from the grip of number 1 to the grip of number 2 and scans the horizon through narrowed eyes.

Loader transfers right hand from grip on number 2 to grip on number 1 and turns half right to eject spent shells and reload. Returns to eyes front with number 1 charged and ready held vertically by the grip in his right hand. Safety catch ON. Re-arms fingers of choice with two spare cartridges.

Repeat until guns are too hot to handle.

A good combo should be capable of twenty rounds a minute by this means. Lord Ripon, that noted Edwardian Shot, once killed twenty-eight pheasants in a minute at Sandringham and is reported to have had seven birds dead in the air at once. He used two loaders for the most part though, and anyway we are not competitive at all nowadays.

The Gun is busying himself too. In each butt are two sticks, like a pair of narrow cricket stumps. He plants one of these at either side of his butt. They are to stop him swinging through the rest of the line on either side. Each Gun's safe arc of fire is between 10.00 o'clock and 2.00 o'clock in front, and to make matters interesting, behind between 4.00 and 8.00 o'clock. When shooting with a single gun it is expected that you take your birds in front and shooting behind is therefore largely redundant. This is especially so at pheasants, for instance. When shooting double guns, however, shooting behind is both normal and expected.

'Aren't there pickers-up behind though?' you cry. And indeed there are, but either they will be so far behind as to be out of range, or, given the undulating contours of moors they will be cached beneath a roll of ground and be safely out of sight; or sometimes they will take up station in some other conveniently safe spot – in the two spare butts on either end of the line for example.

In the butts all is now ready for the off. There is no horn or whistle to start. The beaters probably started half-an-hour ago anyway, two miles away. Two way radios and mobile phones ensure adequate communications between Guns and beaters and ensure that they are both on the same moor and working towards each other rather than away. The combined age and experience of hosts and keepers contributes significantly, of course. For what may be some time nothing happens. Guns stand or sit, resting their barrels on the turf rim of the butt, perhaps enjoying a smoke to keep the midges at bay. Tension mounts. Nothing happens.

A distant blur of black dots could be grouse moving or midges dancing above the butt. They're definitely grouse and even as you watch them pitching in a hundred yards distant on the left, there are two shots from the butt next door. A covey of a dozen or so have hurtled through between you and you neighbour and are now skimming away out of range. Even as you are cursing, the loader says 'Left!' and there are another bunch coming left to right across your front. Swing through the leader and one drops. The rest turn sharply to bisect the butts again. As you turn the loader slaps the spare gun into your hand and ducks down with the other. You pick up the grouse behind and drop another into the heather. Back to the front again and change guns. More birds moving. Two quick shots as they pass and change guns. The traditional Bang! Bang! Bugger! These are coming higher and you get one in front, turn and take another high behind and out to the left. Turn back and change guns again. How many is that? Four, I think. You pick up another covey early heading directly over the butt and shoot twice in front. The first is a miss, but the second one is well dead. So dead that it fizzes straight past your nose to bounce just behind the butt. That would have seriously hurt, if either of you had not seen it coming. A 1½lb bird at 40 mph. Not a comfortable thought. It is not just guns that hurt people on grouse moors. More grouse on the left again. Definitely a right and left there. Change guns. And one more behind. Turn back; change guns. There are beaters in the distance now. Just as you are thinking about safety zones, they vanish into a dip like Zulus in the movie. Coveys are moving right and left now. One down on the right. Change guns. One, two down on the left. Change guns. Now there is a horn. This means that the beaters are about to emerge from their dip and will very much be in range. The horn means no more shooting in front. As if to underline the point a covey now flushes from the heather where you dropped your first bird and which space now appears to be occupied by a beater's head. As the birds pass you pivot, only vaguely noticing the pink faces of the team in the butt slightly above you and thinking how vulnerable they would be if you didn't know exactly what you were doing. And a brace behind. Turn back and change guns. Then there is a whistle. Unload and lay the gun on the parapet. What was that? ten minutes? And how many? Thirteen? Eight in front; four behind and this one right here that nearly took our heads off.

How did we get into this? We are not zillionaires. We are humble novices who do not shoot very often, or very well, with one gun, let alone two. But we can dream, can we not? What does everyone get tipped after a day like this? Lots, is the answer. Crisp £50 notes everywhere. One to the loader and one at least to the keeper. Your host gets a warm handshake naturally and an invitation included in your handsome 'Thank-You' letter to join you at your villa in Antibes for the festival, or to share your box for the Kentucky Derby. Oh, and don't forget to send the jet for him.

Let's go back to where we belong and go rough shooting.

11

ROUGH SHOOTING

Rough shooting describes neither the natures of the folk who undertake it, nor does it imply that they only undertake it in an approximate fashion. The rough in rough shooting refers to the ground over which the sport is undertaken. Which is rough. Tonsured paddocks and furrowed plough is one thing and tended heather quite another. Around the margins however are patches of cover and neglected copses and coverts with a pond or two which together form the staple diet and natural environment of the rough shooter. Rough shooting varies between a bloke and his dog taking a mooch round the fringes with a gun and a pocketful of shells to a half dozen blokes doing the same; sometimes with another handful of blokes with sticks to lend an air of organisation to the proceedings. The bags are not substantial and tend to be varied; somewhat like the blokes and the patches of cover through which they roam. There are no keepers here, dapper in estate tweed. No pickers-up with teams of well trained retrievers lurking in the background. No pens packed with well fed pheasants.

What governs the rough shoot, and the rough shooter, is boundless enthusiasm, the consistent triumph of hope over experience, and a deeply held conviction that winter Saturdays are better spent chasing a pheasant round a wood than redecorating the spare bedroom.

With the increased commercialisation of shooting and the urgent need within agriculture today to press every inch of farmland into remunerative production, the rough shoot is in danger. The times when a bottle of whisky, a genial demeanour and reliably turning out on occasion to chase the pigeons off the newly sown Twenty Acre were enough to secure a landowner's permission to shoot such game as might be found about the place, are going.

On the other hand, there are still some landowners, large and small, who are content to let shooting rights over their ground for a modest consideration. Even faceless bureaucracies, pension funds, offshore corporations and the like, are ready to sign off on a modest shoot, happen the deal is put to them right. This is fertile territory for the incubation of the DIY syndicate to which reference has already been made.

On the basis that a few acres have been secured for the purpose, the question arises of how to make the best of its opportunities. Keepering is a central issue. Thus far keepers have been an essential in our lives. Everywhere we turn in the shooting world there have been keepers organising, governing, shepherding, guarding, tending, rearing and protecting game and generally keepering away diligently in the background. Their contribution is endless, largely unsung, hopelessly under-appreciated by the shooting community and ignored by the wider public. In the absence of a keeper, you begin to realise exactly how valuable they are.

Without the reared bird there is precious little left. Pheasants, partridges and duck are the backbone of the rough shooter's bag and left to their own devices in the wild, without a keeper to look after them, a pretty hamfisted effort they make to survive and flourish. They probably try hard enough, but the odds are stacked against them. There are wild pheasants in this world, but most will be the descendants of reared stock and they have little experience of fending for themselves, particularly when it comes to breeding. At its best the pheasant is a fickle and feckless parent. Cocks mate and push off at once, and hens tend to lay eggs here and there, often in the nests of others and sometimes in more than one place at a time. If they do brood themselves, they are easily shocked off the nest and if they leave for any length of time they can't be bothered to return.

Partridges, the English variety in particular, are far more diligent. They pair up for a season and both parties take equal responsibility for the family and will defend their nest and young valiantly in the face of assault by predators. Too valiantly for their own good, very often. Heroic, but ultimately fruitless. Over the past thirty years the English partridge, which once was so common that it was hardly thought to even need keeping at all, but could be left to its own devices, has declined to disastrous levels. No certain reason has been identified for this collapse. Disease, predation, increased use of pesticides at crucial times in the little partridge's life, changes in the agricultural cycle, climate change and neglect have all been proposed; but no single culprit has yet been fingered. The Game Conservancy Trust is undertaking valuable work in the area and should be supported whenever and wherever possible in doing so.

Mallard, teal, pochard, gadwall, golden eye, pintail, shoveller, tufted, and wigeon are all ducks on the quarry list, although probably mallard and teal are the most likely to be encountered by the rough shooter as opposed to the more specialist wildfowler. Ducks, too, have an awful time in the wild. Pollution is their particular *bête noir*, for obvious reasons, and the lead problem referred to earlier. Duck have also to confront the danger of discarded and broken fishing line which being nylon is virtually indestructible nowadays. Plastics of all sorts are death to ducks. Bottle tops, tubes, tabs, pulls, strings and packaging, carelessly and callously discarded by us, entangle, choke and poison all varieties and breeds of water feeders, as will abandoned cars, cans and supermarket trolleys. Mink, escaped and insanely released, are a voracious and increasing problem.

The commonest threat to all game is predation. And for this, I believe, we are largely responsible. There is more tosh talked about the balance of nature than almost anything else about the countryside these days, but one thing is certain, and that is that the populations of predators are rising progressively. Leaving aside the bizarre preferences expressed by the public for the protection and proliferation of savage killers, through their unstinting support for the RSPB raptor reintroduction programmes and their continuing love affair with foxes and cats, the humbler predators such as crows, magpies and rats, being scavengers and carrion eaters, are provided with a year round selection of delicacies thanks to the awesome effect of the motor car. Whereas once the populations of predators and prey would be equally affected by the changing of the seasons, suffering alike in hard weather and soft; now the scavengers have only to drop onto any verge in any season to find abundant sources of protein to keep them fit and strong. While the tarmac surface of any major road is dotted with the sad remains of this and that, the bulk of the slain, and worse, wounded, are unceremoniously bounced and flung by impact off the highway itself. The verges of a major road are a positive charnel house of corpses. And here the predators feast all year round and wax strong regardless of the weather. Comes the breeding season for ground-nesting birds such as pheasant, partridge or duck, these predators have a field day. Weasel, stoat, fox, feral cat, rat, crow, magpie, hedgehog, mink – all mean only one thing to ground-nesting birds and their eggs and young: death.

What can be done about the problem? Systematic trapping of these threats is the most effective solution. There are approved traps for all these species both in the ground and above it. Traps must be visited at least once in any twenty-four hour period, and this places a considerable strain on the man power resources of any modest rough shoot, and may be impossible for many. However diligent work, especially in the all important breeding season of late April to mid June will repay considerable dividends. Any brood of chicks is likely to sustain losses through bad weather, hunger, disease, and predation. Take any one of these threats out of the equation and the stock improves by a corresponding percentage. Foxes can be shot with a rifle either at dawn or dusk when they hunt or at night, with the aid of a lamp. This is not a treatise on game preservation and there is insufficient space to set out the rules and regulations on these specific areas. There are pamphlets and books aplenty on these topics, though, which will amply repay research both in terms of increasing a stock of wild game on any shoot, no matter how small, and the personal satisfaction to be derived from seeing it there. The same is true of feeding and watering, though these are less labour intensive. Static feeders and drinkers or the provision of rations for ponds and woods will both nourish and retain game on the ground as well as attracting birds from less well tended areas. Nor should feeding stop with the end of the shooting season. Some of the hardest weather may fall after the shooting is over for another year and this is often the hardest time for birds – though not for their enemies. Continuing to feed is not only a moral obligation for those of us who have taken pleasure during the shooting day, but also allows birds to retain strength and vitality into the spring and the breeding season when again the healthy and fit survivors will be retained on the shoot and will be adequately fettled to maximise their breeding opportunities. All of which is to your benefit in the longer term.

Diligent cultivation of your pigeon shooting and beating friends will result eventually in an invite to come hedging and ditching with the rough shooters.

The Rough Shooting Day

The form on a rough shooting day is much the same as for any other organised day, except in miniature. There may be only a few Guns and the same, fewer or none, of beaters. There will be a motley crew of dogs. Things may start later because there is not expected to be as much to do or as far to go to do it. Time is therefore not of the essence. Timing is still important, especially for the novice, and while others may not pitch up until a quarter past the appointed hour, that is their privilege not yours. Anyway, they may be bringing the soup, or the beer, or a dog.

Here we are then, five Guns and four beaters, three spaniels and two Labs and a something which Derek insists is an Abbyssinian Otter Hound called Zebedee, but which shrieks Battersea to the rest of us, who are enjoying a coffee and a smoke at the beet stand behind the barn beside the Christmas trees where Nigel was sconced during the roost shoot back in February. Mention of the roost shoot reminds various of the Guns and beaters of anecdotes concerning that evening and the carouse that followed it, memories of which some of those present are still trying to suppress both individually and locally. Recollections refreshed there is a moment to formulate plans.

Derek is the prime mover in this little shoot and captain of today. As the one remaining employee on the farm, which extends to some 230 acres, it was he who persuaded the elderly owner to let him develop the shoot. In addition to the Christmas trees of sacred memory there is also the neighbouring plantation which housed you and Derek on that celebrated night of pigeons and frolics. There are two decent fields of sugarbeet still partly unlifted and a small wood in the centre of the farm. One side of the wood is set-aside and the other was drilled one width out with maize with the permission of the farmer as part of Derek's benefits package. There is a copse on the other side which contains a pond fed by a stream that runs down the thick hedge. By diligent courtship of the forester in the pub, there is a block of trees on the edge of the farm, which although we are not allowed to shoot in it, can be walked through in the interests of neighbourliness. The fields are variously divided by hedges and ditches. The farm is bordered by keepered estates where good numbers of birds are reared and released. Relations are good between neighbours, not least because since Derek began to take an interest in the farm as a shoot, he has campaigned long and hard against the more obvious predators, principally foxes, which he lamps with a rifle and the crows and magpies, for which he maintains a Larsen Trap. This has prevented the farm from becoming an oasis of predators from which raids can be periodically launched on the neighbouring keepers' stocks. He also beats regularly on the neighbours' shoots. The quid pro quo is that those keepers are perhaps less diligent in securing their boundaries in Derek's direction and consider the few pheasants which slip across to be a modest exchange.

The shoot therefore has five possible drives: the Christmas trees; the plantation; the pond; the wood; the forestry – the plan is therefore straightforward. First the pond. If there are ducks in residence they won't stay long if they hear shots, so it is important to address them first. Four Guns will line out around the edge of the wood and one Gun will accompany the beaters down the hedge to intercept anything from there and will back-Gun the beaters as they go through the wood itself – then we will all line up and blank one of the beet fields into the main wood, which will be drive two. The forestry will be three and then we will finish with either the Christmas trees or the plantation. It doesn't do to shoot every drive every time. Always leave the birds somewhere safe to stay, otherwise they will bugger off for good which seems as reasonable a theory as any.

There is no draw for numbers. The Guns are 1,2,3,4,5 as we are standing in a row just now. Nigel is number 1 and therefore gets to walk on the first drive. You are number 4, since you ask.

A quick word about kit. Although rough shooting isn't rough, nor is it formal. Casual is the order of the day. Suit up, by all means, it is harder to be overdressed than under, but bear in mind that you may be working harder for your shooting than usual. A tie is not obligatory, for example. Thornproof leggings may be a good idea. If you are walking Gun in the wood or the forestry for instance, there will be brambles and thorns aplenty. Walking through the beet will be wet and muddy for sure, so the leggings will be a boon there also. Walking and shooting also means the lightweight slip for the gun and the gamebag to stow it in. You won't want a cartridge bag, twenty shots may be a big day, so a beltful and a few in the pocket to be on the safe side will be ample. Remember to include a handful of bismuth or other non toxic shot shells because duck are on the quarry list today. Gloves, stick, ear-defenders, knife. And this time don't forget your flask. Elevenses will be a self service job today for sure.

So the beaters and Nigel plod off in one direction to the top of the hedge leading down to the pond while the rest of you set out for the opposite hedge to get to the bottom of the pond wood via two sides of the beet field. Don't unship the gun for the time being unless instructed to do so by the captain. The ducks, if there are any, will take wing at any shooting as you move into position and the purpose of the drive will be lost. One of the spaniels and the Abbyssinian Otter Hound are encouraged to work the hedges as you go, however because anything they put out will likely make for the pond wood in any event which is all to the good. As indeed they do and it does. A cock pheasant clatters out of the hedge almost as soon as you begin and skims low across the beet to the pond wood. At least he is there, at any rate. As the party makes its way along the second hedge two more pheasants are rootled out with the same effect. Although pheasants have a habit of vanishing completely when they have been watched doing exactly what was required of them like this, it still lifts the spirits to see them on the move. As you approach the pond wood, Derek signals for numbers 4 and 5 to cross the hedge and stand in the beet on the near side. The other two Guns will dispose themselves on the other corner. Such breeze as there is, is coming across the wood and should encourage the birds towards the line. The beaters meanwhile, seeing the standing Guns almost in position, set off. There are two walking down the edge of the sugarbeet, a third is working his spaniels along the hedge bottom and the stream within, while Nigel is opposite him on the far side. The last two beaters are on the far side of the hedge in the plough beyond.

Unsleeve the gun, and this being a duck drive load up with expensive non-toxic shot. You can put the sleeve and the gamebag on the ground so as not to encumber yourself for the time being.

Nigel has his gun ready since the line is now set round the pond in the distance and he can take any chances that the hedge throws up. Which it duly does, in the form of another pheasant which scampers out of the brambles ahead of a spaniel's nose and after legging it for a few yards with the spaniel in hot pursuit takes off and glides into the wood. That's four pheasants in the wood. One each. This is shaping up to be a big drive.

A minute later another cock lurches out of the hedge and climbing fast across the breeze turns back over the beaters. Nigel lets off two shots without discernible effect and there is a ragged cheer from the beaters. An alarmed quack is quite distinct from the direction of the pond. Good news indeed.

The beaters are now almost at the top end of the wood. There is the squawk of a pheasant and a shot and another cheer from the beaters. Suddenly there is a deal of quacking from within the wood and duck are clearly on the move. Four tiny wine bottles shoot out over Derek's head and seeing him there come hurtling round the corner climbing as they come. Derek gets a shot off as they come and a tailender tumbles. The rest shoot vertically upwards leaving your first shot well behind them, but your second intercepts their new trajectory and a teal thumps into the beet in front of you. There is much quacking now and a pair of mallard are battling against the wind over your neighbour at number 5. One staggers at his first shot, and then collapses very emphatically at his second. Two more mallard are making better headway, well up and with the wind over Derek when he shoots first one and then the other in handsome right and left. 'Right! Right!' comes from the wood and there is a cock pheasant almost over your head, which you have failed to spot while watching Professor Derek's 'How to Shoot Mallard'. With a frantic swing and pull it simply stops and drops. There are shots from the far side of the wood.

As the beaters emerge from the wood, there is some 'Well. Well. Well' –ing, and 'That was a bit of all right!' – ing. Unload the gun and pick up your game. The cock pheasant is no more than two steps behind you and is not a problem, but the little teal seems to have vanished completely, which is incredibly irritating. As you pace back and forth where it ought to be, one of the Labs sets off determinedly through the beet past your legs and emerges some dozen steps away with the little duck in her mouth, its paddles just moving. Huge relief. So you had a teal and a pheasant. Your neighbour had a mallard. Derek had two mallard and a teal and his neighbour number 2 had a pheasant. Nigel caught up with two pheasants. Two brace of pheasants, a brace of teal and three mallard. First drive. Definitely time for elevenses. Flasks out and toasts in all directions. Brilliant start! Marvellous! Fantastico!

Three more drives. More or less shooting for you. Who knows? Let's sprint to the other end. Back at the cars and you're wondering what the form is. Fingering your wallet and wondering just how this is all going to work. Derek keeps but is not a keeper. He is more of the host. Someone must be paying the beaters presumably, but who and how much? There is considerable scope for looking stupid here.

Rough shooting does not conform to any known formality. In this sense too, it is rough. Take it as you find it. Today, perhaps, the total bag was twenty-eight head, being twenty pheasants, two teal, three mallard, two hares as you went across the beet and a pigeon. Which is a pretty good day for five Guns. But as for what it is worth and who should get it? It's a nice question. With luck, whoever invites you will tell you the score when issuing the invitation. If he doesn't; ask. If you don't want to say 'Derek, what do I have to pay for?' then put it in terms of the beaters, and ask 'How will we pay the beaters?' or 'Who will see to a drink for the beaters?' which will probably do enough to prompt an explanation of the financial structure of the day. If the truth be known, he is probably dreading having to bring up the subject himself, not knowing you all that well. This shooting lark costs a ton of money, yet no one wants to be the first to mention it. Weird. British, of course, and frightfully Edwardian. You should also ask about lunch arrangements while you are about it. It may be a catered soup and sausage in the barn affair delivered by someone's long suffering spouse; or it may be bring your own; or perhaps it's 'You're on cheese and pickle sandwiches for ten'. It's as well to know in advance.

There may be any number of variations on a theme, and it slightly depends on the ratio of beaters and Guns, but on a rough shoot it would not be unusual for each Gun to pay for a beater either directly by saying thank you and here's a tenner; or indirectly by putting a tenner in the captain's hat when he asks for a tenner for the beaters. I have been asked for two tenners on the way to lunch in the pub after a splendid little rough shoot, one for my lunch and one for the beaters' lunch, which they got gratis; and a very jolly lunch we had too. The bag tends to go much the same way: assuming there is sufficient to go round, which is always quite a big assumption. Beaters get a brace of birds, Guns get a brace of birds – usually in that order, after all whose fault is it if there aren't enough? – then the spares are offered to the Guns first and then to the beaters. And after lunch, as it might be in the pub, after a pint or three, or four, has been taken, there is a deal of etiquette as to who leaves first or who gets the next round in. This is where shooting legends are made and grow and where shooting reputations are gambled and lost. You are on your own now.

Just because rough shooting is less formal and more easy going than other forms does not mean that any of the fundamental rules can be relaxed. Easy company means safe company and Derek will be no less stern a critic of poor gun handling than the host on a 250 bird covert shoot. Indeed he is every bit as likely to be more forthright, direct and to the point, considering that you are a guest and not a punter paying big money. So always ensure that your gun is unloaded and sleeved at any juncture when not about to be used against fur or feather – and if not sleeved, then open so that others can see that it is empty. When walking across plough or roots ensure that the gun never strays towards fellow Guns or their dogs. If you should stumble, take out the cartridges and check those muzzles. Don't steal birds off other Guns. Rough shooting bags are not huge and you may not have a lot of shooting, but that is no excuse for trying to boost your performance at someone else's expense. Sure, if Nigel blats off twice without effect at some passing pheasant, by all means kill it dead behind him; but not so far behind him as to make it a long shot or a foolish one. Derek has worked hard to create a stock of birds here and you wounding them at stupid ranges will impress no one. If you can kill it dead forty yards away and well up, then so be it. Poaching is a crime much diluted by manifest success; but its guilt is redoubled by failure. Anyway it makes you look greedy and desperate. There may be hedges, ditches, fences and streams to cross, jump, climb and wade. Wait your turn, and offer to hold another's gear while they address the obstacle and offer them yours when you start scaling things. Asking someone to hold your gun for a moment is not an imposition. It demonstrates that you are not inclined to take chances under any circumstances.

Which is reassuring for everyone. Remember always that you are a comparative stranger in this company. A heavily armed comparative stranger with the capacity to maim and kill fellow Guns, beaters, dogs and game. Relaxed and easy-going rough shooting may very well be, but the trust that exists between all the participants is a fragile flower and carelessness or callousness will blow it to kingdom come in an instant. It is simply not polite to scare people out of their wits. Safety is the greatest courtesy of all. There may be a deal of leg-pulling and ribaldry on a rough shooting day which is all part of the fun. It is much less fun if someone is pointing a loaded gun at you. Even if they are laughing.

12

PARTRIDGE SHOOTING

For many sportspersons partridge shooting is, barring the driven grouse which is beyond the reach of normal people, the top of the sporting tree. Perhaps this is because it takes place on the cusp of the changing seasons, between summer and winter; for all the season starts officially on 1 September, October and November are the height of the partridge season. Maybe it is because partridges are little and fly low and quick, almost like grouse. Perhaps it is because partridge shooting has something essentially English about it. Pheasants are, or were, imported from Asia. Grouse are a northern bird, and the north as anyone knows is a foreign country. The partridge is irretrievably Anglo-Saxon. I come from Norfolk, of course, which makes me biased.

All of which is redundant theorising because modern partridges are French. The French or red-legged partridge is so called because it has red legs, and is called French because Napoleon Bonaparte's army wore red leggings. It is also indigenous to France from whence many eggs are now imported to stock manors in this country. Partridge shoots are manors. Pheasant shoots are estates. Grouse shoots are moors. Because grouse live on moors, pheasant shoots are grand and partridge shoots are resolutely yeoman. Probably. There is a rumour that the red-legged partridge is inclined to run when threatened, also like Napoleon's army. If so it is a very old joke indeed.

Whatever the story behind the name the French partridge has largely supplanted the English as the stock of choice on partridge manors. There are practical reasons for this. French partridges are easier to rear, easier to keep, easier to drive over Guns, don't fly far once airborne and have the convenient habit of legging it back to where they started as soon as people have stopped shooting at them. This is in sharp contradistinction to the English bird which is difficult to rear, hard to keep, avoids Guns like the plague and once pushed off its territory is quite likely to settle down where it lands. Since it will fly for considerable distances once launched, this is usually on someone else's manor, which rather frustrates their former owners.

The English partridge has also found it next to impossible to adapt to the early twenty-first century and seems unable to breed with any success in the wild. It is as a consequence a rapidly dwindling resource, which is simply a tragedy. Perhaps the English partridge was more Edwardian than any of us realised. Another major difference between the English and French breeds lies in their defence mechanisms when threatened. Both stocks will initially gather together as beaters approach and have a bit of a conflab about what is going on. The English birds then bail out in small groups of perhaps half a dozen or a dozen and zoom off downwind. When they cross the hedge behind which the Guns are waiting their reaction is to scatter in all directions like an exploding firework and sheer off individually to the discombobulation of the Guns below.

The French birds wait a little longer before lift off and then address the hedge in larger groups of perhaps twenty birds, which will hurtle straight over the line looking neither left nor right. It is difficult to say quite which makes for the most difficult shooting: the starburst Englishmen or the swarming French. Either can leave the novice Gun standing with his mouth open, having let off two shots for no noticeable effect.

Good partridge Shots take their birds very early and shoot very fast. All of which requires them to be very confident and competent indeed, because while partridge shooting takes place further up into the air than grouse perhaps, the whole operation tends to be not many feet above the beaters' heads and fast and furious with it.

Driven partridges are generally shot, or shot at, from behind hedges, and in Norfolk and Hampshire where the great partridge manors are you will see hedges trimmed into a neat 'A' shape about ten feet tall for the purpose. Where partridges are paramount you will also see trees planted in these hedges at one hundred yard intervals. The wind direction when driving partridges is so critical that Guns will be set out not on pre-determined pegs but parked between trees three and five while the beaters aim to drive the partridges between them like goalposts.

The art of driving partridges is arcane in the extreme. They fly down wind, and won't fly into the sun. They will run on stubbles but fly from roots. They will land in roots but not in stubbles. Root fields should contain a bowl or dip; stubbles should be flat. If you happen to have a 5,000 acre partridge beat therefore, you can see how you will have to rotate the crops in order that you don't get your stubbles and roots confused and the morning drives and the afternoon drives arse about wind-wise on a shooting day. There are books galore on partridges. Most of the best ones were written before 3 October 1952, which was the day when Joe Nickerson and a team shot over 2,000 wild English partridges at his Rothwell manor in Lincolnshire. Since then the English partridge has been in steady decline and unless we can find out why and reverse whatever circumstances need reversing we shall lose this remarkable and charming local bird first from the quarry list and finally from our countryside altogether. And if sportsmen won't save it, who will?

The Partridge Shooting Day

Partridge shooting varies only a little from the other procedures that we have considered, but some of these differences are important.

We meet at the house in the usual way, only it might be earlier by half an hour to take full advantage of the longer daylight. Guns will draw for numbers, but it is entirely possible that we may be six or seven as opposed to the eight or more on a pheasant or grouse day. We may be using single or double guns, but probably single. Double gun shooting is rare today, mainly because of the costs involved, but also because of the ambivalent attitudes towards big bags of reared game.

Given that this is early October the Guns will be lightly suited and shod. Shoes or short boots, suit, cap is the order of the day. A pair of sunglasses in the top pocket is a useful adjunct. Partridges simply will not fly into the sun, so the chances are that the Guns will be facing the sun for most of the day and the shades will be a boon, if the early cloud burns off as the sun rises.

The first drive is textbook. Having left the vehicles on a track we walk a little way down the slope with our host dropping the Guns off in sequence on the track behind a tallish hedge. The field beyond the hedge slopes slightly upwards towards a spinney which is fronted by a cover crop. The field itself is planted with low growing kale. Several rows nearest the hedge have been lifted leaving rough ground between the hedge and the edge of the crop. The breeze, what there is of it, is blowing gently into our faces and the sun has yet to rise above the distant spinney. Clearly the partridges will be feeding in and about the cover crop and perhaps sunning themselves on the far side of the copse. The beaters will rouse the sunbathers first and encourage them through the spinney. Some will, should, fly directly from the top of the rise, others will run through the cover and only fly much later when they run out of cover through the kale roots. It is not classic wild partridge driving, but it follows the strategy and behaviour appropriate to the reared French partridge with which the shoot is stocked.

There is no talking in the line. Partridges are wary and if one or a few break out early or in the wrong place, the chances are that they will pick up many more and before you know where you are, the whole driveful is rippling out of the sidedoor and all is lost. No chatter therefore, no car door slamming. No mobile bloody telephones. And no whistle to start either. Load up when you are in position and shoot on sight. Partridges only, that is. And no yelling at the dog.

Thinking of dogs, where are the pickers-up? They will be positioned well behind the line; though not so well behind the line on this drive as they might be. Since we are lined out in a lane, between hedges, our only effective arc of fire is between the two hedgetops. This means that the Guns will not glimpse the birds until they are almost upon us and will lose sight of them a second or so later. The pickers-up can therefore stand safely in the field behind us.

For the Guns the only option is to stand in the middle of the track. One could stand right back against the hedge to our backs, but that would mean only shooting in front. Equally one could stand well forward and only shoot behind. The compromise is to stand in the middle, as everyone is doing. Although you always have a modest discretion about where you stand, it is important that you remain, more or less, where you are put. If you leave your position you will confuse your neighbours and might put yourself in jeopardy. Standing in the middle of the road, we have a sound footing and will be comfortably balanced, but we will have to spin round from time to time to try for birds behind. Now we all know about not swinging through the line, and we know that grouse Shots put canes on their butts to stop them doing so. There are no butts and no canes here. Not swinging across the line is going to be a collective act of will and concentration, and since we are likely to be spinning like dervishes with any luck, it is as well to remind ourselves before the whole thing gets fraught with partridges.

Check your neighbours therefore and rationalise your safe areas of operation fore and aft. 'There to there in front. There to there behind.'

'Bang! Bang!' from your left, and you just see one partridge hit the rear hedge and a second tumbling over it. Your neighbour is not only a known partridge pro but has just come back from two weeks grouse shooting in Scotland. He is loose, practiced and on tip top form. And he's just had two in front which you didn't even see.

'Ba-bang!!' He's at it again. There must be birds moving somewhere. On your right. Three partridges flit across the gap. Didn't even get the gun up. Mark you, neither did the Gun on your right, and they went clear over his head. And again! This time you do see them briefly and manage a slightly desperate shot as they vanish behind. Not sure if you got the tailender. Not sure if you didn't swing across your neighbour's head a bit into the bargain. 'Ba!-bang!!' Old Supergun down the road is getting well stuck in. Again. Abruptly a partridge appears over the hedge in front. With hardly a conscious thought the gun comes up and you shoot it overhead, whereupon it almost disintegrates in mid air. Oops! That's the other reason for taking them early or late. You caught that one stone cold amidships from no more than twenty feet. No wonder a lot of partridge Guns use light guns and light loads for this sort of thing. There are birds moving all along the line now. A covey come through nicely between you and the next Gun. You kill one bird quite straightforwardly but as you pull onto the second another suddenly seems the better chance. Then they are gone. That second of confusion is the great covey defence. Pick a bird and stick with it, come hell or high water. Hit or miss. You never kill the second choice. Partridgeman takes another brace. Also never think that you can overcome the covey defence simply by loosing off both barrels into the middle. First, it seldom works which is remarkable but true; and second, it is called 'Firing into the brown' or 'Browning the covey' and is disapproved off as being both unsporting and amateurish. Quite apart from which everyone knows it doesn't work. Partridgeman takes another brace.

Another bird is coming. The beaters call 'Over!' Well up this time. 'Yours!' calls Partridgeman. Do not be fooled. It is an immature hen pheasant. Before they grow their long tail feathers, pheasants, especially the hens, and especially out of the sun, look very like a slightly slow partridge. The sight of which comes as a huge relief to the struggling novice, because he is fairly confident that he can nail this one rather more effectively than he has been dealing with the little rockets which have been buzzing by and over him up till now. In addition to which everyone seems to be leaving it for him. Pound gets you a penny it's a hen pheasant. Smile knowingly and ignore it. If you are fooled incidentally and you do shoot it, it is not the end of the world. Game laws and regulations apart, I don't think anyone in living memory has been transported to Australia for shooting a hen pheasant in October. It just makes you feel silly, especially if they make you carry it around all day.

There is a horn at the end of the drive. You have got two or three down in the lane and a couple more over the hedge behind. The verge behind Partridgeman is dotted with his slain and the hedge behind looks like a giant flypaper with partridges stuck here and there all over it. Just how do you get to be that good? Consider the reply of a notable Shot to just this question. He said 'Just spend a few thousand a year for the next twenty, and see how well you get the hang of it.' That was in 1960, when you could buy a brand new sports car for £1,000.

The next drive is markedly different. This time we are lined out on a rolling, rising stubble field. Each Gun is placed behind a large round bale. In front of the bales, some thirty paces out are a handful of beaters with flags, fertiliser bags nailed to a stick. The stubble is between two woods which run up to the crest on either side of us and meet across the top. What we can't see is that there is a strip of game cover at the foot of the top section of wood and that this is teeming with partridges. The beating line will have to be gently managed or the whole lot will be out in a single, dramatic and ultimately fruitless storm.

Down below we are trying to work out how to manage the shooting round these big bales. The solution which everyone arrives at seems to be that we stand some twenty feet back behind the bale and shoot over the tops as if there was a hedge between them. Bearing in mind that there are flag men out front and that the beaters will at some point during the drive emerge over the crest ahead, we must remember to keep shooting well up. Well up to a partridge pro means about six feet above the beaters' heads. You and I should stay rather higher or we will gain quite a different reputation. Behind the line pickers-up are visible in the distance a good three hundred yards behind and slightly below the line. Pretty much out of the way, though we had still better not shoot actually at them. As it turns out we don't have to. The birds break in neat coveys of fifteen to twenty and come swooping down the stubbles towards the line. As they do so the flag men flick their flags at the last minute and the coveys rise abruptly and spray over the bales in a very fair imitation of English partridges flaring over a hedge. Since we have practised this very style at the shooting school you are on firm ground here and start giving the birds a right caning, left and right, fore and aft, such that even Partridgeman is having a job getting in on the act. From a full pocket of cartridges at the start of the drive, and a couple of quick handfuls grabbed from your bag on the ground in a lull, there are only three left. The gun is hot to the touch, and there must be twenty birds in the stubble behind you. You should know exactly. It is difficult to keep track in a hot spot of exactly what you have killed; but you should try. If you have someone standing with you, loader, spouse, partner, significant other, friend or bodyguard they should be encouraged to keep count also. After the drive you can compare notes and take an average in the event you don't tally. It is easier, of course, if you are standing on the croquet lawn in front of the house since pheasants and partridges show up quite well on lawn. But on plough or in woodland or in heather or bracken or stubble, let alone in any kind of crop, they just vanish without trace and while the pickers-up and the dogs will find most of them, you do not want to be responsible for leaving dead, or worse, wounded birds to waste.

Five drives before lunch and five after is not an unusual partridge day. Partridge drives are generally quicker than others, and with light until 4.30pm at least it is possible to take a longer day and even a longer lunch, whether indoors or out, brought with you or provided. Sitting in the autumn sunshine beside a barn full of new season hay, with a cold mug of beer and a good doorstop of a sandwich with a bunch of friends and a few dogs in the midst of a partridge manor in England. Where else could a gentleman be at this time of year?

Thinking of beer and gentlemen reminds me; peeing in the shooting field is a matter of individual discretion. Better not to, of course, but if necessary a quiet moment against a hedge between drives. Never, ever during a drive. In the absence of hedges, anywhere but into the wind and avoid as far as possible pointing at others as you do so. Ladies, of course, don't pee and have their own rules about these things I know, and for the rest of us the rule is that a gentleman is always concentrating elsewhere.

Yet again the horny issue of the tip rears its head. Apply the same rules as have been previously described. Has the day been successful? Has it been well and discreetly managed? Have you had a good time? Have you had a blistering moment which will stay scorched in the memory in letters of fire for years to come? Do you want to be invited again? A wodge of notes may seem a high price to pay for a brace of partridges that you can buy in a supermarket for £5, but then if you take a gun into a supermarket you may very well end up shelling out considerably more in the end.

13

DOGS

Dogs are central to the shooting day. From a purely practical point of view dogs fulfil all those functions for which people are uniquely ill suited. Dogs scent. Dogs can probably see more with their nose than you can with your eyes. They know where birds are and they are more than happy to ferret them out on your behalf. In bursts of overenthusiasm they may actually retrieve birds before they have been shot; but this is an understandable error. After all they are only dogs and cannot be expected to understand the niceties of sport which surrounds the more practical objective of bird collecting. Dogs go where no sane human being would venture and are happy to do so – thorns, brambles, freezing water, flowing streams. There is almost nothing a dog won't go through.

After a drive, dogs retrieve the dead and wounded at which they are also better and more enthusiastic than their owners. They can find birds which have rolled into cracks or down holes; they can nose out a wounded bird which has clapped down under the brush and they can run down a bird which has legged it across three fields of plough which would take you or me a week to cross, if we made it at all. And after all of this service, dogs ask nothing more than a rub down, a few ounces of supper and the opportunity to lie at your feet adoringly for several hours. Dogs are, on the whole, just marvellous.

Strictly speaking no one who shoots ought to be without a dog. Which doesn't of course mean that every shooting person has to own one. I've never owned a dog in my puff and I've been shooting for years. No one however should shoot without a dog, mostly because without one you won't see very much to shoot at in the first place, and secondly because you may not be in a position to retrieve something you have shot. And if there is one rule which is writ large in shooting circles, it is that what is shot must be retrieved. Failure to retrieve anything you have shot should be numero uno on your list of sins. Or perhaps duo after shooting your host; but even then he should be properly retrieved. Shooting something and discarding it makes you a callous and unthinking killer and no sportsman. So there.

On posh shoots naturally there are hordes of dogs of all descriptions. Which means that the Guns have no need, really, for their own dogs. The dogs are by way of being rented for the day along with the ground, the beaters and all the other staff and accoutrements. Some Guns even take this enforced redundancy a step beyond irony and arrive with wildly unsuitable dogs to reinforce the fact that they expect to do nothing all day but shoot. A terrier, a pug, a Pekinese or an elaborately coiffured miniature pink poodle all make a certain statement and if that is the statement you wish to make then go for it. Why shouldn't you? Everyone else is making statements with their dogs; why not you? If your pink poodle should happen to pick up something which everyone else has overlooked – and poodles were hunting dogs before anyone considered dying the poor dears pink – then so much the better.

The beaters have teams of spaniels, the pickers-up have platoons of retrievers and Labradors and the Guns usually have a smattering of their own dogs who serve no known purpose other than to demonstrate that their respective Guns know what's what. There is endless debate and not inconsiderable acrimony and rancour about the protocol of picking up after a drive on a big shoot.

Basically those Guns who have their own retrievers, of whatever breed – usually Labradors or golden retrievers, are desperate to show off after a drive and to demonstrate that there is more to them than being a piece of artillery of more or less accuracy. They want to work their dog. The fact that the dog is a complete basket case who will do more to redistribute birds about the park than his Gun ever did, and will take an early romp though the next drive into the bargain, is neither here nor there.

The pickers-up, *au contraire*, are paid by the estate to hoover up as many birds as possible as fast as possible. The Guns have paid for X number of birds and the sooner the bulk of them are in the bag, the happier everyone will feel. A good team of pickers-up is said to contribute twenty per cent of the bag, mainly by collecting birds which the Guns did not even realise were shot. Whether a good number of them actually were shot or not depends very much on the scrupulousness of the shoot in question.

The objectives of the Guns with dogs and the pickers-up are therefore at odds and it is from this basic conflict that the argument emerges. The rational solution which is pursued on the best shoots, is that the pickers-up stand well back behind the Guns during the drive and content themselves with collecting only those birds which are clearly wounded but which pass over the Guns by a considerable distance nonetheless; chasing down birds which are shot but which run upon touching down; and, after the drive, move progressively forward collecting as they go, focusing first on those Guns without dogs and only finally assisting those Guns whose own dogs are still charging back and forth collecting the slain. The logic is straightforward. In terms of politeness; it is as rude to inhibit

'Sit'

The puppy will learn to sit to the upturned hand

'Stay!'

The desire to follow the trainer is very strong and must be resisted

'Fetch it'

The puppy will learn to enjoy his lessons with the dummy

'Peep!'

The puppy will learn to respond to the stop whistle – even when eye contact is broken

'Dead'

When taking game from a dog never lift the head

'Heel'

No dog should be introduced to the field until it has become absolutely reliable at heel

pickers-up from undertaking their allotted role in the day as it is to circumscribe a Gun's enjoyment at seeing his faithful Towser at work. A modicum of mutual respect will resolve these issues in a nonce.

Such mutual respect however will be in proportion to the usefulness of either dog.

Whether picking-up or shooting, dogs should sit, or better still lie, at the heels of their boss throughout the drive. No leads or tethers or other forms of restraint should be required. Dogs attached to great corkscrews, skewers, stakes, weights and anchors are generally signalling bad news on the behavioural front. Dogs attached to cartridge bags are usually worth watching for the fun of seeing them scampering about mid-drive broadcasting ammunition in all directions.

It's funny the first couple of times, but it begins to pall actually, after two or three goes, when the pursuing Gun, yelling lustily, passes in front of you – again – as you are trying to shoot. Any Gun seen attaching a dog lead to any part of himself for the purposes of restraint is a potential killer from whose immediate vicinity you should remove yourself forthwith and with all speed. Even if you have to feign a coronary.

Following the drive, dogs should begin the pick-up with the remotest wounded birds first and foremost and should return with them briskly for quick and humane dispatch. They should not savage them to death on the grass and return with the remains. In the meantime the owner should be collecting those nearest birds, until dog and owner progressively move together onto that corpse which divides near and far more or less equally and to the boundless satisfaction of all.

There is equal debate about sending dogs for running birds during the drive. If the dog in question is wholly reliable, to the point of being an automaton, then yes by all means. Actually it is really cool. You shoot a bird which bounces once and then starts legging it across the field. The dog, natch, gives it a glance and looks to you for instructions. A nod and he's tearing up the ground after it. A sixty yard dash, a body slam, and he ambles back with the bird, and then – this is important – sits with it in his mouth until you have a moment to take it and deal with it.

My god-dog Coco almost got it right. At her peak in terms of experience and obedience (which only periodically collided during her career), she was sent off under just such circumstances and only dropped points on her return because she put the bird down and then lay on it. While addressing the ticklish issue of runners, there arises the question of whether it is acceptable to shoot a running bird on the floor? Definitely thorny. As a novice, probably not. Wave frantically at pickers-up in the distance and indicate that you firmly believe a dog should be sent forthwith; which it should. Some professional pickers-up like to leave runners like this in order to show off later and will feign deafness and blindness in the interim. A charade which is disgraceful when a wounded bird is involved and should be brought discreetly to the keeper's attention at the end of the drive.

If you have a notoriously experienced neighbour you could draw it to his attention. If he is up to it, he might shoot it dead without a thought. If he is uncertain or there are dogs and people in dodgy places then he won't and neither should you. Even on a shoot where ground game is not shot, I would shoot a running bird on the ground, if I was there in my own right as it were, and not as a guest of someone else, when I thought the shot was utterly safe. If I was a guest of another Gun, I would not; to save him any potential embarrassment.

I remember once hearing a senior keeper on a very posh shoot shout 'Someone shoot that bloody deer!' as a roe doe came bounding through a wood. The Guns looked at one another aghast. 'Someone shoot that bloody deer!' as she ran almost along the line in full view. 'Will someone please shoot that beast!' The Guns were all looking in different directions, when a notable Shot near the end of the line, took a pace forward and shot the doe twice in the shoulder and then quickly ran up to where she fell and shot her again at close range. The rest of us were appalled and wondered what to do. As we gathered round the dead deer, which had effectively ended the drive for us all, the keeper pointed out that her muzzle and bottom jaw had been shot away by a poacher's attempt at a shot and turning the body over indicated the two crossbow bolts in her abdomen. I don't know if I'd have the nerve to do it even today and that's twenty years later.

Wonderdogs are one thing, of course; real dogs are quite another. Spaniels, are the brown and white or black and white splotchy ones with the hair. Mostly springers: the English springer is relatively larger than its Welsh cousin, sometimes cockers, which are woollier and squarer. Spaniels are hunters, though they do retrieve, and are uniformly popular with beaters because of their fascination with brambles and boundless energy. Pickers-up usually have Labradors on the one hand (black or golden) or golden retrievers (as their name implies) which are retrievers, although they will hunt given half a chance. Other breeds put in an appearance from time to time, but no one will be surprised if you don't recognise them.

Coco, of course, was a brown Labrador, technically chocolate. This is the third colour and used to be quite rare in this country until Coco and I made it the height of fashion. In fact the brown Labrador predates other colours and is notably bigger than the modern fashion which is for small fast dogs. Chocolates also have a notorious attitude problem in that they think about stuff.

Most dogs, and Labradors are no exception, have boundless loyalty, unconditional affection and very small brains. Chocolates have questionable loyalty, singularly conditional affection and think all the time. At least Coco did. She was very obedient and a great retriever; but was forever commenting on my shooting. She would sigh heavily when I missed things; she would lie on her back and sun her tummy while we waited for drives to begin; she would wander off and sit with other Guns who were shooting more birds than me; she disliked collecting damaged or badly shot game and would collect yukky pheasants by the tip of one wing with her eyes closed. She could be very trying. She didn't belong to me, but to the extent that she actually belonged to anyone, she lived with the Sherpa, and we shot together for several years until the Sherpa emigrated to the south of France and Coco went with her. She was wonderful company on a shooting day and I miss her dreadfully.

Should you have a dog? The modern Gun, occasional guest in the season, town-bound for the most part, chained to the office, seldom sees daylight in the summer, let alone the winter, probably shouldn't.

Consider this. Well trained gundogs are as rare as rocking horse pooh. Well trained gundogs are well trained because from an early and impressionable age they have been in the company of a single person who has spent hours and hours and miles and miles walking with them, playing with them, teaching them the whys and wherefores, explaining what we do and how we do it and practising endlessly with socks and with dummies and with cold game and with warm game and then finally in the field three days a week between August and February. For years. It never stops. They have not walked on pavements, lived in flats, been indulged by tiny tots with sweeties or scoffed a plateful of canapés off the coffee table during drinks parties. If a dog is for life and not just for Christmas, then a shooting dog is for shooting and not for company or guarding houses or for any other purpose other than shooting. And if that seems a lot to live up to then don't. Relationships ebb and flow, marriages founder and dissolve, families disperse and birds leave nests; shooting dogs are still eating the headrest off the driving seat and insisting on being taken shooting.

Of course you must have one. One day. When you do get one, the rules are very simple. Your dog must come when called or whistled; preferably to you. Your dog must sit quietly beside you during drives and only collect such birds as it is directed to by you after the drive is over. It must not run about the place barking and chewing up the game. It should not fight other people's dogs. It should not shit on your host's doorstep nor dry hump his leg, his wife or his dog. If you can achieve these simple precepts you have a wonderdog on your hands who will get more invitations to shoot than you will.

14

SHOOTING AND SEX

D.H. Lawrence has a lot to answer for. Not that there is much shooting in *Lady Chatterley's Lover*, but there is a deal of sex; and a gamekeeper is involved; and it is largely out of doors. Does this make shooting sexy? Does this make gamekeepers strangely attractive? Sadly not. Milkmen used to be sex machines at one point too, but the days of the doorstep delivery have gone forever.

People, however, can be very sexy indeed and places can be very romantic. Take a group of attractive folk and dump them in a romantic setting with a decent Chablis and just stand well back and see what happens. Shooting has often been portrayed as a thoroughly hormonally-charged sport, with gouts of testosterone splurging in all directions, as burly chaps with bristly moustaches and red faces go – *mano à mano* with sundry birds and beasts. We have Ernest Hemingway to thank for this, I imagine. The reality is somewhat different.

Most crucially, the shooting field is not a seething cauldron of testosterone. Yes, there are very often chaps involved and, yes, the atmosphere might be described as clubbable. But there is a marked absence of competition between shooters and it is much more of a team undertaking than individual. For obvious reasons, competitive clay pigeon shooting must be excluded from such generalities. In the field the Guns are on one team and the game is on the other. Which is why shooting has been adopted lately as a healthy management bonding exercise. A function it serves as well as any other management bonding exercise. Money and power are both aphrodisiacs, of course, and since shooting is an expensive sport there tends to be an abundance of both in the shooting field. Guns who turn out to shoot on a big day at the pheasants or the grouse are certainly going to have a hefty wedge of the wherewithal if they shoot with any regularity. It must be said, however, that Guns who shoot regularly will have less available spending money about them for exactly the same reason. You can't spend it twice, after all. But let's not beat about the bush, there are a lot of rich folk in shooting. And rich folk tend to enjoy a certain amount of power to boot. It is arguable whether rock music stars, a startling number of whom have been known to turn out with a gun and some big trousers, can truly be described as powerful in the same sense that leaders of politics or industry may be so described, but they can certainly be forthright when it comes to getting what they want, whether it is a hotel room, 2,000 blue Smarties, or everyone singing along. Are movie actors powerful? They may command astronomical fees and behave like five year olds on set and lock themselves in their trailers for days on end, but their function, after all, is to be told what to do by directors and what to say by writers. Their agents do the negotiations too. Lots of movie stars shoot.

Captains of industry shoot too and politicians sometimes do. The life of the politician is now so governed by vocal single issue groups that they can scarcely do anything at all without pissing off some crucial segment of the electorate, to the point where they can scarcely cross the road without offending someone. They do less and less of everything and become even more diminished as a result.

Sad but true. There was a time when most of the Cabinet of the UK would be unavailable on 12 August for anything other than a declaration of war.

I have a theory about powerful people. They like being bossed about. Mettlesome Steed Theory. When you are constantly the centre of attention and for ever making momentous decisions and everyone defers to you the whole time and staff are buzzing about hither and thither waiting for the next decision and it is always up to you; alone; at the top; and the whole thing is hanging in the balance and the knives will be out if you shove things the wrong way, just once, it is nice from time to time to shrug off the mantle of power and become a footsoldier once more. Under the circumstances it is actually a very good feeling to be told what to do for a change. Some powerful men visit houses in the suburbs where they are dressed in nappies and bossed about by ladies of a certain age who dress as nurses or governesses for the purpose. Some powerful women like to be spanked. Others – of both sexes – more sensibly, go shooting; where a keeper in tackety boots and bigger trousers still tells them 'Stand you just beyond the oak in the middle of the paddock and stop any birds breaking out that side.' The very clarity of the instruction simplifies life. For the next thirty minutes or so, the Gun, be he captain of industry, government minister, rock star, film star, mover or shaker, be he a she, all that is required is to stand beside the oak in the paddock and stop birds breaking out that side. No time to worry about interest rates, or international ramifications, or chord changes or motivation or whatever. Just stand in the paddock and defend the tree. What bliss that must be for someone whose mind is a constant seethe of contradictory and conflicting ideas and confused advice. What a strange and particular pleasure to just not think for a half an hour.

Once in position, the Gun may be a bag of nerves. After all, out in the paddock all alone, there is a sense of being on display. The beaters and the other Guns will clearly be able to see what is happening on the flank and if a major cods is achieved then much comment and mauling is likely to result over lunch. Tension therefore in abundance. And excitement. And as the birds begin to move, whether a few or many, no Gun, whether a comparative novice or a seasoned veteran will fail to feel the tingle of anticipation. This is not testosterone, this is adrenalin. And if, during the next half hour, this Gun should defend his, or her, patch with some diligence and skill and should the paddock, when the horn finally sounds, be dotted with the slain including that stonking right and left both stone cold dead in the air, and should some old beater emerge from the wood to assist with the pick-up and comment that 'That was a tidy old drive you had there. Ve-ry ti-dy. Especially the right and left.' Then there will be a very relaxed and deeply chuffed Gun indeed, who quite besides being rich and powerful, is now about as happy as a Gun can get, and who laughs at your jokes, whose eyes dance with excitement, whose face is ruddy in the cold air, and who is ready, in short, to charm your socks – and more – off; and to be charmed in return.

In addition to which since the whole party is staying in a very grand house, which is only a battlement or so short of a castle, complete with four-poster beds and agreeably dark corridors, and …Well, stuff is bound to happen.

It has been suggested that in the midst of so much death in the shooting field that at some unconscious level there is an urgent need to procreate in order to counterbalance the mortality which is inevitably confronted during the shooting day. It would make some sense if we were shooting each other rather than the pheasants, I suppose. Professional shrinks more learned than I will assert that there is something fundamentally attractive about a manifestly efficient hunter-gatherer. A Gun who can kill dinner on a grand scale in a matter of minutes appeals to the fundamental need to be provided for with meat and skins. This genial killer with the slack handful of birds is clearly such a one.

Tosh. Stuff and nonsense. This is no caveman, or indeed woman. This is a fit, charming, very rich, distinctly available individual with good hand eye co-ordination, an easy laugh, a flat in town, an estate in Scotland and a house in Mauritius. Bugger psychology, you don't need Sigmund to find that attractive.

Even without the material fringe benefits, the shooting field is a place where folk are likely to be near, if not at, their best. It is almost impossible, however, to bedazzle in damp tweed in the pouring rain. Shooting folk though will always have shooting in common just for openers. From time to time Guns will turn out with lovers who are not enthusiasts. These relationships seldom last. Shooting wins every time. Eventually they turn up with someone who watches and admires or who participates also. There is an immediate bond, a sense of shared purpose and relish and enjoyment. There are no rules in love, but these relationships will last longer.

The countryside where most of this sort of stuff goes on is almost painfully beautiful, of course. I defy anyone sitting in the sun on a west Highland hill watching the shadows run across the purple heather of the moor and the ripples sparkle on the loch below and the grouse calling 'Go Back! Go Back! Go Back!' not to feel like kissing someone. Fresh air and exercise naturally increase the blood flow and we all know where that leads. Sex in the field is unusual but not unheard of. Lowland game shooting offers rather less opportunity because of the constraints of time and space. Pheasant drives are seldom long enough and the Guns are, in any event, in full view of the beaters, pickers-up and each other for the most part. There is also the cold to contend with. Partridge shooting is probably worse still in terms of time, since there are more drives and quicker. In late September though the balmy weather makes for more favourable conditions. The grouse, it must be said, offer everything. Opportunity, privacy, time, temperature and inclination. Dammit, heather is even comfortable. Grouse drives can be very long and at the start, very little may happen for some time. Butts can be a fair way apart, and if on a slope, for example, while those lower down are inevitably exposed to the view of those higher up the slope, the events inside the top butt are invisible to the rest of the party. There is no doubt that the capital act has been undertaken in a grouse butt. What is less certain, thus far, is whether anyone has managed to shoot a grouse drive and execute a sublime union at one and the same time, and if so whether a right, left and centre – as it were – was successfully secured.

There has long been a tradition in Scotland of achieving the McNab in honour of John Buchan's mythical poacher. To achieve the McNab is to shoot a stag, catch a salmon and shoot a brace of grouse between dawn and dusk, in a single day. The original poacher did something quite different, but that is neither here nor there. And he was poacher, to boot. In recent correspondence in *The Field*, it was confirmed that a Royal McNab included a stag, a salmon, a brace of grouse, and the lodge cook in the same day, although it was not made clear whether the cook had to be achieved between dawn and dusk or just within the same twenty-four hour period. I remember that where the lodge cook was also the spouse of the sportsperson, it didn't count, though why not wasn't explained. I can't imagine there are any guarantees in this life. There was also the suggestion of an Imperial McNab which included the owner of the lodge, though I don't think anyone was claiming one. One imagines that grouse, salmon, stag, cook and owner would have to be a very busy day indeed, and anyway there isn't a name for it. An Improbable McNab, perhaps. Stalking is a very serious occupation where long periods are spent lying in the heather waiting for something to happen. If something is going to happen, then it is probably going to happen here, as long as the stalker is out of the way; unless the stalker is what is happening in which case you had better get rid of the pony man. And that's enough said, I think.

I know that there is much talk about engraving on certain guns which is rude, not to mention explicit. Suffice it to say that I have seen some of these wretched guns and like pornography in

'A right, left and centre?'

general it is ultimately an unrewarding experience. I also have it on good authority that the person who commissioned some of the engraving concerned, and who was himself a principal in some of the scenes, had paid the engraver a bonus over and above the agreed commission price wildly to exaggerate certain features. So there. Love, on the contrary, sometimes appears on the locks of expensive guns. I know of a man who had his wife's likeness engraved on the locks of his number 1 gun and his favourite retriever on the number 2. Or perhaps it was the other way round.

Shooting has been used a good deal as a subterfuge for sex. There is the story of the syndicate that ran very happily for several seasons without the eighth Gun, who happily paid his subscription each year but spent every shooting weekend with his mistress in a nearby cottage. Following each shoot day the keeper would drop a brace of birds on the door handle so that the Gun would have something to show for his efforts when he got home. History does not relate whether the keeper received an additional tip for his trouble. The rest of the Guns thought the whole arrangement perfectly sound since they were able to invite guests free of any additional cost in the absence of the lover. For that matter, I once shot in a line of Guns each of whom had a wife standing with him. None of the wives were their own. Once or twice a season, I gathered, the men would leave their own wives to go shooting with the boys and the ladies would leave for a weekend away with the girls, on what pretext I never discovered. The two teams would meet at an hotel for two days of extra-marital sex and shooting and then return to their families in due season. I imagine that the shared communal burden of guilt surrounding this mass infidelity somehow diluted any individual misgivings anyone felt.

During the several seasons that the original Sherpa and I shot together with a regular syndicate, there was an occasion when I was abroad on business and sent along a friend to shoot in my stead. The Sherpa went along as usual both to guide my friend and to exercise her dog – which was her usual preoccupation in any case. The arrival of the Sherpa with a different Gun caused no little consternation among the regular Guns, a situation not helped by her cryptic comments about my declining performance, both shooting and otherwise, through the season and the need for occasional changes of diet.

Upon my return there was a good deal of boot staring and eyebrow raising before the shoot captain blurted out to me that the Sherpa had brought another man to the previous shoot. Despite my protestations that he was my guest and that everything was above board, I think it was generally concluded that I was showing a stiff upper lip about the whole thing and apart from occasional sympathetic looks, the matter was never discussed again.

Shooting is not particularly sexy. Some of the people who shoot are very sexy indeed and some of the places where shooting is undertaken are undeniably romantic and can turn a chap's mind to other things; but the activity itself is not erotic, I fear. The whole undertaking is quite raw and fundamental in many ways though, and while formal game shooting is far from being a coarse affair there is an essential earthiness about it, which, like any form of hunting, is noticeably stimulating.

Death in the field is dealt with in a similarly stalwart manner. On one occasion when our host slipped the leash mid-shoot he was taken back to the house in a Land Rover and laid in the game larder for the time being until the shoot was concluded – as he would doubtless have wished. It was strange though to be hanging up the birds at the end of the day, as we awaited the funeral director, with our late host lying on the slate bench along the wall. For good order's sake we also put him down on the game cards.

When one of the Guns in a shooting party in Scotland dropped dead in his butt, much as that great Edwardian Lord Ripon did in 1923, it was decided that since having to return to Scotland for the inquest would be likely to disrupt the shooting arranged later in the season, it would be better if he died at home. Accordingly he was propped up in the passenger seat of his own motor car and duly driven back to England where he died again later in the night and was very properly enquired after by his local coroner with the minimum disruption of shooting dates for the other Guns.

One of the beaters died in the field on a shoot I attended and there was some question as to what should be done. Since another beater was also a senior police officer in the area the suggestion that the corpse might spend the rest of the morning on the game cart was quite properly dismissed, and it was decided that someone should drive the body to the hospital. One of the pickers-up volunteered, but in the end one of the Guns was deputed to go. As the headkeeper opined, 'We've got eight Guns and only four pickers-up; and he was only to be at number 1 next drive, anyway, so he wouldn't have got much shooting.'

Sex and death. Death and sex. – All part and parcel of a shooting day.

15

DOMESTICITY

Once you have got home after a shooting day you will have two or more birds or even possibly a hare which require you to do something constructive, or more exactly, deconstructive, with them. Cook books tend rather to gloss over this aspect of things and shooting books definitely skate right past the topic. 'Take a large hare…'' Yeah. Right. You can take the birds and beasts to your local friendly butcher, of course, who will squeak in alarm at the thought of having something as unhygienic as dead game in his smart, clean and EU approved stainless steel premises. Take a couple of brace of pheasants to the prestige meats counter (butchery seems not to take place any more; packaging has replaced it) of your out of town supermarket and see what response you get. You may be lucky and have an old fashioned family butcher and game dealer who will pluck and dress your birds for you, but he will charge you the price of a couple of oven readies for the job, which seems to defeat the object of the exercise. Ultimately you have to do the job yourself.

Mrs Beeton said that you should hang a pheasant by the neck until it dropped off the hook. Mrs Beeton must have had her taste buds surgically removed. You should however hang a brace of birds for a day or two because it does make them taste better, or specifically it makes them taste more which is better, and because it makes them easier to pluck.

Pheasants come in pairs – a brace – of a cock (orange; large) and a hen (brown; small) tied at the neck by twine. The obvious thing to do is to hang them on a hook by the string. Which is fine. Better though to hang them the other way up, by the legs. The reason being that the flesh at the bottom is thin and taints quickly and easily, while the flesh at the top is thick and fatty and will not taint as quickly or easily.

If you have a large and commodious country house then you hang game in the game larder. If you have a generously proportioned residence in town you hang them in the cellar. If you have a flat, you hang them on the balcony; and if you don't have a balcony you sling them from the window. My mate Hobbs hangs his on the washing line; or did until he woke up one night to find three foxes giving each other leg ups after them. You can get very smart game hangers now which have a sort of bee keeper's mask over them to keep the flies off which in these mild and globally warmed days is a splendid idea. If it is very cold indeed, pheasants won't begin to deteriorate for several days. Before Christmas, I would venture forty-eight hours tops. Then comes the moment of truth.

Plucking

I'm not a pheasant plucker
I'm a pheasant plucker's son
And I'll be a pheasant plucker
Till the pheasant plucking's done.

Step 1: cut the twine.

Step 2: position the bird (either one) over the top of a swing bin lined with a fresh binliner

Step 3: starting on the back take two or three feathers and yank them smartly towards the head; against the grain of the plumage

Step 4: drop feathers into bin

Step 5: continue until bird is naked from neck to toe, wings excepted.

Some parts are easier than others. The legs are a doddle. The tail feathers are a one at a time job, otherwise you'll really tear the arse out of the poor thing. The breast is tricky – the key is not to tear the skin. If the bird is very cold this makes the skin tight and the whole procedure much easier. If you do tear the skin, the only answer is to reduce the number of feathers you are yanking to one at a time. Pulling great handfuls of plumage out at a time achieves very little except sticky hands and a very *manqué* looking pheasant indeed.

A professional pheasant plucker would pluck the wings too. We however, are not professional and there is little to eat on a pheasant's wing, less still on a partridge's and nothing flat on a snipe's or a woodcock's; so just forget it.

Having reduced both birds to a state of naked immodesty, the time has come for a spot of pruning. Poultry scissors are marvellous things. Savage to look at, but a joy to use. If you are going to do this sort of thing regularly, then you should definitely have a pair. If not, secateurs will do the trick. Failing which a cleaver. Wings off. Feet off just below the knee. Head off just below where you stopped plucking leaving about a thumb's length of neck.

Your bird is now looking much more at home in the kitchen. The cognoscenti will now waft the bird over the gas hob or give it a bit of a singe with those blowtorches with which you *brûle* your *brûlée* these days. Not turned up full though. What this does is to remove the last of the emerging feathers here and there and any hairs and bum fluff which might be loitering about the place.

Now before the gruesome part, there is a last job. At the neck end where the neck joins the body, there is a bulge. If you haven't discovered this already, it is the crop, which is where birds store food prior to digestion. It is a sac and is likely to be full of corn or maize or pine nuts or greens of some description. Whatever it is full of will be quite fresh still. What you have to do it to get two fingers inside the skin of the neck, up and over the crop, and draw the sac out without spilling chick peas or whatever all over the place. Having done which you can now trim the neck as close to the body as you can.

Now down to the business end.

Just above the 'Parson's Nose', above the tail, where the bird's breast falls to a point, where you would be putting stuffing if someone else had done this for you, is sheer skin. Put a sharp knife through there, point first, blade outwards and cut a slit. Take a grip on the breast with the left hand, and with a deep breath, insert two fingers of the right as far as possible, grab as much of everything as you can and extract. A lot of gubbins is now parked on the work surface; some of which is still attached at the arsehole. First go back in again, to make sure everything came out first go. Very often the heart, which is the size of a pistachio, is still attached to the cavity floor. Get everything out. Then with the shears or a sharp knife, snip off the Parson's Nose, the arsehole and all its assorted sordid attachments and dump them in the bin.

Repeat for second bird.

Rinse the carcasses and relax. Tie up the binliner and discard, but not if there are cats or foxes in the vicinity who will have pheasant guts all up and down the street in no time. Wash knives and shears. Partridges should not hang for more than twenty-four hours unless it is very cold indeed. Everything happens much the same, except that partridges are easier. Grouse should be dealt with the day they are shot, which is still summer after all. Pigeons are a doddle, and you can pluck the breast with little more than a brisk rub. Champion pigeon pluckers can undress a pigeon in less than a minute. Not very tidily though. There is nothing on a pigeon bar the breasts so you simply slice the fillets off either side of the breastbone.

You can do much the same for any bird in fact, and it is quicker and easier, and if you are not roasting your birds, then filleting them off the bone is as good a way as any. For real speed they can be skinned to boot. Here's how.

Put bird on work-surface on its back. Lay left hand firmly on the breast and gather a pinch of skin towards the tail between the thumb and forefinger. Take a sharp knife in the right hand and snick the pinch. Hold down legs with right hand and peel back plumage and skin from breast. The whole shirtfront comes off in one go. Fillet what is thus exposed and store. Discard remainder unless you want the legs too, which take about a minute each to pull inwards from the skin and amputate with shears top and bottom. Five minutes a bird – tops.

More stylish than fillets and quicker even than filleting, is to skin the breast as described and snip around the front of the breast bone with your shears, severing the collar bones, in effect, and then simply wrenching off the entire breastbone with the fillets still in place. Cooking on the bone imparts a better flavour to the meat and cooks it more evenly and this is a very satisfactory compromise between presentation and speed. Don't overdo the wrenching until you have had a little practice or you may inadvertently redecorate the kitchen.

Duck, mallard anyway, are bigger and more boring by far, not least because they have a tremendous amount of plumage, and even when that is out of the way, there is another layer of down and fluff still to go. The plucking itself is easy enough, it just goes on and on and on and on. Teal are the same only smaller; while geese are the same only larger. Never shoot a goose unless you have the weekend free for plucking.

Woodcock and snipe, should you encounter them, are eaten whole. They have a continuous digestive tract, which contains no faecal or other toxic waste matter, so they are merely plucked from top to toe, pinned by their own little beaks and roasted for fifteen minutes in a hot oven. It sounds outlandish and bizarre but it's true and it works. Gourmets and connoisseurs also eat the eyes and the brains as being peculiar delicacies. They got the peculiar right, anyway.

Take a good long pull on your whisky glass and turn your attention to the hare.

Dressing Out Game

If you are squeamish this is the moment to bail out. Dressing out game of any type affects folk in different ways. Some find no difficulty in it at all; some reach a point where they can do no more; some wouldn't touch dead game with a long pole under any circumstances. Wherever you stand on the sliding scale of disinclination to get messily involved, no criticism is implied or intended; but be aware that hares fall into a different league from pheasants.

There are two things to remember when first given a hare: hold its front paws and run your thumb down each side of its belly. This will drain its bladder of urine which might otherwise leak into the body cavity when the hare is hung. Unlike rabbits which should be gutted (paunched) forthwith, a hare should be hung complete for a day or so. Second, tie a plastic bag round the hare's head. Hare's blood does not congeal, for some reason, and a good deal of it will end up on the floor underneath the hare unless preventative measures are taken. Then you can hang it up by its heels until you are ready to proceed. When you are, this is how you do it. Take a small sharp knife, a plastic carrier bag, and a cleaver and board.

Lay the hare on its back and take a pinch of fur just below the rib cage. Snick this with the point of a sharp knife. Having snicked, you will see the wall of the abdomen under the fur. With a thumb either side you can pretty much peel the fur away to reveal the skin on the hare's front. Take a pinch of this and with the blade of your knife cut across the hare's body until there is a clear hole in the abdomen wall. Insert the point of the knife, and with the blade uppermost cut up and out for the full length of the abdomen, from ribs to crotch. Be aware that there will be a good deal of blood sloshing about in the cavity, which will now be finding a way out, so the draining board is a good place to undertake all this, rather than, say, the dining room table. Also be aware that there are various bits and pieces inside, the gall bladder springs to mind, which if punctured will release stinks that will clear the street. This is why it is important to cut up and out and not go stabbing anything.

As with birds a lot of stuff is going to come out of this hole, much of it singularly unappealing. It should however still be attached at both ends. The thing to do is to find the north end of the tube and follow it up to the diaphragm, which you must cut through to get into the chest cavity, where more blood will be sloshing about, and as far as the hare's throat. Get a good firm grip on the tube between finger and thumb and cut it with the other hand. You can then drag everything from that point south and dump it in a pile between the animal's back feet. Now move to the south end, and following the final tube as far as possible, cut it as close to the exit point as you can. The hare's insides are now out, with the exception of the kidneys which will be stuck to the top back of the abdominal cavity. Take the insides and put them in a plastic carrier bag.

To return to the beast. It will now be possible to continue to peel away the skin from either side of the incision around the back of the hare. Pull the fur with one hand and wiggle the fingers of the other around the flesh with the other. Once right round, cut the skin round the back, such that it is, in effect, jacket and trousers. Reach for the cleaver. Wrists, ankles, neck. Into the bag.

Taking off the jacket and trousers is straightforward and follows the logic of the situation. Peel where peeling is easy and where not, the application of the sharp knife will help matters along. It might facilitate things for example, to slit the sleeves and trouser legs and the jacket up the back. Do mind out for bones sticking out of the corners. They can be cruelly sharp and it is never too late for the Rabbit's Revenge. Once undressed, the fur goes into the bag too.

What remains is a series of connected joints with a fluffy white tail. Take it off with the knife. It is the final entry into the bag, which can now be tied and discarded. If the cats and foxes get at this one, you will be in real trouble and will have visits from the RSPCA, Social Services and the police, so the usual dustbin rules apply.

Hares and rabbits and deer, for that matter, are six joints. Two legs at the back; two shoulders at the front; basket - which is rib cage and upper back; and saddle which is the lower back. Shoulders are attached only by muscle and can be detached by knife. The back legs are ball joints which may take a chop, if fiddling about with the knife point doesn't work, although it should. Chop the remainder in half below the rib cage.

Bag up joints. Wash down tools, surfaces and self. Pour further whisky and relax.

16

DISASTERS

We have had some high old times through the season thus far and enjoyed ourselves enormously. Books always show the best side of things. Life, sadly, is not like that. Sometimes it all goes horribly wrong. Very real disasters lurk all about the shooting field and accidents, as we all know, are waiting to happen. The greatest disaster of all is when someone or something, other than the quarry of choice, is shot.

There used to be a rule that if someone was shot - not dead obviously where a whole legal infrastructure swings inevitably into action - but peppered and wounded, that the Gun responsible handed over his gun or guns to the victim, left the field and never shot again; and no more was said. I doubt if that rule is much applied today. The least that should happen, though, in the event of a peppering incident is that the perpetrator is publicly dismissed from the field forthwith. Any more serious incident is already out of the hands of those present.

All responsible Guns are insured against damage to third parties. Membership of the Countryside Alliance or the British Association for Shooting and Conservation both confer such insurance and every shooting person should join one or other. If they shoot game at all, they should join the Game Conservancy Trust while they are about it too. Shooting accidents are mercifully rare. Loads of people around the world are constantly shooting one another under some pretext or other and their actions are consistently used by those who would interfere with others' sport as a club to beat the licenced and legitimate sportsman. That can't be helped, though it must be resolutely resisted. On a less grim note what happens when someone has an incident? As it might be an accidental discharge or a dangerous or foolish shot?

The accidental discharge can be the result of mechanical defect as well as carelessness. A malfunction of triggers or firing pins can, rarely, cause a cartridge to explode apparently of its own accord. If the Gun in question has been following all the rules of safe gun handling the result will be an ounce of lead somewhere in the stratosphere and down again, or a hole the size of a soup plate in the ground just in front of him. In either event no material damage has been done, but the Gun in question will, quite properly, be extremely shocked and upset, not to mention relieved that he has got away with it. None of these conditions are actually conducive to relaxed and effective shooting and the responsible Gun will excuse himself from the field for the drive or the morning or the remainder of the day at the very least. If he doesn't he should be encouraged to do so. Following which if he has a spare gun, or a spare gun can be found for him, he may, after a discreet period, be welcomed back into the line.

In the event of carelessness there can be no such reconciliation. The Gun must leave the field forthwith and not return. How long this exile is likely to persist is a matter for the host and the remaining Guns who may be more or less friends of the host or the careless Gun. I will admit here to such an accident in my teens. Nervously fiddling with the triggers at the start of a drive, I blew a hole in the ground. I didn't think anyone saw it. Certainly no one mentioned it at the time. My next invitation to that shoot was five years later – to the day – and that was family. I might have got away with less if I had owned up. A careless shot requires a word from the captain. If someone is taking birds unreasonably low or swinging through the line or jeopardising the beaters or pickers-up, it should be brought to the attention of the captain. As a first step, the captain should explain quietly but firmly to the miscreant that he should take more care and be more polite. On a second occurrence the captain should issue the rebuke loudly, roundly and publicly. And another failure and the axe must fall forthwith, even if it means stopping the drive. In the event of a dangerous shot, go direct to-step three. I have captained teams for more years than I care to remember and have issued first warnings twice. I have never sent someone home. I have one guest presently on suspension.

If the captain won't do anything, you are faced with a choice. Either do it yourself or leave. If you have brought the matter to the captain's attention but he is unwilling to proceed – 'Because he's our biggest client, for Christ's sake!' – you either take matters into your own hands, if he'll let you, and address the guilty party yourself or make your excuses and leave. If you are in a line with a dangerous shooter, the risk simply isn't worth the day's sport, which will be no fun anyway. If he isn't really being dangerous, you have just grievously and gratuitously insulted your host by suggesting that one of his best friends is a raving psychotic and you might as well pack it in anyway.

Shooting the wrong thing is embarrassing. Hen pheasants on partridge days are a legitimate mistake, at least after 1 October they are. Potting a sparrow hawk or an owl (which can look very woodcocky in a tense moment) is much more serious and puts your host in a thoroughly tricky position. Apart from abject apologies there is not much that can be done. Really you should just pack up and hope no one peaches on you to the Feds. I'm not sure what the response would be if you turned yourself in to the constabulary for owlcide, but I suspect that they would take a dim view of it. The answer is not to shoot in the first place if you are not confident about the species. There are odd things about the place which you can shoot, such as magpies and jays, which the keeper especially will applaud. He will be less keen on your shooting his pet guinea fowl which flounder through the line from time to time, despite the fact that they are legally shootable. White pheasants are not particularly rare but do attract fines on shoot days. These range from a bottle of port to £100. Sometimes it is a joke to spice up the day, sometimes it isn't. If someone asks you not to shoot the white pheasant, then don't. If they tell you that if you shoot the white pheasant you will have to shoot the next drive stark naked, that is a matter for you. Pheasants and partridges are easily recognisable even to a novice and other species will become so in time. Stick to what you know, leave the rest and avoid the whole question is my advice. Better an opportunity foregone than a reputation shattered before it has even been established.

Foxes are an especially thorny area. Some hosts actively encourage vulpicide, even when ground game is not being shot, while others abhor it. You don't often confront a fox in a shootable situation, and if you do it is best to be caught looking in the opposite direction. A shotgun is not really the best thing to shoot foxes with and all other risks aside, you will feel dreadful if it is not killed outright. Leave well alone and claim your uncle is a Master of Foxhounds and would disinherit you if he found out. No one will criticise your decision.

On a more practical level what happens if the day's sport isn't up to much? *Caveat emptor.* Was ever a Latin tag used to cover such a multitude of sins? If you are buying shooting, by the day, by the season, directly or through agents, you are always going to be in for the occasional disappointment. Much has to do with the management of expectations. The host who mutters darkly about 'Rounding up the odd cock or two here and there' and yet delivers a perfectly reasonable, if modest, day's sport has a significant advantage over the host who confidently predicts 250 plus head of game, and then

Never shoot anything you are not prepared to carry

fails to break a hundred. It is not that a bag ninety-nine on the first outing was especially good, or that ninety-nine on the second was actually poor; it is a question of where expectation and outcome coincide.

If you are buying a day's sport, whether individually or as a team, some reasonable leeway must be given. Shooting is a sport, after all and not a machine. Ten per cent either side of the quoted expectation is the norm, and beyond this, financial arrangements must be adjusted. It is always worth checking the small print in any agreement to see what provisions are made in this respect. If you are expecting game and end the day with more pigeons and magpies than pheasants you have some right to be aggrieved. You may have enjoyed some wonderful shooting, but you have nonetheless been legged over. The bag should be calculated on the intended quarry and not incidental bonuses. The weather is also critical. You can shoot in rain, though it is never very much fun, and if it is torrential the whole thing is fairly pointless. Bright sunshine is hardly an ideal shooting day, but it is hard to claim it as an excuse for cancellation. Fog is a killer. More particularly, fog makes shooting even more dangerous than usual and is a surefire disaster. There is no hard and fast rule about weather cancellation, but generally the estate will postpone the day until later in the season, or even to the following season. It is also possible to insure days against weather cancellation and this is sometimes prudent. If the shoot and the guests are fairly local and popping back the next weekend is not out of the question, then perhaps there is no need. If it is a top day on a top moor and guests are flying in for the purpose from all over the world, then it is probably easier to call the whole thing off and take the insurance money. On the whole, grouse shooting should be insured because it is logistically complex and very expensive; wild English partridges probably because there is no guarantee you will ever get another chance; wild pheasants perhaps; and rented shooting of reared and released game probably not.

There is also the sticky issue of who pays what and when. Most shoots require a deposit, usually of some twenty-five per cent of the expected total, when a day is booked, and expect the rest of the money either at the end of the day or subsequently. Some ask for the balance before the shoot date. It is a fine balance as to who should be at risk. The compromise position is fifty/fifty. The Guns stump for twenty-five on booking and another twenty-five a month before the shoot, and pay the balance on the day or on receipt of an invoice afterwards. Discussing money on the day always seems somehow distasteful and, if the team captain has quite honestly left the chequebook on the hall table, it can lead to real embarrassment, so afterwards is most convenient.

If you shoot regularly on an estate as a paying guest, these issues diminish over time; but the first meeting is always a bit fraught. The host has a team of unknowns maundering about his estate with guns; and the Guns are in a strange place which might be Jollity Farm on the one hand or something out of Deliverance on the other. Poor and unsporting birds are a disappointment, but are also something of a subjective matter. One man's miserable hedgehopper is another person's soaring archangel. And if a line of Guns stand resolutely silent and stony faced as hordes of pheasants or partridges flutter round and by them, it is quite hard to retain the contractual high ground at the end of the day, however solid your moral and ethical sporting position might be. If the birds simply don't put in an appearance at all, you are in better shape contractually. If you have followed the fifty/fifty route, you are unlikely to be too much at risk in any case, but if you are well below even the halfway point of what you expected, then I can only recommend a huge and very public fuss and if anyone approaches you at the end of the day with his hand out tell them where to stick it. Unless it has got a large cheque in it.

If the Guns are unusually hopeless, the estate is entitled to calculate a fee based on the number of bangs. There are generally a couple of beaters with clickers who are counting the shots throughout the day and the average of these two will form the basis of the calculation. A normal team of normal Guns should address normal game under normal circumstances on the basis of about three to one. There are a lot of normals in that sentence because there are some shoots which pride themselves on delivering birds which are so impossible that top Shots average nearer six to one, while a visiting team might loose off five hundred rounds on a drive for three pheasants and a crow. With experience comes wisdom. There are ways in which you can reduce your exposure. References may be offered or asked for. I always offer a new estate where we are thinking of visiting the name of someone who will vouch for us on safety, for example, or accuracy or general agreeableness. I can't think of anyone who has asked for one. I use any network I can pump for information about a new shoot, before I commit. The shooting community is not huge and word of mouth gets around like wildfire in short order. A word with a beater on a neighbouring estate, a pint offered or accepted in the village pub on a shoot day during the season before you visit, may well pay dividends.

Or you can use an agent. With the growth of commercial shooting has come a corresponding growth of a plethora of firms and individuals who will mix and match Guns to shoots and back again – for a fee. As a novice this is not a bad way to start out in your shooting career. The agent is the buffer between the aggrieved Gun and the aggrieved host and both sides can have an agreeable tantrum at the agent betimes and tell him to sort out the problem. Nine times out of ten there is no problem, but when there is, it is good to have an agent to do your arguing for you, and someone to sack if he doesn't win.

17

A Summary of the Rules

What exactly have you learned from all this? You should have learned by now that the key to good shooting, on the one hand, is lots of practice and the expenditure of not inconsiderable sums of money and the foundation of proper shooting etiquette, on the other, it is simply good manners and the distribution of a whole lot more.

The worst thing you can do to your host on a shooting day is to shoot him or one of his other guests, and the second worst thing you can do is insult him by your crass incivility to his staff by failing to shake his keeper's hand with sufficient generosity at the end of the day.

The rest of the list of possible sins flows directly from these precepts and while impoliteness does not diminish on a sliding scale and rudeness is an absolute concept not measurable by degrees you will muddle by if you absorb all or most of the following:

When invited to shoot, respond immediately and stick resolutely to your decision.

Ask whatever questions you must to ensure that you understand what is required of you.

Turn up in the right place at the correct time, on the proper day.

Be properly equipped with guns and cartridges that match.

And with such additional gear as you may require to be self sufficient without having to beg, steal or borrow from other people who are too busy looking after themselves to be nannying you.

Dress. Not up necessarily, nor to impress; but certainly put something on. Then add enough clothes to suit the formality or otherwise of the day, so as not to make other guests feel either over or underdone.

Remember the names of the Guns either side of you in the line.

Don't gossip.

Clearly identify your safe angles of fire on arrival at your peg, including spotting pickers-up, stops and back Guns.

Stay awake and alert.

Check barrels.

Don't load before the instruction to start the drive. In the absence of a whistle or whatever, don't start shooting at anything other than the game of choice.

Be safe. Be safe. Be safe.

Don't point your gun, either by accident or design, at anything you don't mean to kill.

Hit or miss, never mock or curse birds.

Don't poach birds from in front of your neighbour.

You can kill one behind him if he misses. Once. Just to prove you can. Otherwise a bird that has been missed twice already has done its bit for the day.

Don't shoot after the signal to end the drive.

Unload and sleeve your gun immediately after the signal.

Collect your birds, beginning with any wounded. Dispatch these discreetly.

Then help to pick up your neighbour's birds by all means but publicly acknowledge the fact that they are not yours.

Collect your empty cartridges.

At elevenses do not lug out a bottle unless you are confident it will not be unwelcome.

Don't drink too much either here or at lunch.

Don't pee into the wind.

Be civil to beaters and pickers-up at every opportunity.

At the end of the day thank the beaters and other shoot staff.

Tip the keeper with single denomination notes.

Thank everyone in sight orally and later in writing.

Take your birds home.

Clean your own gun.

Keep your Game Book.

Be content.

Always concentrate on the game in hand

APPENDIX

Useful Addresses

Countryside Alliance,
The Old Town Hall,
367 Kennington Road,
London,
SE11 4PT

Tel: 020 7840 9200

The Game Conservancy Trust,
Fordingbridge,
Hampshire,
SP6 1EF

Tel: 01425 652321

British Association for Shooting and Conservation (BASC),
Marford Mill,
Rossett,
Wrexham,
LL2 0HL

Tel: 01244 573000

Sporting Seasons

January 31st	*Snipe, Woodcock & Wildfowl (inland)* **seasons close**
February 1st	*Partridge and Pheasant* **seasons close**
February 15th	*Red & Sika Hind and Fallow Doe* **seasons close (Scotland)**
February 20th	*Wildfowl (foreshore)* **season closes**
February 28th	*Red & Sika Hind, Roe & Fallow Doe* **seasons close (England & Wales)**
March 14th	*Coarse fishing* **season closes**
March 31st	*Roe Doe* **season closes (Scotland)**
April 1st	*Roe Buck* **season opens**
April 30th	*Red & Sika Stag & Fallow Buck* **seasons close (England & Wales)**
May	
June 16th	*Coarse fishing* **season opens on some waters**
July 2nd	*Red & Sika Stag* **seasons open (Scotland)**
August 1st	*Fallow Buck* **season opens**
	Red & Sika Stag **seasons open (England & Wales)**
August 12th	*Grouse, Snipe & Ptarmigan* **seasons open**
August 20th	*Black-game* **season opens**
September 1st	*Partridge, Wild Geese & Duck* **seasons open**
	Woodcock **season opens (Scotland)**
September 30th	*Autumn Hunting* **season opens**
October 1st	*Pheasant & Woodcock* **seasons open**
October 20th	*Red & Sika Stag & Roe Buck* **seasons close (Scotland)**
October 22nd	*Red & Sika Hind, Fallow & Roe Doe* **seasons open (Scotland)**
October 31st	*Roe Buck* **season closes (England & Wales)**
November 1st	*Hunting* **season opens**
	Red & Sika Hind, Fallow & Roe Doe **seasons open (England & Wales)**
December 10th	*Grouse, Ptarmigan & Black-game* **seasons close**